WITNESS
TO
POWER

AMONG OTHER BOOKS BY MARQUIS CHILDS

Sweden: The Middle Way
Washington Calling
I Write from Washington
The Cabin
Ethics in a Business Society (with Douglass
    Cater)
Eisenhower: Captive Hero
Walter Lippmann and His Times (Editor, with
    James Reston)
The Peacemakers
Taint of Innocence

WITNESS
TO by Marquis Childs
POWER

McGRAW-HILL BOOK COMPANY

New York   St. Louis   San Francisco
Düsseldorf   Mexico   Toronto

123456789 BABA 798765

Library of Congress Cataloging in Publication Data

Childs, Marquis William, date
   Witness to power.

   Includes index.
   1. Childs, Marquis William, date
2.   Journalists — United States — Correspondence,
reminiscences, etc. I. Title.
PN4874.C514A38   070.92′4 [B]   75-5727
ISBN 0-07-010763-7

For
Catherine,
Diana,
Christina,
Marquis,
Amanda,
our grandchildren

Acknowledgments

My publisher, Joseph Pulitzer, Jr., made possible many of the assignments that provided the material for this book. I am indebted to him for his friendship over the years. Jeannette Hopkins, as editor, has given me invaluable help as she has with other books in the past. My colleagues in the Washington bureau of the St. Louis *Post-Dispatch* have been unfailingly helpful, particularly Richard Dudman and Helen-Marie Fruth. Cindy Hamilton was remarkably patient in preparing a manuscript that underwent various vicissitudes. I am, most important, grateful to my wife for her critical judgment and for her cheerful acceptance of what have sometimes been hardships in our travels around the world.

Contents

ACKNOWLEDGMENTS   *vi*

PROLOGUE   *1*

I

THAT MAN ROOSEVELT   7

II

POLITICS AND THE SUPREME COURT   *30*

III

HERO AND ANTIHERO   *53*

IV

THE CONQUERED AND THE CONQUERORS   *70*

V

WINNERS AND LOSERS   *91*

VI

EUROPE FULL CIRCLE   *111*

VII

AFTER THE KINGS AND THE CAPTAINS   130

VIII

EAST OF SUEZ   146

IX

TRIUMPH AND TRAGEDY: THE KENNEDYS   163

X

HOPE LONG DEFERRED   185

XI

THE GIANT AND THE SLAVE   205

XII

CHINA: THE GREAT WALL BREACHED   222

XIII

THE MAN, THE SYSTEM   241

EPILOGUE   263
INDEX   271

Power is poison. Its effect on Presidents (Prime Ministers, Secretaries of State, Generals) had always been tragic, chiefly as an almost insane excitement at first, and a worse reaction afterwards; but also because no mind is so well balanced as to bear the strain of seizing unlimited force without habit or knowledge of it; and finding it disputed by hungry packs of wolves and hounds whose lives depend on snatching the carrion.

The Education of Henry Adams

Prologue

I was seventeen when I first discovered the power of the printed word. A barnstorming pilot in a World War I flying Jenny had put down in 1920 at the Clinton County Fair in De Witt, Iowa. He was taking up the adventurous for five dollars a ride. My father was campaigning for county attorney with the crowds at the fair. Carrying a bundle of handbills proclaiming William H. Childs for County Attorney, I paid my five dollars and boarded the plane. As we circled over the fairgrounds, I scattered the handbills out of the open cockpit. My father and mother were astonished as the leaflets came fluttering down. Dad won the election. I was sure it was that snowstorm of handbills, which made news in the local newspapers, that had turned the tide.

In the intervening years I have had a close look at that power as it operates in politics at every level. The press plays a part in the brokerage of power. The role of Thomas Jefferson's Fourth Estate is unique. In no other Western nation do reporters and commentators exert such an influence. Theoretically they are in the bleachers keeping an objective eye on the field, but, impelled by a sense of righteousness or merely by the love of the game, they become participants. The consequences astonish the foreign observer when he first encounters that brokerage of power.

I would estimate that James Reston of the *New York*

Times is the equivalent of, say, three United States
Senators — and not those passive entries from the wide-
open spaces but big city Senators with visible force.
Joseph Alsop could be equated with a Deputy Secretary
of Defense; he filled his column with dire warnings of
America's military weakness as though he were a Pentagon panjandrum before a Congressional committee.
Leaking to Jack Anderson is like treating with a foreign
power; as an apostle of all that is holy and virtuous he
assumes at times the position of a sovereign state. Dan
Rather, at the height of his role as Nixon devourer, was
Mr. District Attorney. James Jackson Kilpatrick herds
the conservatives in the direction he wants them to go.
Walter Lippmann presided through the years as a supreme pontiff, revered by many, and resented by others,
for his magisterial style.

In the early thirties I was writing for the feature
section of the St. Louis *Post-Dispatch*. The derisory
term for my writings was cornfield murders. I encountered a great deal of human nature I would not otherwise have known. I recall a baby born in Tennessee
with a tail, thereby suggesting something, whether up
or down, about William Jennings Bryan, the theory of
evolution and the "Monkey Trial." The parents of this
phenomenon were understandably reluctant to discuss
it since they had already moved to have the tail, if indeed
it was that, removed by surgery. But, chiefly, I had a
strong interest in politics and occasionally got into
political reporting by the back door. In Louisiana, the
Kingfish, Huey Long, had already begun his reign as
Governor. I managed to insinuate myself into his bed-
room in the new executive mansion in Baton Rouge,
where he was holding court as a monarch in the corn-
pone style. He was lying on the bed informally dressed,
and that is an understatement; a half dozen henchmen
were paying court. Seated beside him in an armchair
was the charming young woman, Alice Grosjean, whom
he had promoted to Secretary of State. The subject under
discussion was the formal ball which that evening would

inaugurate the mansion. Miss Grosjean wanted him to invite a friend from New Orleans and the Governor, in a somewhat surly mood, was having none of it. With a diplomatic skill that showed her obvious qualification to be Secretary of State, Miss Grosjean persisted and, in the end, the Kingfish yielded as gracelessly as possible. I suspected that the young man was already downstairs, confident of the verdict.

Although I was never given the royal treatment, one or two favored reporters from up North would sit drinking with the governor until he was seized with a desire to go to New Orleans. Summoning the Chief of the State Police on the phone, he would roar, "Clear the tracks." This order meant that traffic was to be kept off the eighty-mile-long route as the governor's car, speeding at eighty-five to ninety miles an hour, bore down on the city where he had demolished the rule of the Bourbons who had so long presided over red-clay and hookworm poverty. For all his clownishness, I came to feel that of the demagogues, North and South, in the Depression years, he had the best chance to overthrow the Establishment. Moving into Arkansas, he put over against the Old Guard mousy little Mrs. Hattie Carraway as United States Senator, and that was only the beginning. Then came his assassination in the flamboyant state capitol he had built as a monument to his greatness.

During a leave of absence from the *Post-Dispatch* I had made two trips to Sweden, and the book I was ultimately to write, *Sweden: The Middle Way*, had begun to take shape. Swedish welfare, the cooperatives, the system of collective bargaining with compulsory arbitration as a last resort, the high level of education and civic responsibility all seemed to me to add up to a way of life that was an alternative to fascism or communism. As the Depression deepened throughout the world the choice increasingly was assumed to be between the extremes of the totalitarian Left and the totalitarian Right. This was a naive view, at least as far as the United States was concerned; yet, at the time, with totalitarianism spreading like a plague, people in the West struggled to believe there was a humane and decent way out. The response to my Sweden book attested to this wistful hope.

When I returned to the feature section of the paper and the cornfield murders, I discovered I wanted something else. A Rabelaisian character named Harry Niemeyer, theater and motion picture critic, was about to retire. When Ibsen and Shakespeare came to St. Louis the task of reviewing the productions had been delegated to me and, as a consequence, Niemeyer suggested I apply for his job. It was a way out.

O. K. Bovard, the managing editor, was a great editor who knew what he wanted in the paper and how to get it—in my view the primary requirement. Without benefit of privacy he sat in the city room, surveying the scene with an unfailing eye for the bustle around him and the proofs that flowed across his big desk. He was regarded with awe if not fear. Having fired an incompetent reporter (the Guild was still to come), he listened to the man's plea that after all he did have to eat. Bovard's answer was, "Not necessarily."

I approached Bovard with trepidation. I understood there was to be a vacancy and I hoped to be considered. He looked at me with shock and dismay. "But Childs," he said, "you don't want to write about the movies!" He told me he had something else in mind.

Three weeks later I was on my way to Washington as the third man in the small bureau the *Post-Dispatch* then maintained. I could hardly have been happier. It was what I had scarcely dared to hope for: Washington in 1934 in the flood tide of the New Deal each day presented some extraordinary happening. I plunged in with the eagerness of the innocent I was. Whether in the lobby just off the floor of the Senate, at one of the many press conferences held by Cabinet officers and ambitious politicos, or in the sanctum of one official or another, the atmosphere was incandescent. The administration was so open that when the weekly Cabinet meeting broke up Cabinet members could not wait to disclose to favored reporters waiting in the West Wing reception room their own version of what had transpired. The mysterious center was Franklin Roosevelt; mysterious because, although he saw many men and women of one kind or another, he responded to each with words that seemed to suit the hopes and fears of that individual. Each would leave the Oval Office believing the great man had been won over to his cause.

I was very soon at ease in this atmosphere, surprised to discover how readily those who had been merely headline names became, if not friends, useful acquaintances. The embassy party, however minor the embassy, the late afternoon drink with the Senator, the whispered exchange at the crowded reception—this was the setting for the game, and the temptation to be a player, not just an observer, was irresistible. It went against objectivity, or the *myth* of objectivity. I saw it happen so often in my colleagues' and in my own relationships with the men of power. How does the Fourth Estate rank with the other three? It is impossible to say since the record is unwritten and it is likely that it will never be set down in its entirety. But here is one small piece of that record: how the game went, who the players were, and who the score keepers. As it soon became clear to me, we all joined in that game to one degree or another. We were players without numbers on our jerseys, arrogating to ourselves a power never contemplated by the men who framed the First Amendment to the Constitution. In the turbulent seventies this fact was to come into an ever sharper focus. The Fourth Estate sought to compensate for the sins of the executive. It was a stirring adventure. Whether this hot pursuit on the field of glory will be welcomed by a grateful public it is too soon to say, but for the players, drawn in increasing numbers, the game itself has been the reward.

That Man Roosevelt

The press conference was over. It was in that comfortable time when seventy or so reporters could crowd around the President's desk in the Oval Office to hear and be heard. I had been told to stay behind with the promise of a private talk. Steve Early, Roosevelt's press secretary, was taking a last phone call. I stood in the doorway until he came forward to lead me through the inner corridor to the President's office. Just before we went in he turned to say, "You know he'll probably go after you about that article you wrote about Willkie in *Look*. He's got a memory like an elephant." I had only a vague recollection that I had expressed Wendell Willkie's resentment of Roosevelt's public condescension.

Then as Early ushered me in, pausing only briefly before departing, I sat down beside the President's desk for what was to be the last private talk I had with him. Here was the commander-in-chief of the greatest force ever fielded by any nation. At the center of the

storm he was comfortable, easy, in a soft, grey flannel
suit that looked a bit the worse for wear. It was April 7,
1944, shortly before he began to reveal his gradually
unfolding intention to seek a fourth term. Even in this
brief interval, he was Merlin the Magician. The absolute
quiet of his office was the most conspicuous quality of
that innermost center of control; it was so quiet I could
hear the ticking of the electric clock in the clutter of
memorabilia on his desk.

"Will you have a cig [his expression]?"

Holding out the opened silver case he took a cigarette himself, inserted it in a long, discolored ivory
holder, and I lighted it for him. There were lines of
fatigue and perhaps strain around his eyes, but he
looked hardly older than when I had first begun to ob-
serve him. A well-preserved artifact of a nearly vanished
era, he was a composite of his past: the rather priggish,
stiff-necked young man who would always remember
that he had never made Porcellian at Harvard; the devoted son of Hudson River Bracketed, the mother's
boy; the vestryman at St. Thomas's church; the phi-
landerer; the heroic invalid; the statesman.

What he wanted to convey in a friendly column that
I would write—no direct quotations—was his desire
to put down power, and the many things he wanted to
do if only he could be free. This may well have been
true at that very time when he was also thinking of a
fourth term, responding to a nation convinced that he
must be kept at the helm so long as the war went on. I
could admire the subtlety of his performance, repeated
as it must have been for visitor after visitor in the weeks
before the inevitable declaration of his decision. Just
beyond the window I saw his scotty, Fala, lying quietly
outside his doghouse.

I told him I had been around the country and I
found people wondering why he hadn't gone on the air
to discuss the hopes for peace, the shape of the world
after the war. They were puzzled by what had seemed a
long silence. "It works both ways," the President said.

"Some people would have me go on the air at least once every two weeks, while another set of people work just as hard to keep me off the air altogether. I think I will make a radio talk in which I will say that my one real desire is to go back to Hyde Park. We can look at this in a detached way. We can know what history will say fifty years from now. On the other hand I wonder if we can afford to take that point of view at this time."

Although he did not put it in so many words, his sense of responsibility for the record history would write ran through much of what he said. It tempered the detached attitude, which seemed to be deliberately assumed. He talked about what he could and could not tell the public.

"Now you take Poland, for example. What if I had said a year ago that the boundary should be here," he marked with his forefinger on the brown desk pad before him, "or here?" marking again. "The Russians are in Poland today. They might not agree to that. Then what could I do? We are not going to fight Russia over the boundary of Poland. I told Stalin that at Teheran. I said, 'We're not going to war with you over Poland.'" The President tipped back his head in laughter at this.

"Or take France. What can be said about France? People come out of there and tell me that all of France feels this way or all of France feels that way. How do they know? I don't think that anyone going into France today could tell. You take Pete Brandt's question at the press conference today." (Raymond P. Brandt, chief Washington correspondent of the St. Louis *Post-Dispatch*, had put a question about General de Gaulle and American support for the Free French once France was liberated.) "I can't give a final answer. No one knows.

"I remember in 1918 I was in the Château-Thierry sector, up where the Germans had been pushed out and the country had been reoccupied. There was one particular man—his name eludes me—who had done a magnificent job. He had resisted the Germans from the very beginning, and effectively. Now what if someone had

come in there and had said, 'No, we are going to over-
look this man and select, for political reasons, old
M. Labouis to be mayor or take over the administration'?
How do you think the other man would have felt? Or
take the Balkans and Greece. We can't go ahead and talk
about what will be done there. We might arouse their
hopes far beyond anything that can possibly be fulfilled.
That would be a mistake."

Almost exactly a year from that day the President
would be dead. But he spoke then as though he would be
directing destiny into an indefinite future, helping to
put together a stricken world once victory had been
won. It was as though by decree he could abolish mor-
tality. That is one of the consequences of the exercise
of power: the tragic illusion of those who are so addicted
they cannot give up the drug. I have observed in other
men in other countries the assumption that if only time
can be held off and the great leader spared all will be
well. With FDR this was particularly true when he
began to talk about the Far East.

"We have to be extremely careful there. The white
man is more and more in disfavor. His position is becoming increasingly difficult. I know that Churchill is very
concerned about Burma and what is going to happen
there. We are going to have to take some positive steps
or find ourselves pushed out completely.

"Some time ago I worked out a form of trusteeship
for French Indochina. You know that colony was governed very badly. For every dollar the French put
in they took ten dollars out. Those little people had a
culture of their own . . . Cambodia . . . their kings. But
they were badly treated.

"Now my idea is for a trusteeship to administer
Indochina. I put this up to old Chiang—of course he
isn't really old but he looks old; he isn't as old as I am,
as a matter of fact—and he was strong for it. The idea is
to have one Chinese trustee, one Philippine trustee,
one French trustee, one British and perhaps one American. It would work out just as it does with a woman
whose husband has died and left some property, let's

say. She knows nothing about money. Perhaps she hasn't ever signed a check—there are women like that, you know. So, her property is put under a trustee for her to use. That's exactly what we'd do with Indochina. At Teheran I asked Stalin about it. I said, 'Mr. Marshal, what would you think of such a trusteeship?' Well, he thought it was excellent. So then I asked Churchill what he thought. He didn't like it. I said 'I suppose you have Burma in mind.' He said, 'Yes, yes, thinking of Burma.' I said to him that after all there were three votes against one and he had better look out. He didn't like that at all."

And he had not forgotten Wendell Willkie and my article. It was not like that, he said. He had not meant ridicule, he had not mocked Wendell's pronunciation of reservoir. On the contrary he had great respect for his friend Wendell. In attempting a comeback Willkie had been badly defeated in the Republican primary in Wisconsin. With his sly half-smile Roosevelt said, "I thought of sending him a wire, 'If you don't succeed, try, try again.' "

The pixie persisted despite the trauma of eleven years in power; the sheer force of his personality, the wiles and stratagems. It seemed only natural, inevitable, that he should preside over the peace. He developed for me the way he had simplified his life, hoarding and replenishing his energy, so that now he took things much easier. His personal chief of staff, Admiral Leahy, came in every morning before the President was out of bed to give him the overnight news from every front. Then, on the way to his office he stopped in his map room, and it was a much better map room than Churchill's, even though Churchill had begun his much earlier. He spent at least two hours a day in the map room where the bright young men, army and navy, kept moving the illuminated battle lines of the fronts. It was of a piece with Roosevelt's own past, his love of the navy, his service as Assistant Secretary under Josephus Daniels, his love of the sea and ships.

There had been about him always an ambience of

calm, even bland and irritating assurance. The quality
was not arrogance because he wore it with such non-
chalance. For his political enemies it was singularly
frustrating. Hostile cartoonists showed him as King
Franklin I at the center of his court—and what a court
it was, that oddly assorted company he brought to Washington! It was a family, too, an intimate neighborhood,
and he was the squire in the house at the top of the hill
who knew by birth and breeding his role as pater-
familias. Although unemployment stayed at an appalling level, the atmosphere in Washington was almost
buoyant. Anything could happen in that curiously assorted group, which made it fascinating and entertaining to a young reporter. A kind of happy innocence
summed it up, an innocence that persisted against all
odds in believing, as Rexford Tugwell had put it, that
America could be made over by bold young men and
women rolling up their sleeves and getting down to the
job.

The President's Secretary of the Treasury—they
were all the President's friends and fiefs—was Henry
Morgenthau, a Hyde Park neighbor, whom the President called Henny Penny. His wife, Ellie, was an intimate friend of Eleanor Roosevelt. A cautious man who
looked out from behind his pince-nez as though they
were a protective device, Henny Penny had in 1937
come out for budget balancing and a curb on deficit
spending. The resulting downdraft, for the time being
at least, put an end to progress. John Maynard Keynes,
visiting Washington at about this time, took a certain
sardonic amusement in what he considered the naive
belief of the President that he was practicing Keynesian
economics. Whether it was $3 billion or $4 billion a
year, pump priming, as it was called, fell far short of
what was required for recovery. Others knew this, too;
among them was Sen. Robert M. La Follette, Jr., a keen
counselor and critic fully aware that little had been
done to restore the economy to health.

Nowhere was FDR's ambivalence more evident. In
his first campaign he had advocated a balanced budget

and an end to reckless government spending; now he was acutely sensitive to the charge that he was a squanderer responsible for a disastrous national debt. The Hyde Park squire, earnestly wanting the family at the bottom of the lane to prosper, was pressed hard at one press conference after another to give an official estimate of the number of jobless; he responded with a rather lengthy discourse on the difficulty of telling just who was unemployed. Here was a family in which the father, to be sure, was not employed, but the mother took in sewing and the daughter gave piano lessons. They lived fairly well. Was this unemployment? One really could not say.

Miss Frances Perkins was the Secretary of Labor. Her cultivated speech matching that of the President, she had come out of an upper-class background to go the social service route. Child labor, the sweatshop, the Triangle shirtwaist fire: these were evils to be eradicated. She presided in her own fashion over the painful transition from craft to industrial unionism. With courage and intellect and a deep religious conviction—she attended Anglo-Catholic mass almost every day of the week—she stood up to the huffing and puffing of John L. Lewis, that old Shakespearean lion. In all my encounters with her, in her official life and on rare social occasions, her style never varied: the tricorn hat, her trademark; the careful, beautifully articulated speech that so irritated tough union bosses; the intellectual precision brought to bear on deeply emotional issues. With an invalid husband living in New York, she commuted weekends, but she never, as far as I can recall, spoke of her personal life. Her concession to the frailties of humankind was a dry, yet tolerant laugh. She had, I felt, come to terms with the human condition; she had achieved a detachment that stood her in good stead in the turbulence of her office. She was a close friend of Eleanor Roosevelt, sharing as her time permitted in the good works and the high jinks that were Eleanor's life, but always, I felt, with a certain reservation.

James A. Farley was the squire's political lieutenant. Postmaster General and Democratic national chairman, he knew his trade as few before or since. In his map room, the congressional districts from Maine to California were starred with the names of bosses and their henchmen. Traveling tirelessly around the country, chewing gum his only indulgence, he would return to Washington to give the President an acute, realistic analysis of just how things stood at the ward and precinct level. Far from an amateur, FDR knew that map quite well himself. His fireside chats were tuned to those feelings with a mastery so subtle it was almost imperceptible. He might have been talking to two or three people in a living room rather than to the millions who heard him on the radio. Until FDR and Farley broke in 1940 over the third term and Farley's own ambitions, they had a partnership designed in some political heaven, surviving even the slight condescension the Roosevelts felt toward Farley and could never quite conceal.

Harold Ickes, the Secretary of Interior out of Chicago, chosen to his own surprise because of his new-Republican, Bull Moose background, deserved the title of Old Curmudgeon he had given himself. He was constantly and jealously fighting to enlarge the empire of Interior and to keep all intruders off his domain. Roosevelt once remarked that Ickes required more coddling, more nursing, more attention than any other member of the family, and he got it. Scowling at all comers, he fought to take the Forest Service away from Agriculture, and Henry Wallace at Agriculture fought back in his own way. It was disorderly, lively, an often comic scene.

But Ickes' principal enemy was Harry Hopkins, the Marat of the innocent revolution, suspected by the rich of plotting to set up a guillotine on the White House lawn. As head of the Works Progress Administration, Hopkins caught the abuse for the leaf raking, the boondoggles, as he tried to find work for the millions of jobless. Ickes, who suspected him of encroaching on his own Public Works territory, was not above secretly joining his enemies. Hopkins was perfectly typecast. Gaunt, almost emaciated, a chain-smoker, he gave press conferences that were a form of bear baiting. Snarling at hostile questioners, he gave back as good as he got. His untidy office, with no pretensions to swank, was in a rundown building two blocks from the White House. He enlisted under his banner some of the most creative people in the arts, theater, and literature. In the WPA theater project Orson Welles was only one of many who brought new and vigorous life to Broadway. Painters who had suffered severe hardship in the Depression were given commissions to do murals in government buildings in Washington and in post offices around the country. Guidebooks covering every region, prepared by talented writers, were a notable contribution to understanding of American life. Hopkins believed in these people and they believed in him even though their political and artistic zeal now and then caused him trouble with conservatives in Congress. When I caught him off guard I never failed to elicit sulphurous invective aimed at the smug and the rich who said the poor didn't want to work and cared only for a handout. In his own person he was no Marat; he came to enjoy the company of those same rich at the races or at chic restaurants in New York.

Whether it was a deliberate stratagem or simply a reflection of his relaxed, almost carefree approach to administration, the President was quite content to let Ickes and Hopkins skirmish on the recovery front.

A similar overlapping of authority could be found in the area of foreign policy; the rivalry and infighting was more intense and, in the end, brought tragedy. Cordell Hull, the Secretary of State, had, as a legacy of his years in the House, a hold on Congress that FDR found useful. But his limitations, his fixation on a few narrow issues, such as tariffs and trade negotiation were severe handicaps that became more and more apparent as Nazi Germany rearmed and Hitler reoccupied the Rhineland. The Under-Secretary of State,

Sumner Welles, could not have been more different. A graduate of FDR's own alma maters, Groton and Harvard, Welles had a far-reaching grasp of world trends. When I went to have a background talk with him in his office in the State, War and Navy Building across from the White House (housing, incredible as it seems in today's sprawling bureaucracy, the three departments with room left over for General Pershing's ceremonial quarters), I learned a lesson in diplomacy delivered in concise, elegant fashion. Welles' office was one floor below that of Hull but communication between the two men had all but ceased. Hull's partisans were only too happy, in a fine old Washington tradition, to aggravate the feud. Once or twice I tried to sound out Welles on his feelings about the Secretary of State. Each time he was politely unresponsive.

The building itself—outsize beaux arts, handsome in its very ugliness, with the wide corridors, the high ceilings, the air in summers of that pre-air-conditioned era stirred by the whirring of ceiling fans—seemed an ideal setting for the proper men of State. Welles' secretary had the same, elegant quality. When she showed me into his private office I had the impression that I was being properly ushered into a presence. Welles was extremely helpful to Roosevelt, but it was all bootlegged on a sort of "Don't tell Cordell" basis.

Welles had an enemy who, as it turned out, was also FDR's enemy: William Christian Bullitt, an Iago of Iagos. Bullitt was FDR's first ambassador when relations with the Soviet Union were renewed; he quickly became disillusioned with communism and concluded that he deserved a far more important office. Even France did not satisfy him. At about this time Welles fell from grace, and his careful, reserved surface cracked. According to a story that went around Washington, he was drunk on the funeral train *en route* to Alabama to inter Speaker William B. Bankhead, and, the story continued, he had made an improper proposal to a Pullman porter. Through an executive of the railroad, Bullitt

managed to get an affidavit from the porter and circulated
it wherever he could find anyone who would listen.
Frustrated in his ambition, Bullitt as Iago had brought
Welles down. Hull's partisans were not unhappy. For
a while Welles maintained his usual facade as though
nothing had occurred, but finally he resigned, his use-
fulness destroyed. It must have been a considerable loss
to the President. FDR's final comment on the matter
to Steve Early, as Early relayed it to me, was, "Poor
Sumner may have been poisoned but he was not, like
Bill, a poisoner." After his retirement, Welles lived as
something of a recluse on his very rich wife's handsome estate across the Potomac in Oxon Hill, Maryland.
He nearly lost his life when he walked out in the middle
of a bitterly cold night and failed to find his way back
to the house. There were few men in or outside the
government with as clear a perspective as Welles had
on foreign policy, and the loss was not only to an administration but to the nation.

The most incongruous figure on the Rooseveltian
scene was the Vice President, John Nance Garner, who
had been picked at the Chicago convention in 1932
when it appeared that Roosevelt might be stopped and
that the Garner delegates, largely under the control of
William Randolph Hearst, could put over the nomination. A Texan of the simpler days before big oil and big
money, Garner concealed with rusticity the political
shrewdness that had brought him far in the House of
Representatives. He had fostered the recovery measures that called for spending what then seemed large
sums of money, thereby incurring the wrath of President
Hoover. With a ruddy complexion and a thatch of silvery
hair, Garner resembled a genial St. Nick. Having nothing
else to do as Vice President, he welcomed visitors. Henry
Hyde, a veteran Capitol correspondent for the Baltimore *Sun*, first introduced me to Garner, and the two of
us developed a pleasant ritual: At about ten or ten-
thirty we would go into his office just off the Senate
floor. After brief preliminaries he would say, "Well,

time to strike a blow for liberty." He would go to a
medicine chest over the washstand—this was before the
imperial splendor in the suites of the reigning dukes
at the Capitol—take out a bottle of Bourbon, and pour
three stiff drinks. We would chat a bit and he would
occasionally talk about "the boss," his name for FDR.
There was usually time for a second blow for liberty.
A tumbler of whiskey in mid-morning was hardly preparation for alert coverage of the Senate. Garner was
said to drink a bottle of Bourbon a day. Around five-
thirty or six he would climb, slightly mulled, into his
limousine and go downtown to the Washington Hotel,
where he and Mrs. Garner lived. That forceful lady was
said to take charge when the Vice President had ex-
ceeded the day's quota. If it was winter and time for
the routine of formal White House and cabinet dinners
he would climb reluctantly into his tailcoat and white
tie. He viewed the boss and the White House whirlwind
with a skeptical yet amiable eye. But he seemed to
have little contact with it all. Breaking with FDR over
the third term, Garner returned to his pecan groves in
Uvalde, Texas. Now and then a reporter went to see
him, and he wisely refrained from passing any heroic
judgments on a troubled world. He lived for nearly
forty years after he left Washington, proof that alcohol,
if used in proper amounts, can be a beneficent drug.

Cohen and Corcoran were FDR's operatives on the
legislative and political front. Ben Cohen was one of
the wisest and gentlest of men. In later years he served
other administrations in the foreign policy field, always
with modesty. Tommy, as he was known to practically
everyone in government, or Tommy the Cork, as FDR
liked to call him, was outwardly an ebullient Irishman
who played the accordion and sang, often his own satir-
ical songs. At court he was jester with a shrewd knowledge of how to get things done on the Hill and where
the bodies were buried. Beneath the surface he was
more ambitious and more ambivalent than his casual
laughter revealed. I found him miserly with information

as though it were pure gold, which indeed it was for his later schemes. As the New Deal began to run down with the coming of war, Tommy left the President and began a law practice in Washington. He amassed a sizable fortune with help from his political connections; that clutch of personal power substituted for intrigue in the public weal at the highest level. During his tenure in power he had made notable contributions to the New Deal, drafting the Securities Exchange Act, the Public Utilities Holding Company act as well as other legislation and lobbying tirelessly for his boss in the White House.

Like a woman possessed, as indeed she was, Eleanor Roosevelt was everywhere. Resentful of anyone who came too close to her husband, she directed her animus at Corcoran and later at Hopkins. She had been a plain young woman rescued by Franklin the white knight, and when everything she valued crashed around her head she set out to remake her life. Washington then was a small, self-contained city with the houses of the rich clustered on a few streets and circles, and the rest of the city *terra incognita.* One of the survivors of this cozy, long-gone era was Leila Pinchot, widow of the great conservationist, Gifford. An eccentric, who kept her flaming red hair well into her eighties, she continued to live in the great house just off Scott Circle even when it was in such disrepair that squirrels had invaded the long second-floor drawing room. It was Leila Pinchot who told me about the summer of 1916.

The Roosevelt children, their nurse and the servants were at Campobello. Eleanor and Franklin, then the handsome Assistant Secretary of Navy, had gone to the Chevy Chase Club for a dance. Franklin danced a great deal with Eleanor's attractive social secretary, Lucy Mercer. Before the evening was half over Eleanor said she had a headache and would go home. Typically, she had forgotten her keys and there was no one in the house. Hours later Franklin found her sitting on the front stoop. He told her he wanted a divorce so that he could marry Lucy. She pleaded the case of their five young children. Couldn't he wait for a year? If he still wanted a divorce at the end of that year, she would agree. A series of events swiftly altered their lives. The United States entered the war in April 1917. Roosevelt carried much of the burden in the department as the venerable Secretary, Josephus Daniels, was content to see him do. Eleanor was knitting, rolling bandages and doing canteen work for the Red Cross. After the war Roosevelt rose in Democratic politics in New York and was nominated as Vice-Presidential running mate for James Cox in the 1920 election. It was a hopeless campaign from the start, but as Roosevelt trooped across the country he made friends with important Democrats who were to stand by and serve him well in later years. The notebooks of the disciples who traveled with him began to fill with names, affiliations, anecdotes.

At Campobello, tempted by the frigid water at the end of a hot day, he came down with a crippling illness diagnosed as infantile paralysis. But with this adversity Eleanor came into her own. She used all her resources to help him physically and to rally his spirit. Gradually, as he came to accept the bitter condition of his infirmity, with only a dim hope of walking again, she became his legs, his ears, his eyes. She overcame the class prejudices of her sheltered upbringing and developed a natural instinct for politics.

My own feeling was that he underrated her. Once, after I had started writing the column an appalling five or even six times a week, he said to me, "You know, you write too much." Yes, five or six times a week was too much, I admitted but added that his wife wrote that often. His response: "Oh, the missus just writes a kind of diary." A kind of diary it might have been, but she managed her personal and public life with great skill and now and then sly humor. She once reported that, during the visit of King George VI and his queen to Hyde Park, her mother-in-law's butler had dropped a heavily laden tea tray in the presence of the royal couple.

One great burden for Eleanor Roosevelt was the

possessive mother-in-law who held the purse strings. On a trans-Atlantic crossing I found it fascinating to hear Sara Delano Roosevelt talk about "my son, Franklin," as though he were still the young man on whom she must keep a watchful eye. To gain independence and to raise funds for her causes, Eleanor took on radio broadcasting with a commercial sponsor, provoking savage criticism from the Roosevelt enemies. She moved with outward serenity through tireless days of lectures, broadcasting, inspirational trips to "work projects" in trouble and back to the White House to report to Franklin on what she had seen and heard. Ruthless when someone stood in her way, she needed friends who needed her. I found her remote but polite, perhaps because I had no need of anything she might have to offer, and because I was an ally of Hopkins.

As the President prepared to go to Philadelphia to accept the renomination of his party, a ceremony as predestined as the coronation of a pope already chosen by the College of Cardinals, the number of unemployed was still between 10 and 12 million; no exact figure was available. Industrial plants and men were idle. But bread lines and the apple sellers had vanished from the streets. The unemployed might be raking leaves and work project income might be low, but they had respectability and, even more important, they had hope. All of us bandy around the world leadership too freely. Roosevelt was the apotheosis of that abused word. Out of his complex personality, the conquest of his infirmity, the absolute assurance of his own identity and his role in life, he spoke to the great mass of Americans and they heard and understood.

Philadelphia, the scene of the 1936 Democratic convention, was the field of Agincourt on which the princes of the realm gathered to pledge their fealty before going out to do battle for their king. The power brokers were gathered from around the country: Edward J. Kelly of Chicago, Frank Hague of Jersey City, Tom Pendergast of Missouri, Ed Flynn of the Bronx—power brokers who had benefited hugely from the New Deal. (The smell of graft was now and then discernible. In the course of a long interviewing session at his winter residence in Miami Hague let drop: "Why there's fifty thousand a year in honest graft in that job.") They held open house in their lavish hotel suites and waited for the moment when they and their henchmen could roar obeisance.

That June night at Franklin Field was memorable not so much for what FDR said—we shall go on to win not just an election but a victory over poverty and greed—as for the occasion itself: the outpouring of mass support with radio carrying his words across the nation. It had begun badly. Waiting backstage for the cue to go on, the President had fallen flat on his face. There was always a danger of that since when he stood, with his braces locked, he always needed support. The reading text of the speech he had been holding went flying. Deeply concerned that he might have been injured, his son James, Garner and others picked him up, dusted him off, and retrieved the speech. He went on before the vast crowd as though nothing had happened. A prolonged shout went up. Anxious as always to conserve the radio time, he brought silence and began to read the text with the skill that made it sound almost like an ad lib.

Roosevelt crisscrossed the country by train in the campaign that followed, sounding to me like a bishop visiting the people of his diocese. He spoke of issues almost tangentially. How much better off we were than we had been four years before, he insisted. The pronouns were almost always we, us, you and I . . . This was a part of his legerdemain—the smiling, kindly bishop sharing the blessings of his gentle rule. At each stop local references to recovery projects were carefully spliced into his text. Eleanor's appearance beside him on the back platform always drew cheers. Rarely did he speak of the opposition, but when he did it was in condescending terms, as though it were a negligible matter that should be treated lightly.

His Republican opponent, Alf Landon, the Governor of Kansas, was an able and an honorable man who suffered under several handicaps, not the least of which was his total unfamiliarity with big-time politics. Among his principal advisers were the newspaper publishers who had helped to build up his candidacy. Publishers are notoriously bad mentors. These moguls of the press would get on and off the Landon train, there would be conferences in the rear car, and the campaign would continue downward. The chief mogul was Roy Roberts, publisher and editor and one of the major owners of the Kansas City *Star*. He was a grossly fat, genial man, with a homespun manner almost too good to be true, who behaved at times as though he had invented Landon and intended to maintain his proprietary rights.

I went with Landon on a swing into New England. An important address had been planned for Portland, Maine. The setting was a large park with the speaker's stand a considerable distance from the bleachers where the crowd assembled. As the candidate began to speak a fog rolled in from the sea. For much of the audience he might have been speaking from the moon. Photographers wanting to get better closeups climbed a rather rickety structure over his head while he started to read his text. "Get down, get down from there, I tell you," Landon said in what was meant to be a stage whisper, but his words were broadcast on the national radio network and startled his listeners. It was a bad omen. Still in effect at that time was the Maine law setting the presidential election two months ahead of the date for the rest of the nation. And Landon carried Maine. It gave the campaign a much needed but deceptive boost. "As Maine goes so goes the nation" became a new political battle cry.

The men running Landon's operation struggled to keep the stuffier and more plush benefactors from attaching themselves to the campaign. During a campaign trip in upstate New York, Paul Block, Sr., an imperious publisher, gave orders that his private railway car be coupled to the Landon train. Word of this reached the candidate's entourage as the car was about to be shunted into place. How would that look: a private railway car, the symbol of the very rich, hooked on just behind the candidate's car? Standing foursquare in the marshaling yard, a loyal Landon manager defied the switching crew to run him down. It was a comic scene that we of the press appreciated.

As for Roosevelt, one after the other the princes of the realm vied to show the visiting monarch the splendor of their homage. He rode into Jersey City with Mayor Frank Hague at his side as bombs went off in the air and sirens and whistles shrieked. A holiday had been declared and thousands of school children lined the way, waving flags and cheering. Hague waved back, smiling like a jack-o'-lantern, next to the President in the open car. New Jersey would go Democratic in November. Hague could give him that assurance without fear of contradiction.

It was Ed Kelly of Chicago who, in mid-October, put on the greatest spectacle of all. I never expect to see anything like it again. Before the President's departure from his hotel for the Chicago Stadium, a long parade had snaked through the streets where he would pass. Marching bands of every kind—fife and drum, country music, piano accordions—dressed in every kind of ethnic costume, were joined by celebrants of the New Deal and FDR in the long procession that drew half the city into the streets. By the time the President's open car turned off Michigan Avenue onto West Madison Street, only a narrow passage had been left between the solid crowds. A continuous roar could be heard as the President passed by. People leaned from tenement windows; banners and posters were raised high, children were held on their father's shoulders to see the man pass; and in the half light of an exceptionally warm evening, a rain of torn papers fell on the streets. Photographers clinging to the cars in the rear advertised the presence of the press. The tone of the crowd changed immediately.

"Where's the Chicago *Tribune?*" "The hell with the *Tribune.*" Sticks to which posters had been fastened slapped at the cars. The hostility toward the invincible Republican *Tribune* was fueled by the charge of a doctored picture of a beggar picking up discarded Roosevelt buttons.

Chicago Stadium looked like a massive fort under siege. An estimated 100,000 people were gathered outside. Calcium flares lighting the night gave it the look of a lurid, unnatural day. Giant bombs went off overhead. Police and Secret Service men locked arms and formed a double line to open a path into the stadium for the President. I felt for the first time fear of the mass. We in the press corps were nearly crushed between a phalanx of police and the surging crowd. We were barely inside when the doors slammed shut.

I had often seen the President as master of crowds. From the rear platform of his campaign train, looking out over a crowd of 15–20,000 stretching into the distance, he could hold it in silence broken by cheers and applause only when, at an appropriate pause, he invited such an interruption. Chicago was the only time I saw FDR temporarily awed. The capacity of the stadium was 20,000; at least 5,000 more had squeezed in. The roar as he approached the speaker's stand was overpowering. Although Mayor Kelly had pleaded for quiet in deference to radio time, it was several minutes before the President could make himself heard. Looking stunned at the outset, he finally came through. Under powerful lights sweat poured down his face in the jungle heat of the packed hall.

He talked about the necessity for free enterprise. This was in response to the charge being circulated by the Republicans that he was against all business. He was for individualism in the arts, in business, in every field. Only monopoly was bad. Half of the industrial wealth of the country had come under the control of fewer than 200 huge corporations. But what he said made little difference; they had come to roar, and roar they did. Many of the more ardent of his followers are reported to have climaxed the evening by relieving themselves on the *Tribune's* gothic tower on Michigan Avenue. As for the President, he went directly from the stadium to his private railway car which would take him to Michigan, the next stop on this extraordinary road show.

We of the press following him across the country wrote the familiar burble. Doubtful states? Could he carry Michigan? After all, Michigan was normally Republican. And the crowds? They meant nothing. People would go out (this in the pretelevision era) to look at a dead whale on a flatcar. The Republicans were sustained by the *Literary Digest* telephone poll showing that Landon would win by a comfortable majority. Some of us left the train—it may have been after Michigan—to join Big Jim Farley *en route* to Washington. How would it come out? He'll carry every state but Maine and Vermont, was his reply. Of course, we didn't believe him. He then expounded Farley's Law: Nothing that happens in the last two weeks of a campaign can affect the outcome.

The grand finale was in New York's Madison Square Garden just as the campaign ended. Although the 20,000 who packed the Garden were more restrained than the crowd in Chicago, they were nonetheless determined to give their all. The trade unions were concentrated in New York. The International Ladies Garment Workers, the Amalgamated Clothing Workers, the Hillmans, the Dubinskys, the highly sensitive Jewish vote, the intellectuals in the publishing and writing fields, the borough bosses—here was the amalgam generated by the New Deal. Differing in kind from Chicago and Jersey City and Detroit, it was nevertheless the same variegated pattern, the same weaving together of the separate strands. FDR was never more confident, more buoyant.

"I should like to have it said of my first administration that in it the forces of selfishness and lust for power met their match. I should like to have it said of my second administration that in it these forces met their master."

An article I had written entitled, "They Hate Roosevelt," had appeared in *Harper's* magazine in the summer. It was based on a fortunately brief weekend my wife and I had spent with rich cousins in Connecticut. The head of the household, through his brokerage firm, was a beneficiary of the New Deal, yet the hate they spilled out was venomous. Reprinted in a pamphlet, the article was circulated in hundreds of thousands of copies. I thought I heard an echo of it when FDR rolled out this thunder: "Never before in all our history have these forces [of big business] been so united against one candidate as they stand today. They are unanimous in their hate for me and I welcome their hatred."

Roosevelt's election in 1936 was a famous victory. Still he could not resist a thrust at his critics afterward. At the Gridiron dinner on the night of December 21 he gave one of his most pixieish speeches. It has never been made public. With a graceful compliment to Governor Landon, who was the other speaker at the dinner and with whom he had spent the morning talking about politics, sport fishing and hunting, he went on to pay his respects to the press and to the newspaper men who were his hosts:

"In a great serial which ran for several months in the papers, one of the characters bore the name of Franklin D. Roosevelt. Whether this character was to be a hero or a villain I could not at first make out. But as that magnificent work of imagination developed, I decided that this character Roosevelt was a villain. He combined the worst features of Ivan the Terrible, Machiavelli, Judas Iscariot, Henry VIII, Charlotte Corday and Jesse James. He was engaged in a plot to wreck the American Constitution, to poison the Supreme Court, to demolish capitalism, to destroy old age security, to get us into war, and to assassinate all the men in the United States who had red hair or, as newspaper publishers claimed, the rank of colonel [Col. Frank Knox, publisher of the Chicago *Daily News*, was the Republican candidate for Vice President]—in short to blot from the face of the earth the United States as we have known it.

"I began to believe it myself. Didn't I read it in the

columns of our great papers? . . . Yes, I began to believe
it myself. One morning, about the middle of October, I
became curious about this man Roosevelt and I went to
a beautiful old mirror of the early Federal period and
took a careful look at him in the glass. He smiled. I
remembered that one of the most damning indictments
that had been brought against him was that selfsame
smile. I smiled back. And after a careful examination I
decided that all that this villain looked like to me was a
man who wanted to be reelected President of the
United States.

"He was reelected, and the great 1936 campaign
serial turned out to have a most surprising ending. On
the morning of November fourth the editors decided that
this villain was, after all, a reasonable person. He was
deluged with editorial advice—suave advice, friendly
advice, advice based on the apparent assumption that
this man was really a reincarnation of a cross between
Little Eva and Simple Simon.

"May I recommend this habit of standing in front of
a mirror? It is a good habit. It restores perspective. It
brings out all the blemishes one ought to know about."

A widely reprinted cartoon of the time showed a
stout, frock-coated figure standing on the shore complaining because, though he had been saved, his silk
hat was floating out to sea. I knew that it was one of
Roosevelt's favorites. He had saved the system from the
almost total bankruptcy of 1933. He was a traditionalist
in nearly the same sense that his mother and most of his
Roosevelt relatives were traditionalists. Why his own
class, the privileged, the well born, were so venomous
toward him he could never understand. Outwardly he
was amused, or professed to be. Certainly they were
useful as a political target and he could take deadly aim
at their foibles. Although they could not touch him in
any meaningful way, I sensed that he was hurt more
deeply than he showed. His role, as the haters would
never understand, was as a power broker between the
many with so little and the few with so much. In that

role he had no rivals in this century. His critics on the left said that his program was a mere palliative, leaving profound inequities that would sooner or later do great harm to the system. He listened, he smiled, he nodded in seeming affirmation, and then he went his own way as he always had.

Politics and the Supreme Court

The imperial prerogatives, the lines of force and power, are quickly perceived in Washington. The Supreme Court is a textbook institution: the pinnacle of the judiciary, one of the three coordinate and independent branches of our government of divided powers. The Court has again and again been at the center of the political struggle. I became fascinated by the way that power was exercised in a grave test of the Constitution and the system, and I soon learned that the veil of sanctity was fragile and easily torn to expose the all too human beings on the high bench.

We had learned in a trivial yet revealing incident one imperial prerogative. While my wife was driving the family car she was rammed from behind at the intersection of Massachusetts and Wisconsin Avenues. She got out and was confronted by an indignant gentleman who demanded to know why she had got in his way. In his way! She pointed to the damage done to the rear of the car and reminded him that she had stopped for a traffic light. He turned his back, climbed into his own car and drove off. But she had written down the license number, and I found that the car belonged to Justice James McReynolds. From his appearance and his manner we concluded he had been the driver. A cantankerous, obdurate man, he was appointed to the Court by Woodrow Wilson, whose Attorney General he had been. With some difficulty I finally got him on the telephone to ask him whether his insurance would cover the damage done, particularly since he had been at fault. "Do you believe your wife?" he asked, his voice crackling with anger. I replied that I did and that her reputation for veracity was very good. "If you believe a woman then you can believe anything," he said and hung up the phone with a bang. I consulted a lawyer friend about possible legal action, but that obviously would be futile and his advice was that I find my reward in the knowledge of the temperament of one of the nine untouchables.

That temperament was in full fig when the Court handed down a majority decision to uphold Roosevelt's action invalidating the clause that required the government to pay gold on demand for government securities. Dissenting from the majority, McReynolds delivered an oral jeremiad denouncing practically everybody from Roosevelt on down, not excluding his brethren on the Court. He hurled Jovian thunderbolts at a faithless and failing order as the other justices sat by in silence. The setting was the old Supreme Court chamber in the Capitol. With the rather modest marble columns, the high bench and subdued light, the simple room was in marked contrast to the Roman splendor of the great temple soon to be built. The McReynolds tirade was good copy, and scribbling a few paragraphs at a time I dashed out to put them on the wire.

The aged justices, looking like a row of roupy black crows, were soon to be drawn into the vortex of politics. Justice Willis Van Devanter had been appointed by William Howard Taft in 1911. The Chief Justice, Charles

Evans Hughes, whose luxurious beard in that beardless age prompted the irreverent H. L. Mencken to call him the feather duster, was named an associate justice in 1910. He resigned in 1916 to run for President, and was restored to the bench as Chief Justice by Herbert Hoover in 1930. At eighty-one, Louis Dembitz Brandeis was the oldest member of the Court. Confirmation of his nomination by Woodrow Wilson had been delayed by a bitter dispute with overtones of anti-Semitism. With a liberal view of the law and the power of government to regulate certain aspects of national life, Brandeis had been one of three dissenters when the Court struck down the Agricultural Adjustment Act. The AAA, the dream of Henry Wallace, agronomist, philosopher, mystic, attempted to restore prosperity to the farms with scarcity economics, and as such was crucial to FDR's recovery program. The majority of the Court had dealt the President a severe blow. Rumors and speculations about what he would do circulated in the overheated atmosphere of the capital. I went over the speeches he had made during the campaign to confirm my recollection that he had never once referred to the Supreme Court or its power to invalidate legislation. At his twice weekly press conferences after his reelection he was coy, cunning, evasive. He was just cute as hell and we filed out of his office frustrated and resentful.

The AAA decision stirred widespread protest, particularly in the prairie states where drought had added to the hardship of farmers facing mass foreclosures. Speaking at a Jackson-Jefferson Day fund-raising dinner in January 1937, Roosevelt denounced the dead hand of tradition that was inhibiting the nation's recovery. The loyal Democrats in the dining hall took this to mean the Supreme Court. They jumped to their feet and whooped and hollered until he was able to restore quiet, but FDR remained the smiling sphinx who gave no clue as to his intentions.

Then on February 5, the President sent to Congress a proposal to enlarge the Court. His plan would give the

President power to appoint an additional justice whenever any current member of the Court who was over the age of seventy declined to retire or resign. The maximum number of justices was to be fifteen. Six justices were then past the seventy mark. The uproar that followed the President's message to Congress has seldom been equaled. Cries of alarm and rage went up from the opposition, the traditionalists, the conservatives, and other quarters, as well.

I had made the acquaintance of Justice Brandeis and I realized he might offer a view, as indeed he did, on the fierce controversy. He had the look of an Old Testament prophet with an aureole of silver-grey hair and eyes that seemed to see beyond the immediate and the trivial to an eternity holding promise for the redemption of frail and corruptible man. His belief in Zionism and a homeland for the Jews was a motivating force. Although in background he and Holmes were quite different, he had formed a close friendship with the Yankee from Olympus with whom he frequently joined in dissent. It was a pleasure to see these two sages walking, as they often did, to and from the Capitol.

Justice Brandeis and his wife lived in an apartment in an old building just off Connecticut Avenue. The furniture must have been put in place when they first came to the capital and I doubt that it had ever been moved. The stiff-backed walnut chairs and sofas upholstered in faded tapestry might have been used on the set for a Eugene O'Neill play. I cannot recall a single beautiful or distinctive object in the apartment. The Brandeises were dedicated to the life of the mind and the spirit.

In "the season" when the Court was in session they gave solemn dinner parties that ended a little after ten, and a series of Sunday teas. Nothing stronger than sherry was ever served. To the teas they invited a varied company, including the young. Mrs. Brandeis skillfully managed to see that most of the guests had a brief conversation with the Justice. On the first occasion that we had been invited she whispered, "The Justice is very interested in your book on Sweden. Won't you come and talk with him about it." Presiding over the tea table, she had the help of Poindexter, the Justice's door opener and general factotum at his office in the Capitol. Poindexter was an institution. When you arrived you said, "Good evening, Poindexter, and how are you?" He replied with grave dignity, invariably remembering your name. Over the years he had absorbed the ritual and demeanor of the Court. Coming from an ardent abolitionist background in their native Kentucky, the Brandeises never would have thought of Poindexter as an Uncle Tom. He was a valued friend and assistant.

In outward appearance a benign prophet, Justice Brandeis had a serpent's guile. We began to work closely together as the controversy over what became known at once as the "court packing" proposal developed into an elementary struggle between the executive — that is to say Franklin Roosevelt and his Attorney General, Homer Cummings — and the judiciary and a large part of the legislature. Our work was secret, the exchanges being by telephone or a late visit to the Brandeis apartment. Believing it would mean the end of an independent judiciary and therefore a grave threat to the American form of government, Brandeis was too wise to make any public expression of his conviction. That was the dilemma of the Court: how to give vent to the intense feeling shared by all nine over the assault, as they saw it, on their very existence.

At the same time I had come close to Sen. Burton K. Wheeler, who led the Senate opposition to the Roosevelt plan. As the hearings progressed before an increasingly hostile Judiciary Committee I was the intermediary between the Justice and the Senator. A greater contrast between two men could hardly have been imagined. A hard-bitten populist who had risen from the brass-knuckles era of Montana politics, Wheeler chewed off his words with tightly clamped jaws. In 1924 he had been the Vice-Presidential candidate on a third party ticket with Wisconsin Senator Robert M. La Follette, Sr. Fighting the copper corporations in his own state, Wheeler was a radical who, in the aftermath of the court fight, became a handsomely paid lawyer for some of those same corporations. He had been a Roosevelt ally in the first phase of the New Deal, and had been instrumental in passage of the utility holding company legislation with the "death penalty" clause for the ultimate removal of corporate control over the nation's utility systems. Now he was marshaling the opposition witnesses before the Judiciary Committee. He spoke bitterly as I sat in his office and listened by the hour to his recitation of the iniquities of the scheming Roosevelt. He was convinced that the Roosevelt brain trust, with Corcoran and Cohen in the forefront, had betrayed him. It was for me a salutary lesson in political enmity.

Wheeler was pressing hard to persuade Chief Justice Hughes to come before the committee to refute Roosevelt's most telling charge: that the Court was far behind in its work, the aged judges so in arrears that litigants had to wait months to have their appeals heard. Brandeis was equally determined that Hughes should not make a public appearance. His argument, which I passed on to Wheeler, was that, however convincing the Hughes presentation, it would be beneath the dignity of the Court to descend into the sweaty arena and be subjected to cross-examination by committee members favoring the President's plan. Wheeler called on Brandeis, who suggested a compromise: Why not a letter from the Chief Justice? The Senator from Montana went that same Saturday afternoon to call on Hughes. The letter asserting that the Court was ahead of its work schedule was dictated on Sunday and read by Wheeler before the committee on Monday. It was carefully documented and highly effective. The Court had spoken in its own Delphic fashion.

Six weeks later I brought word from Brandeis to Wheeler that Justice Van Devanter was about to resign. He had served for twenty-six years, and had voted

against fifteen New Deal measures, most of them principal acts on which the Roosevelt program depended. He
was one of the six who had killed the AAA. The Van
Devanter resignation, with the likelihood that others
would follow, resulted in a ten to eight vote in the
Judiciary Committee for an unfavorable report to the
Senate, but the way was open for the President to appoint
a new justice to the Court.

The master power broker had circumvented the
Supreme Court. He might have said that he lost the
battle but won the war. The cost of this brokerage was,
however, very high. Roosevelt had alienated Wheeler
and others in the populist wing of the party who harbored a deep sense of betrayal and fought him step by
step as war loomed closer. Social Security, the Labor
Relations Act, and other measures at the heart of the
New Deal were securely locked in, but no further social
legislation of any moment was enacted during the remainder of his tenure in the White House. And not
until the first orders for war matériel came from France
and Britain was there any real erosion of the great mass
of the jobless.

Much later I saw at first hand another encounter
between the Congress and the Court. Rep. Kenneth
Keating was chairman of a subcommittee looking into
the Department of Justice and reports that influence
had been used to free convicted criminals from federal
prison. His target was Tom Clark, who had been promoted by President Truman from Attorney General to
Associate Justice. Keating showed me his file of allegations that while Clark had presided over the Justice
Department convicted Mafia criminals had made large
payments to Clark's former law firm in Texas and had
not long thereafter been released. Several times he
asked Clark to come before his committee, each time in
vain. The wall of the separation of powers was impregnable. In his taped interviews with Merle Miller, Truman was to say that his appointment of Clark to the
Court was the worst mistake of his Presidency.

The balance Roosevelt had maintained on the three-legged stool of government in his first four years was further shaken when he filled the vacancy of the Court. His choice was Sen. Hugo La Fayette Black of Alabama. Black was in the middle of his second term in the Senate and had been a vigorous proponent of the New Deal. Investigations he directed into various big business practices laid the groundwork for New Deal legislation. Having come up the hard way, with a sharp awareness of the inequities in post–Civil War Alabama and of the devastation of the depression, Black was a New Dealer and a libertarian, his politics clearly defined. Respected in the Senate for his ability, although regarded as something of a loner, he was confirmed without question, if only because of the clubbable spirit in that comfortable club. Then, while the new Justice was on a visit to London, a Pittsburgh newspaper ferreted out the fact that in his beginning years in Alabama politics he had joined the Ku Klux Klan. Hounded by reporters, he could say little since it was the truth. As the outcry grew, the demand arose that he be forced to resign or in some way be prevented from taking his place on the bench when the Court convened in October. His defenders responded by saying that before the First World War joining the Klan was, for an ambitious young politician, like joining the Elks or the Odd Fellows. To be sure, it had been a mistake, but he was young and ambitious and this early error should not be held against him. He atoned for this mistake by establishing in nearly thirty-five years on the bench one of the most distinguished records in the history of the Court. During the furor over the Klan, students of the judiciary raised a serious objection to the appointment, Black's lack of judicial experience. Justices should be named from the lower federal courts after extensive knowledge of procedures. Except for nineteen months as a police judge in Birmingham, the new Justice was without judicial experience although he had considerable experience as a lawyer.

One of those most concerned about Black's quali-
fications was Justice Harlan Stone, a scholar of the law.
I was fascinated with the function of the Court and the
men, and had cultivated Stone. And it was here that,
unwittingly, I did a great disservice to both Stone and
Black. Stone and I were in the habit of walking together
once or twice a week. I would call for him at his home on
Wyoming Avenue where, in a book-lined study, he did
most of his work. We would customarily trudge up the
Massachusetts Avenue hill in the early winter dusk;
he gradually unfolded his worry about Black and the
Court. I was flattered that this slow-spoken judge with
the solid quality of the New Hampshire mountains
from which he came should take me into his confidence.
Each Justice has to carry his share of a heavy load, he
told me. He must know the intricacies of the Court and
the ways of opinion writing. To take his place on the
bench without knowledge or experience could mean
serious delay, and that was the problem with Justice
Black. In retrospect I believe that Stone, without animus toward Black, was trying to telegraph a message
to FDR so that he would be influenced in his subsequent appointments. I wrote a rather lengthy article for
the St. Louis *Post-Dispatch,* setting out some of these
views without attribution to Stone. It was an example of
the journalism of remote view; I quoted "sources close
to the Court," employing the kind of ambiguity that was
to come increasingly into use. Stone had read it and in
effect approved it. He suggested that presenting the
same case in a publication with national circulation
would be helpful. It might even be possible to accentuate
the problem that a Justice without prior experience
would present to the highest court with its crowded
docket. After all, one of FDR's chief arguments for the
court packing plan was the law's delay. The article
appeared in *Harper's,* and I was immediately the center
of a storm of criticism. A clamor arose from liberals,
New Dealers, defenders of Justice Black. I was roundly
denounced for poaching as an amateur on ground where

I had no right to be. The tempest would have quickly passed had it not been for an unfortunate coincidence.

I had discussed at length with colleagues in the Washington bureau of the *Post-Dispatch* my friendship with Stone and had explained his outlook as reflected in my articles. Paul Y. Anderson, one of the most brilliant reporters ever to write from Washington, was then a member of the bureau. He had run down the leads on the Teapot Dome scandal so persistently and with such telling effect that he was credited, as much as any single individual, with exposing the malefactors who had abused the public trust. He wrote for the *Nation*, as well as for the *Post-Dispatch*, in a mordant style infused with sharp, satiric humor. His description of individuals on the political beat was often devastating. He would be sober for weeks or even months and then go off. O. K. Bovard, who had worked closely with Anderson throughout the Teapot Dome exposé, often giving direction that led to new revelations, finally found his patience at an end. Anderson was fired. As I later learned, Anderson took his stand in the National Press Club to tell all passersby that Stone had inspired my article. The first I knew of it was a call from Justice Stone's secretary, Miss Jenkins.

"I'm calling," she said, "from a telephone booth. There are fourteen reporters in the judge's outer office and he wants to know what to tell them."

"Tell him," I said, "to deny that he had any connection whatsoever with the article. That is his only option."

I met the Justice once again in his home. It was a somber occasion. I sensed that he felt he had been wronged and that he had been wronged by me. It was summed up by the acerbic Miss Jenkins sitting nearby: "I always told the judge he talks too much."

Thereafter we encountered one another but rarely, usually at large public gatherings, and we did not speak. Once every six months or so Drew Pearson wrote that Roosevelt would never name Stone Chief Justice because he had blotted his copybook in the Black affair. This distressed me since in making an error in judgment—and it was that—I had apparently helped to deny him his life's ambition. It was, therefore, particularly gratifying to me when, upon the retirement of Hughes, the President named Stone to head the Court.

If Stone's intention had been to persuade FDR of the need for Justices with knowledge and experience in the law, he was in at least one instance successful. Reshaping the Court as one resignation followed another, Roosevelt made as his second appointment a lawyer with impeccable credentials. Stanley Reed, a Kentuckian who had come to Washington before the New Deal and stayed to serve in several New Deal offices, became Solicitor General in 1935. In that important post, in effect the practicing lawyer for the Attorney General, Reed represented the government in cases vital to the new dispensation. Upon his appointment to the Court in 1938, he merely changed from one side of the bench to the other, and the brethren welcomed him as one of their own who knew not only the law but the proprieties.

It was not to be so when the next vacancies were filled. Roosevelt had a sometimes impish taste for the surprising and the shocking. By appointing Prof. Felix Frankfurter of the Harvard Law School he got what he must have anticipated. Frankfurter became a controversial figure when he helped defend Sacco and Vanzetti, the shoemaker and the fish peddler, who were finally executed for the Braintree, Massachusetts, holdup/murder. With FDR and the New Deal he came into his own. He was a frequent visitor at the White House and a brilliant conversationalist who never failed to entertain the President. A close adviser and a sponsor of Tommy Corcoran, he was a brain truster without portfolio. This was one reason for the opposition to his confirmation. Was this not an invitation to break down the barrier separating the executive and the judiciary, and was there any assurance that once on the bench he would cease to be an intimate counselor of the President? It was a rational objection, but there were others that were not so rational.

By 1939 the Communist scare had already begun to take hold; the Dies Committee was pillorying witnesses and making sensational headlines. Although damped down by the war and the propaganda that flourished during our alliance with the Soviet Union, the committee's activities were a prelude to the McCarthyism of later years. The chief instrument was Sen. Pat McCarran of Nevada, a large, solemn man who breathed suspicion from every pore. His workout on Frankfurter was a warm-up for subsequent inquisitions. As a member of the Senate Judiciary Committee passing on the confirmation, McCarran demanded that Frankfurter appear in person to answer his questions. This was unprecedented. Stone had gone before the committee at the time of his confirmation, but at his own request, to clear up a matter relating to his service as Attorney General for Calvin Coolidge. Preceding Frankfurter's appearance, singularly obnoxious witnesses had spewed out the poison of anti-Semitism. The nominee was an alien-minded Jew and so was Justice Brandeis, said one witness reading from a Brandeis declaration on the loyalty of Jews to Zionism. That could be dismissed as the mouthing of the lunatic fringe, but McCarran was something quite different, a Senator of the United States with considerable rank and authority.

Frankfurter had come to the crowded hearing room, flanked by his personal attorney and long-time friend, Dean Acheson. Acheson was out of government at the time, having resigned as Under-Secretary of the Treasury in disagreement with Roosevelt's spending policies. The two men were in striking contrast: the tall, aristocratic-looking Acheson with his guardsman's moustache, Establishment and Episcopalian in every lineament and the almost gnomic professor whose parents had brought him to America from Vienna at the age of ten. At the beginning of the interrogation Frankfurter was visibly nervous, his normally high-pitched voice rising even higher. As the hearing went on he seemed more at ease and replied in a clear, firm voice to McCarran's questions.

"Were you ever a Communist or a member of the Communist Party?"

"No, I never was." This reply, given under oath, seemed to disappoint McCarran.

At the outset the witness had expressed his sense of humiliation at having been called to testify, but as he gained confidence he seemed almost to enjoy the experience. The interrogation went at some length into Frankfurter's connection with the American Civil Liberties Union. In his serious, professorial manner he undertook to explain the function of the ACLU. It stood for the freedom of the individual. His friends on the committee from time to time gave him eloquent support, and this drew applause punctuated by hisses from the standing-room-only audience. The committee voted unanimously for his confirmation. McCarran was not present when the vote was taken but whether he deliberately absented himself was never known. By a voice vote the Senate followed suit, and after the swearing-in Frankfurter was ready to take his seat.

He was to see himself as the conscience of the Court. In this role he had rancorous exchanges with later Chief Justices. During his years on the bench, he arrived at a view of the law and the Court so limited that it excluded broad social objectives as the Court's prerogative. He believed that political reform and social change must come from the political branches of government—the legislative and the executive. His brilliance and his flair for language—often convoluted and complex language—remained undimmed. Something like a Frankfurter cult developed; his letters and his opinions were enshrined.

One of the Chief Justices harried by Frankfurter was Earl Warren, an Eisenhower appointee. On one occasion they exchanged angry words, to the acute embarrass-

ment of the Court and of the counsel who had been subjected by Frankfurter to an interrogation the Chief
Justice had thought unwarranted. He was normally
calm, stoical, and the public anger was out of character
for Warren, who had succeeded in uniting the Court in
his first year on the bench with the unanimous *Brown*
decision that overturned the doctrine of "separate but
equal" black and white public schools. I had known
Warren when he was Governor of California. He was a
moderate who had sought to draw the sting from the bitter quarrel over the loyalty oath at the state universities.
He had come early on to know the perfidy of his fellow
Californian, Richard Nixon. On the eve of the 1952
Republican convention in Chicago, Warren had the
support of the California delegation. His long experience in government, his skill in putting together a moderate party in his rapidly growing state, and his wide
support from Democrats and independents made him a
candidate to be reckoned with. As the California delegation came across the country on a special train,
Nixon flew to Denver for an intensive lobbying campaign in behalf of General Eisenhower. His argument—
Ike is bound in any event to get the nomination and you
had better get on board—had made many converts by
the time the delegates reached Chicago. Warren, who
had flown on in advance, soon learned that his delegation had been suborned. The delegates were whoring
after a popular hero. Without their support his candidacy
was done for. I talked with Warren in the sitting room of
his suite at the Hilton Hotel just after he had learned of
his loss. I wanted to draw him out on the betrayal. Although I could see how strongly he felt, he was his customary, unflinching self. Loyalty to party ranked above
his certain knowledge that his last chance for the Presidency had vanished.

Not long after his retirement as Chief Justice he told
me how Lyndon Johnson had turned the screws to make
it impossible to say no to a service off the Court that
Warren felt was improper. After the Kennedy assassina-

tion Johnson phoned him to say it was imperative that
he serve as chairman of the commission investigating
the crime. Warren refused on the ground that no member of the Court, and particularly the Chief Justice,
should be drafted for duties off the bench. That same
afternoon the President asked him to come to the White
House. You wore the uniform of your country in the
First World War, Johnson said, now I'm asking you to
wear it again. How could I refuse a request put that way?
But I knew, he added, that it was wrong.

FDR's fourth appointment to the Court, after Frankfurter, was William O. Douglas, a New Dealer who
owed his selection to the Roosevelt sweep in 1936 and
the resignations in the aftermath of the court packing
plan. Before his stroke he was still carrying on, the
banner of his liberalism undimmed, speaking at forums
around the country, assailing big business, the corporate
stranglehold on the economy and a government supine
before conglomerate wealth. He lectured, he climbed
mountains, he married four wives, and in one venture he
was as close to a vote of impeachment as any Justice
since early in the last century. The irony is that twice he
could have left the shelter of the Court to be part of the
rough struggle of politics. Whether Douglas's name was
on the list of possible Vice Presidents that FDR submitted to his political lieutenant, Robert Hannegan, has
long been debated. The choice, in any event, was
Harry Truman at that strange convention in Chicago in
1944 which Roosevelt never even attended. Having
inherited the Presidency less than a year later, Truman
was in trouble. An enemy was the quarrelsome Secretary
of Interior, Harold Ickes, whom Truman had retained
along with most of the Roosevelt cast. One fine spring
day several of us were invited by the President for a
luncheon cruise on the Presidential yacht, *Sequoia,*
then called the *Williamsburg.* We sat before lunch on
the afterdeck in warm sun. The President was in a
somber mood and appeared to be oppressed by his
heavy responsibilities. One of us asked a question about
Ickes.

"Are you referring," Truman asked, his voice charged with emotion, "to shitass Ix?"

For the time being this put a damper on further discussion of the Secretary of Interior. In fact, it dampened any exchange until, finally, the President said in a slightly more cheery vein, "Well, it must be five o'clock somewhere; let's have a drink."

Determined to remove Ickes, the new President telephoned Douglas to ask if he would be interested in becoming master of the vast domain of Interior. The Justice had long been an apostle of conservation and the out-of-doors. No sooner had the offer been made than he went down to the Interior Department to sound out his close friend Ickes, who strongly counseled him against accepting. Within twenty-four hours Truman had heard of the visit and it was no surprise, it was perhaps even welcome, when Douglas refused the post, saying it was his duty to remain on the Court.

A far larger opportunity came three years later as Truman was preparing, against the opposition of most of the certified liberals, to run for reelection. He could not win. That was the verdict of the party Left who were Douglas's closest friends. With extraordinary naiveté, they believed they could draft Dwight Eisenhower to run at the head of the Democratic ticket. In planning for the convention at Philadelphia, the President consulted with Oscar Chapman, then Under-Secretary of Interior and a loyal friend who, from the first, believed that Truman could against all odds win a full term on his own. About two weeks before the convention the question of a Vice President came up. Truman told Chapman he intended to ask Douglas to take second place on the ticket. I can tell you, Mr. President, Chapman said, exactly what will happen. He will respond by saying he would like twenty-four hours to think it over. During that interval he will leak it to the press and then he will say no. It happened just that way, headlines told first of the offer and then of the rejection. From his retreat in Goose Prairie, Washington, the Justice had opted for the safety of the Court against the chance of running with a President judged a sure loser by the liberal Left. Truman tapped Sen. Alben Barkley of Kentucky for the second place and confounded all the prophets and pundits by winning in November.

A secure place on the High Court for life, short of impeachment, does not erase the prejudices and predilections of the past. Indeed, with Douglas as a cardinal example, they may even be accentuated. Nor is the power struggle foreclosed by reason of the seemingly rarefied atmosphere in the marble temple built more as a monument than a functional building. (The acoustics in the lofty courtroom were so poor that various devices had to be employed to make the words of the Judges on the bench audible.) The antagonism, the conflict over place and position, between two of the brethren erupted once in such an acute form that it determined the outcome of a case with far-reaching consequences.

FDR had appointed his Attorney General, Robert H. Jackson, to the Court in 1941. Jackson had won his reputation when, as counsel to the Bureau of Internal Revenue, he had prosecuted the tax case against Andrew Mellon, directing the investigation into the ramifications of the enormous fortune that Mellon had put together in aluminum, oil, sulfur and an infinite number of interrelated interests. Proceeding for weeks in a Pittsburgh courtroom, Jackson had presented a skilled exposition of the amassing of one of America's greatest fortunes. He had won his place in the New Deal pantheon for having held up to public view corporate aggrandizement that defied the laws intended to impose limits on corporate reach. Jackson and Douglas were destined to be rivals. Coming from a small town in upstate New York, the new judge had a genial, easygoing manner that contrasted with Douglas's brusque, sometimes combative approach. This was particularly evident in the privacy of the Saturday morning conferences when, with the assignment of opinions by the Chief Justice, differences of view were debated.

After he had been on the Court only five years, Justice Jackson made a grievous error. He was persuaded by Truman to serve as the American prosecutor at the trial of the German war criminals in Nürnberg. By temperament and background he was ill-equipped for a leading role in an experiment of uncertain validity and dubious outcome. Crimes of the most monstrous magnitude had been committed, but whether, in the immediate heat of the fall of Germany, the path to justice lay in a trial by Western jurisprudence, rather than a firing squad, was a troubling and unresolved question. Jackson had difficulties with the men in the dock, conspicuously that diabolical genius, Hermann Göring, who, in the end, foiled his captors and the court by committing suicide, with poison he had concealed in his rectum, two hours before he was to be hanged.

With the death of Chief Justice Stone in 1946, speculation began at once over his successor. Douglas and Black, the two liberals on the Court, were hostile toward Jackson and the prospect that he might be named Chief. Partisans of Douglas sought to reach the President with the claims for their man. Involved in the legalities of the Nürnberg trial, Jackson heard with dismay what his detractors were saying. He believed that more than any other Justice on the Court he was qualified to be Chief. And his skill in writing opinions, his ability to express the law in clear and understandable language, convinced at least some of his colleagues that he was the logical choice. But with the Black-Douglas partisans carrying on their campaign more or less openly, the rivalry embarrassed the President. He ended by naming Fred M. Vinson, a poker-playing Kentuckian who had had a successful career in the House of Representatives. In his seven years on the bench Vinson left only a slight imprint.

A little later, when the lesson of Nürnberg should have been plain, Truman once again came close to breaking down the wall between the Court and the executive branch of government. This was at the moment

when Stalin had dug in to balk any settlement of the
German question, and the threat of open conflict hung
in the troubled air. The President had suggested to
Vinson that he fly to Moscow to try to persuade the
dictator to accept a compromise course. The proposal
was leaked, and the publicity put a stop to it. It was a
time when the belief still persisted that if only one could
talk to the great khan, reason would prevail.

The choice of an outsider as Chief Justice did little to
ameliorate the antagonism between the Douglas-Black
alliance and Jackson. It was to come to a climax in a
case that shook the nation with the angriest of passions.
Julius and Ethel Rosenberg were convicted of wartime
sabotage for passing the secrets of the atomic bomb to
Communist agents. The revelations of Communist
treachery; the defection of Klaus Fuchs, who had
worked on the nuclear secret at Los Alamos; and the
prosecution and conviction of Alger Hiss following sensational hearings initiated in the House by Richard
Nixon had sent shock waves throughout the country.
Perhaps the ugliest scene I ever witnessed in Washington was the mass demonstration in Lafayette Park across
from the White House. Signs held up by the demonstrators demanded that Julius and Ethel burn. Shouts of
intense anti-Semitism ran through the crowd, for the
most part a well-dressed, middle-class crowd. These
were the dark forces released by the cataclysm of war
and its aftermath, a revolution that broke loose the old
America which had seemed so secure in caste and creed.

The Rosenberg case came to the Court on a writ of
certiorari two years after they had been convicted. The
last of six appeals was taken to Justice Jackson, who by
geographical assignment presided over the Southern
District of New York. This was in June 1953, when the
Court was about to recess for the summer. Jackson recommended that the full Court hear oral argument on a
stay of execution on the last day of the term. Frankfurter
agreed with his position and so did Justice Harold
Burton, a former Senator from Ohio named to the Court

in 1945. Justice Black was in favor of a rehearing on the issues, but since that was impossible he was willing to listen to the argument for a stay. With one more vote, a majority of five would have given counsel for the Rosenbergs their day in the highest court of the land. As Jackson told it to me, word came from Douglas's chambers that he was not interested. The official journal recorded his position as follows:

"Mr. Justice Douglas would grant a stay and hear the case on the merits, as he thinks the petition for certiorari and the petition for rehearing present substantial questions.

"But since the Court has decided not to take the case, there would be no end served by hearing oral argument on the motion for a stay. For the motion presents no new substantial question not presented by the petition for certiorari and by the petition for rehearing."

So the appeal for a stay was denied. Then, two days later, to the astonishment of everyone on the Court, Douglas acting alone stayed the execution until the full Court could consider the Rosenberg case, presumably in the fall term. His action caused a sensation. The Justices had already begun to disperse for their summer holiday. Vinson moved immediately to call them back for a special session to pass on the Douglas orders. Douglas himself had left with a friend to motor across the country. Finally located by the Pennsylvania state police, he returned to Washington. The vote rejecting the stay and postponing a hearing on the issues until the fall was eight to one. The Rosenbergs were executed at Sing Sing prison on June 19. The bitterness within the marble temple of the Court was a reflection of the atmosphere in the nation. When the Soviet Union exploded a hydrogen bomb in August of the same year, it was taken as proof that the betrayers had succeeded in destroying America's supremacy far in advance of the estimates made by the administration. It made no difference that those with scientific knowledge discounted the importance of the so-called secrets since both the fission and fusion processes were available to physicists of the first rank.

On October 29, 1973, Douglas surpassed the service record of thirty-four years, six months and twelve days previously established by Justice Stephen J. Field, who sat on the Court between 1863 and 1897. But before that milestone Douglas was the object of an historic confrontation. Gerald R. Ford, then leader of the Republican minority in the House, initiated in 1970 a resolution calling for his impeachment. Republican critics had long been fuming over Douglas's extracurricular activities, his marriages, his free-wheeling lifestyle with writing and lectures said to bring more income than his judicial salary. The move to impeach had been touched off by the disclosure that Douglas was being paid $12,000 a year by the Parvin Foundation with its Las Vegas gambling connections. Just how this first became known is a mystery. Douglas suspected that his enemies, notably J. Edgar Hoover, had brought it to light. In a case of great sensitivity that involved the FBI, Douglas believed that his vote in the conference room was known in advance of the announced decision. He went to Chief Justice Warren to ask how recently the conference room had been swept. At first Warren understood this as a reference to the janitorial function. When Douglas enlightened him he said he did not know whether the conference room had ever been inspected for electronic devices.

The Parvin Foundation had dubious connections, it was reported, with figures in organized crime. What function Justice Douglas performed was not clear as he kept his own counsel after the revelation. In 1805 the House of Representatives had voted eight articles of impeachment against Justice Samuel Chase, who had been appointed to the Court by George Washington. Chase, the first and only justice to be impeached, was acquitted on all counts in a two-month trial before the Senate. Politics between the Federalists and the Jeffersonian Republicans had played a large part in the Chase impeachment as did politics in the case of Douglas.

Gerald Ford's hard-line conservatism reflected his Republican constituency in Grand Rapids, Michigan. He had risen to the office of minority leader by strict adherence to the cause of conservatism. His voting record was almost 100 percent for budget cutting and economy in government, with the exception of armaments for which he could be counted on by the Pentagon to go all the way. As a minority member of the subcommittee on military appropriations he was committed with an almost automatic response to what the Generals and the Admirals wanted. I had seen little of him since I felt that anything he might say would be so predictable, but we did have one encounter after a White House dinner. I forget what it was about. It may have been the Vietnam War, which he supported with a fine bipartisanship that earned him high marks with Lyndon Johnson. The argument was coming close to a quarrel when we both realized how inappropriate was the setting, the East Room where dancing was in progress.

The minority leader's flock, or most of them, would have taken the greatest delight in seeing Douglas driven off the Court. Undoubtedly Ford was responding to this pressure, which conformed with his own convictions about Douglas's conduct. Ford obtained 123 signatures to the resolution of impeachment. A crime or a misdemeanor justifying a vote to impeach was anything the House decided, Ford announced. He amended this four years later to say his dictum applied to Federal Judges and not to Presidents. A special committee of the House conducted an inquiry that went on for many weeks. The conclusion was a 924-page report holding that, "There is no credible evidence that would warrant preparation of impeachment charges."

The Supreme Court has never lapsed back into the somnolence of the early years of this century. From the Pentagon Papers to the subpoenaed White House tapes, the Court was repeatedly drawn into the power struggle. It was a bone of contention between the executive with the power of appointment and the Senate with power of confirmation. Richard Nixon tried to reshape the Court in his own image and was partially successful after two grievous failures with second-raters who were rejected after prolonged and angry combat on the Senate floor. The Court was the mirror of a nation torn by internal strife which the political process seemed unable to resolve. It would have been miraculous if the Court had escaped the general disarray.

With the four Nixon appointees the Supreme Court has become a strange melange of new and old, yes and no and, perhaps, maybe. Though he looks every inch a Chief Justice in dignity, poise and handsomeness, Warren Burger has in fact added little to his own stature or that of the Court. Lewis Powell, sixty-seven, is a scholar of the law and a former president of the American Bar Association. Harry Blackmun has the distinction of having written the most controversial opinion of the new, or half-new, Court, that which declared unconstitutional state laws outlawing or narrowly restricting abortion. The most avowedly Nixonist Justice, William Rehnquist, is also the youngest man on the bench — forty-seven at the time of his appointment. He has taken to lecturing around the country espousing the conservative cause much as Douglas preaches the liberal-radical orthodoxy. If Rehnquist should approach the Douglas record, he would at seventy, be expressing his philosophy in dissents and opinions in 1995. Not votes but death alone, or the rare process of impeachment, sets the course of the highest court, and diminishes its power.

Hero and Antihero

The windows at his back looked out to the city across the Potomac. Seated behind the broad desk that had been Gen. Phil Sheridan's in an earlier time of conflict, the chief of staff of the United States Army, George Catlett Marshall, was the epitome of the soldier. It was a desk without gadgetry, Spartanly bare with only a thin sheaf of papers at his right hand.

A group of correspondents, twelve to fifteen of us, had met with General Marshall from time to time during the war. We admired his candor, his simplicity of style, his grasp of the action in multiple theaters of war. Now the war was over and the extraordinary power exercised by the military was yielding swiftly to civilian demands and civilian controls. We in press and radio were responsible, with considerable assist from an unparalleled PR operation that pervaded every rank of the military, for stimulating the cult of the hero. As in earlier wars, the military hero held the public eye. Having created our hero, we were in the years ahead to bring the antihero into being. By essentially the same process Pygmalion endowed almost legendary attributes to a Marshall, an Eisenhower, a Joe McCarthy. The hero to confront the antihero in the tumult of a new cold war.

Marshall had none of the posturing of other generals we had observed, none of the bravura of a Patton, nor the theatricalism of a Montgomery. We had given him a dinner just after VE Day to thank him for the trust he had put in us, for his courtesy and consideration in those frank sessions during four years of the war. As spokesman I had wanted to make it a relaxed and informal occasion. To put him at ease, I remained seated for my own remarks which tried to sum up the feeling we had for a great man we had been privileged to see at close range. That was not the general's style. Responding, he stood ramrod straight, called on the waiters to remove the candelabra from the center of the table, and spoke in crisp, soldier-like accents. He talked about current intelligence estimates that put American casualties in the final assault on the main island of Honshu in the hundreds of thousands. The general took these estimates seriously. He told us the Japanese would to a man and woman fight on the beaches with every weapon they could lay hands on. This was before the decision had been taken to drop the atomic bomb.

Later he asked to see me to discuss the pressure on him to demobilize. Disbanding the 7 million Americans under arms with reckless haste meant abandoning vast military stores, he said. Supplies worth billions were being bulldozed under the earth or dumped into the sea. What am I to do? he asked. This is an advertisement to the world that we are giving up our positions of strength everywhere. The cry had gone out that the boys were being kept in uniform so that the brass could hold their wartime rank. An army of citizen soldiers, fed up with four years of war in faroff places, wanted nothing more than to come home. Riots had broken out in several encampments where men waited for shipment home. A rumor circulated that the unrest was partly Communist inspired; it suited our one-time ally to see our strength ebb away. But Marshall made no reference to these rumors. I had no answer to the question he had put. I would write about the need for orderly demobilization, but the great tide of feeling of a civilian-minded people demanded immediate release from uniform.

In the postwar era, Marshall was to be faced with one trial after another. President Truman had discerned his integrity and his response to the call of duty, however onerous, which for a besieged President counted more than anything else. The task Truman asked of him was almost preordained to defeat. He was to go to China with the rank of ambassador to try to persuade the Nationalists under Chiang Kai-shek and the Communists under Mao Tse-tung to agree to a coalition government. The alternative was civil war. Ill-equipped for the assignment, Marshall was to be constantly undercut during the long and fruitless negotiations between Chungking and Yenan by Americans who were no more eager to see his mission succeed than was Chiang. Roosevelt had sent as ambassador to Chungking, the remote city on the Yangtze where Chiang had established his government, Gen. Patrick J. Hurley, a vain and pompous man with a limited mind. It had been a terrible mistake. After floundering about in an abortive attempt to persuade the Communists to accept the Nationalist authority, he had become a partisan of Chiang with no critical reservations. Hurley had resigned with a savage sideswipe at the foreign service officers who had tried to tell the truth about Chiang's weakening position, the inflation and corruption riddling civilian and military life.

Histories of generals tend to be formalized and dull, especially when they write their own. The sober history of Marshall marching on in volume after volume is the best we can expect. General Marshall was a reticent man with an aversion to personal publicity. But we had created another, less reticent hero in General Eisenhower. Much was to turn on the relationship of Eisenhower and Marshall, two heroes so dissimilar in temperament but whose lives were curiously intertwined. One was to end in conspicuous public triumph, the other in private sorrow and a sense of humiliation and betrayal.

As the war was coming to an end I went to Europe with a troupe of writers, editors, and various oddly assorted characters. At the invitation of the Chief of Staff of the Air Force, Gen. Hap Arnold, we went in our own C-54. Like some aspects of the war, the trip was a bit farcical. Nancy Wilson Ross gave it the best caption: Aunt Polly's Visit to the Front. In London I had a close look at the devastation of the V-2s, the weapon developed by the German scientific community on the Baltic island of Peenemunde that had ushered in the missile age. Unlike the V-1s, the buzz bombs that roared over the city, V-2s, fired from Antwerp without guidance and tracked by British radar across the channel, dropped without warning and without sound until they struck. I had arranged with the War Office to go to one suburb immediately after a V-2 had exploded. A block of cottages had been flattened, bodies were being carried off, and survivors were picking through the ruins. During the total blackout the prostitutes in Piccadilly, with their small flashlights, had grown bolder in the expectation of victory. After midnight at the Millroy Club the crowd was so dense that dancing was all but impossible. Here was Evelyn Waugh's handful of dust: a duchess or two, countesses by the score, lovers on leave, husbands on the loose. Claridge's, the Ritz, the Berkeley were bravely carrying on though a bit worn at the seams.

Three of our troupe were invited to a weekend at Cliveden, the Astor estate where Munich and appeasement had been enshrined. The weather was cold winter wet, the halls dimly lit, but Lady Astor's determined and acerbic monologue brightened the gloom. The guest of honor at Sunday lunch was Joseph C. Patterson, Jr., designated American ambassador to Yugoslavia. He talked about a planned visit to King Peter, who was staying not far from Cliveden. He would be a unifying force once the war should end, so Patterson said. He made it sound as though he were going to a Graustarkian capital. The British had already written off the playboy king, and listening as long as her patience endured, which was not long, Lady Astor broke in to say in a voice audible the length of the table, "Waffled again, waffled again."

In a half whispered aside she asked me if I would tell her husband, Waldorf, how much the Americans wanted her to be back in Parliament. Seated at the opposite end of the table, Lord Astor looked a weary old man who wanted nothing so much as to be left to himself. After lunch I dutifully made the appeal, saying how gratified Americans would be to see Lady Astor representing not only her own constituency of Plymouth but all of us across the sea who saw her as the herald of Anglo-American friendship. Her husband shook his head wearily and made no response. The large sums of money that had supported his wife's political career had been drained away in the war.

The troupe moved on to Paris. We were billeted at the Ritz as simulated (I think that was the word) brigadier generals, since only officers with the rank of general had the privilege of the Ritz. The first evening at dinner a real general, an air force major general, came over to our table to say, "After you've had your chow come on up. I've got Göring's suite and a case of Old Crow." I have only a hazy memory of that evening spent in those splendid rooms in the front of the Ritz on the Place Vendôme.

I stayed on in Europe after the rest of the troupers returned. Gen. Ira Eaker, whose swank headquarters was then in the gardens of the palace of the king of Naples, put a plane and crew at my disposal. The generals were doing their best to be obliging. We went first to Belgrade. Here was a scene out of Dante's First

Circle. Down the front of one windowless building was a long smear of red. You see, someone explained to the visitor, a fellow popped his head through the window frame just as the firing began; got it cut off neat as anything, that's his blood. Gen. Lyman Lemnitzer and his aide, Col. Charles Thayer, were waiting in Belgrade for a long-deferred invitation to visit the Russians' Hungarian front. When it came, they were escorted to what was obviously a Potemkin front, devoid of any evidence of fighting either near or far. Their arrival was the occasion of a staggering Russian banquet. In Belgrade Soviet troops were an occupying force prepared to stay forever, or so the Yugoslavs feared.

Back in Paris at press headquarters in the Hotel Scribe, I put in my petition with the high command to see the Supreme Commander, General Eisenhower. I was to hold myself in readiness. The alert came one evening, and early the next morning, with a young lieutenant colonel as escorting officer, I set out for the two-hour drive to Reims. The little red schoolhouse, Eisenhower's headquarters, still top secret, was already famous with the press. It was impressively simple. On one wall of the General's neat private office were etchings of President Roosevelt and Prime Minister Churchill, each inscribed with friendly warmth. On a bookcase across the room, at eye level, was a photograph of Ike's mother. She was seated in a rocking chair on the front porch of her home in Abilene, wearing a gingham dress, bright sun shining on her white hair. Two maps hung on the walls, one of them a relief map of an important sector of the Rhine. The General's forehead was perhaps more lined than it had been when I saw him three years earlier. He seemed balder, with only a few graying wisps of sandy hair on his big-domed head. He talked about friendship with the Allies and how important it was to keep up this relationship in some form of united nations after the war. His insistence from the start was on close cooperation, and he had often dealt sternly with officers who preferred to fight a unilateral war. He decried the currents of optimism at home and stressed the need to get on with ending the fighting soon. He had rebuked a trade union delegation that had come from America to talk about reconversion. In the background was his own public prediction, which he had not been allowed to forget, that the war would end in 1944. The talk was warm and earnest, but his sensitivity to criticism came through. He resented the charge of a "deal" with Admiral Darlan after the North African invasion. In the circumstances, he said, some kind of negotiation had to insure stability. He insisted he had ruled out any censorship in his theater of operations that might have meant blanking out critical comment. He was solemn until that big smile broke through. It was to be his greatest political asset.

The atmosphere was of snap, crackle, spit and polish. His three aides were constantly on the alert, running through an unending procession of visitors from the allied world, tense when anything happened to throw off the Commander's schedule. With two caravans, one for office and one for living, they could have the show on the road in half an hour, and it took little longer to summon up the General's plane on the nearby airstrip. He was a military man first, last and always, and in politics the habits of that lifelong career would prevail, though the public image would be of the boy from Kansas. That Abilene version of Whistler's mother, blown up to life size, was to have a prominent place in the Eisenhower family home when it was converted into a national shrine. What he said was not nearly so important as the presence: Ike, the warm, friendly, unassuming man who had won the war for us. For all the continuing disclaimers of any interest in high political office, he was already positioned by those who saw him as a future President. He was a natural, good old Ike, the hands raised aloft in that familiar gesture. The shrewd men attracted to him could parlay that image as far as the White House.

Observing him as he rode down Pennsylvania Ave-

nue in a triumphal parade in June, 1945, I thought of
what part luck had played. While on the staff of General
MacArthur in the Philippines in 1939, a sequel to his
service with MacArthur at army headquarters in Washington, he was sent home for reassignment after the
imperious General had found fault with his conduct. If
this had not happened he would have remained throughout the war a comparatively obscure member of Mac-
Arthur's staff. He had come to Marshall's attention
following a brilliant staff performance on maneuvers in
Louisiana, and his first assignment in Europe followed.
On FDR's word he became supreme commander of the
invasion force and a national hero who understood perhaps better than the professional politicians at the war's
end that the mood of the country was for respite, for
quiet, yes, for normalcy.

Marshall's lifelong ambition had been, if another
war came, to command American forces in the field; his
model general was John J. Pershing, who led the American expeditionary force in the First World War. As a
young colonel he had been one of Pershing's aides, and
they had been close ever since. What he may have felt
privately when Roosevelt told him, on their way to the
Cairo conference in 1943, that he had tapped Ike for the
invasion is likely never to be known. He was too much
a stoic to confide in anyone, unless it was his wife. Roosevelt said he needed Marshall at his side in Washington. That plea may very well have been the simple
truth since Marshall's integrity, his honesty, his ability
to come to a hard decision without flinching had been for
the mercurial Roosevelt a valuable asset. So Marshall
continued as Chief of Staff of the Army until he went off
on the thankless mission to China.

His successor as Chief of Staff was the returned
hero, Dwight Eisenhower. Caution was the rule. Demobilization was far less a problem than had been anticipated; with a pent-up demand for goods of every kind,
industry quickly absorbed the returning GIs. In one of
those background sessions to which we had become ac-

customed during the war, the new Chief of Staff made a startling statement: The United States was dangerously overextended in the Pacific. It might be necessary to pull back to a defense line on the Philippines or even as far west as Hawaii. This heresy, it is hardly necessary to add, was never spoken in public. MacArthur, the proconsul in Tokyo, would have been outraged as would those fervent Senators who were to become Asia-firsters. In any event, the assignment as Chief of Staff was an interlude to end with the transition to civilian life carefully engineered by the General's powerful promoters on the Eastern Seaboard.

In that transition he was to be President of Columbia University, a metamorphosis that must have afforded his comrades-in-arms private laughter. Ike President of a great university! For the deans and the faculty it was no laughing matter. They learned that to get an appointment with the President they had to go through his aide, Col. Robert L. Schulz, who out of long experience with the General took a protocolaire view of who should and who should not see him. At that time I was coming up from Washington every few weeks to lecture at the Columbia University Graduate School of Journalism, and whenever it was possible, with Colonel Schulz's blessing, I saw the great man. The atmosphere in his spacious office in the Low Memorial Library building was different and yet oddly the same as the one I had known during the war. It was a command post and he was the commander. He grumbled a bit at the expectation that he go to and fro in the country and raise money for the university. He wouldn't go around passing a tin cup. I often wondered how he did see his role. During his stay in the groves of academe he discussed philosophy and the state of the world with great intellectuals. Nothing could have been further from the role the President of that university would fill when the troubles that were already beginning erupted in mass violence little more than a decade later. Eisenhower had never cared for opposition on the intellectual plane or any other.

The most vivid incident I remember occurred the time Kay Summersby's book, *Eisenhower Was My Boss,* appeared. He suddenly asked me, "Have you read that book?" In light of the gossip about their friendship, accentuated by the appearance of the book, I would never have brought up the subject. I replied I had read only one or two excerpts that had appeared in a magazine. He then proceeded for five or ten minutes to hold forth about Kay Summersby. They had gone through every kind of experience together—in air raid shelters, in the turbulence of the first weeks in North Africa, at various headquarters, relaxing at bridge or golf—but that's all there was to it, nothing more. What could I say? I nodded my head in appreciation for having been taken into this confidence. You know, he said as a postlude, I told her I would give her $25,000 to help me write my book when she came over. He added that though he understood she was in New York, she had never come to see him.

Her own book had undergone, or so it was reported, several transitions. The initial version, it was said, had begun with the sentence, "They say I'm a bad woman." She ends her book abruptly by simply stating that Ike said he was going to Washington the following day but he would be back. "He didn't come back." Eisenhower mentions her once in *Crusade in Europe* when he tells of putting together his personal staff in Algiers. "Kay Summersby was corresponding secretary and doubled as a driver." But he pays a warm tribute to women in wartime and to the magnificent performance of women in uniform in Britain. Kay Summersby was a member of the British Women's Auxiliary Corps, which later became the Women's Army Corps.

The election campaign of 1948 had begun with the Democratic convention in Philadelphia. That convention offered one of the most ludicrous spectacles in American political history. Many of the liberals in the Democratic party were convinced Truman could not be reelected. James Roosevelt; Joseph L. Rauh, the distinguished civil libertarian lawyer in Washington; Philip Murray of the CIO and other important labor leaders made no secret of their views. As the delegates assembled they announced that the party must find a winner. And who was their candidate? Eisenhower. No one knew, of course, whether he was a Democrat or a Republican nor what his views might be on the issues of the day. But that he would be a winner on whichever ticket he might choose was the conviction of the liberal Democrats disillusioned with their President.

Ignoring the clamor, Truman went ahead with preparations for his renomination. He hadn't the slightest doubt that as a sitting President he would be chosen to run for a full term. The regulars who were the day-in and day-out mainstay of the party and were now assembled in convention would see to that, but few in Philadelphia could have had a rosy view of his chances. Henry Wallace, who had broken with Truman over the President's foreign and domestic policy, was nominated as the candidate of a third party. And Strom Thurmond intended to rob the Democrats of the Solid South.

I decided to try to see the General to find out, if I could, what he thought of the effort of liberal Democrats to draft him as their leader. Colonel Schulz made an appointment late on the opening day of the convention. I went to see the General in his study in the President's house on the Columbia campus. In the early evening darkness, the General sat with the light of a desk lamp on his Roman head. The image was unmistakably that of the conqueror returned from the wars. I put the question to him: What was his view of the Draft Eisenhower movement? You know, he said, I don't think the way those fellas do. I guess it would be Harry Byrd who comes as close to what I believe as anybody.

This was indeed candor. Senator Byrd of Virginia was one of the most conservative men in public life, an eighteenth-century figure living under the happy illusion that the future could be held back. It was his later opposition that as much as anything else raised up the

South against integration of the schools called for in the unanimous Supreme Court decision of 1954. Eisenhower's views were Byrd's views, and as I followed Ike over the years I saw no reason to believe that his stand on domestic policy underwent any change whatsoever. His ardent liberal proponents were startled when, back in Philadelphia, I told them of my conversation with the General. In any event, the Draft Eisenhower movement blew out like a candle in the windy proceedings of the convention. With some awkward hitches, the delegates renominated a President whom almost no one except Harry Truman himself believed capable of victory. To top off his achievement, the President announced that he was calling a special session of Congress to pass what he claimed was much needed social legislation that the Republican-controlled legislature had ignored. The session would begin on what he said was known in Missouri as Turnip Day, the day you planted turnips whether the ground was wet or dry.

In May 1946 I had lunched with Sen. Robert M. La Follette, Jr., heir to the great tradition of his father, Fighting Bob. Young Bob, as he was still known at the age of forty-eight, was sensitive, highly intelligent. He had survived the unfailing intensity of his famous father, though he had been catapulted into politics almost against his will. He had delayed returning to his home state to campaign in the Republican primary because of his duties as codirector of a joint committee working out reforms of congressional procedure. Now the primary was only three weeks away and he was worried. They've been after me to come back, he said, and I know I should have gone, but we were finishing this report and it just wasn't possible. It's about to come out and I'm going back tomorrow.

It was too late. A young unknown named Joe McCarthy was barnstorming around the state, raising the cry of communism and attacking young Bob as the tired heir of an outworn dynasty. With his square jaw, his black beard showing even after his morning shave, his

raucous voice, McCarthy was a demagogue of demagogues. His narrow margin in the primary was partly
the result of the backing of pro-Communists in one of the
big unions in Milwaukee because young Bob's background was isolationist, and he had taken a critical view
of postwar relations with the Soviet Union. McCarthy's
power lay in outrage, the big lie, distrust, all political
goods that could be brokered in an atmosphere of fear
and suspicion. He made sensational headlines with his
pronouncement over a Wheeling, West Virginia, radio
station that there were 210 or 215 or however many
Communists in the State Department. The press printed
whatever he said as though it were gospel, only rarely
checking or including a statement from one of the victims of his assault. There were those, of course, eager to
create the antihero. Adulatory commentators on the right
were his lieutenants. Edward R. Murrow, who later
broadcast the full score on McCarthy—his distortions,
his falsehoods—was an honorable exception to the prevailing timidity, and, as his reward, was savagely
attacked with the intimation of procommunism.

Republicans in the Senate welcomed this scourge
from the back country. From Robert A. Taft, Mr. Republican, came the advice to keep on hitting since if he were
wrong on one target he could be right on the next.
Embittered at having missed the goal of the Presidency,
Taft remained skeptical of Eisenhower. Too liberal!
What did he know about government and politics. Not
long thereafter, suffering from the cancer that was to kill
him, Taft walked onto the Senate floor on crutches—
the majority leader, resolute to the last. Not all of his
Senate flock were submissive. Sen. Ralph Flanders of
Vermont was to become one of the opposition preparing
the way for McCarthy's censure and downfall.

Those who opposed McCarthy hardly knew how to
stand up to the gutter fighter. I was asked to go on "Meet
the Press" with him when he was riding high. My wife
and I met Joe and Mrs. McCarthy in the dining room of
the Sheraton Park Hotel where the NBC studios were

then located. I made a flip remark, greeting him as "the victim." That remains to be seen, he said, with sardonic contempt. With the program under way, I had just put a question when he demanded to know whether I was the one who had written thus and so about Communist China, about the Soviet Union, about Alger Hiss. He reeled off one alleged quote after another, all taken out of context by a researcher on his staff. In the absence of Lawrence Spivak, a substitute moderator did nothing to halt what was a clear violation of the format of the program. Taken aback and failing to respond, I looked like an idiot. Score one for Joe. Later, James Rowley, head of the Secret Service, told me he had reason to know that McCarthy's performance had been framed up in advance with the substitute moderator.

For all his quick successes, McCarthy was a second-rater given to carousing. Comparing him with Hitler, as some of his critics did, seemed to me far off the mark. He had nothing like the discipline or the fanatical belief of a Hitler. The sad commentary was that with so little he could do so much damage. Here was a power broker who knew how to exploit fear and distrust.

As for the two heroes, the one in the White House took no stand against the antihero. Grumbling privately over McCarthy's excesses and the harm his administration suffered, Eisenhower nevertheless rejected the counsel of those who urged him to take on the rampaging senator. General Marshall steadfastly went about his duty, first as Secretary of State and then as Secretary of Defense during the Korean War and the uproar over General MacArthur's dismissal. Cultivated by McCarthy, who set the tone for lesser men such as Sen. Albert Jenner of Indiana, the legend of Marshall as a traitor began to take hold.

The Presidential campaign of 1952 had fallen to perhaps the lowest level in America's political history. General Eisenhower traveled the high road, reading carefully prepared speeches on national issues, with only occasional lapses into irritation over the attacks of

his opponent, Adlai Stevenson. But Richard Nixon,
McCarthy, Jenner and lesser lights raised the Communist charge against Dean Acheson, Marshall, and
others in the Truman administration. Masters of innuendo, slander and distortion, they stopped at nothing.
Through it all Eisenhower appeared the cheery apostle
of a righteous America who would clean up the mess in
Washington. At times it almost seemed that he was
being manipulated by clever men in the shadows. But
as the Republican candidate was campaigning in Illinois
and preparing to go into Wisconsin, word got out that
he meant to defend General Marshall in McCarthy's
home state. Before his train arrived in Wisconsin he
had a visitor, Thomas Coleman, a powerful Wisconsin
Republican leader from Madison, and an ardent Taft
man never reconciled to Ike's nomination at the Chicago
convention. Coleman had a long conference in the rear
car with the candidate. He is credited with persuading
Eisenhower to omit the paragraph praising Marshall.
In any event, it was excised, although the wording was
later disclosed. I had known Coleman on his home
ground. Silver haired, carefully dressed, he was the
essence of respectable, worldly success in the law. Yet
beneath this front was a desire for revenge against those
whom he blamed for the changes threatening his secure
world. McCarthy was the crude instrument for this fight.

There was an even lower moment in that schizo-
phrenic campaign. A report reached Democratic headquarters that McCarthy was to make a nationwide television attack on the Stevenson campaign. He had been
boasting he would say it was made up of pinks, punks
and pansies. This last was a public reference to the ugly
whispering campaign about Stevenson's personal life.
The Stevenson strategists were determined to fight back.
They had come into possession of a copy of a letter
General Marshall had written to General Eisenhower
when the Supreme Commander had returned to Washington for a brief interval while still in command in
Europe. He had come ostensibly to inform his wife that

he intended to seek a divorce when the war was ended. In blunt military language Marshall informed him that he was aware of the reasons for his return, that he was absent without leave, and that if he did not resume his post immediately he would be relieved of his command. Notice was privately served that if McCarthy used the gutter language the letter would be released. The resulting McCarthy broadcast was, for McCarthy, comparatively innocuous. I am sure General Marshall had no knowledge that a copy of his letter had somehow been obtained from the Pentagon files. It would have shocked and angered him that it was put to a political use. But I am also sure that such a letter existed. Six years after he left the White House, Truman told Merle Miller that he had ordered the Marshall letter destroyed. Those familiar with the whole circumstance question whether this was done.

Not long after the inauguration of President Eisenhower, I went out to see General Marshall, who was living in retirement on a small estate near Leesburg, Virginia. The white frame house was sprawling and undistinguished, but the big livingroom had a comfortable air of peace. General and Mrs. Marshall received me and I quickly got down to the purpose of my visit: to impress on him the extent of the interest I had found in his writing his memoirs. He quickly dispensed with this and went on to talk of other matters. For a few minutes the General left the room. Mrs. Marshall, who resembled him in her poise and quiet dignity, said in an earnest voice, "George will not tell you but I will. He sat in front of that radio," gesturing at an ancient table radio against the wall, "night after night waiting for General Eisenhower to say a word in his defense."

On a more relaxed occasion, at a family birthday party at his brother-in-law's place nearby, I again brought up the question of his memoirs. Half-joking I said he undoubtedly knew that General Eisenhower was completing a history of the war, for which he was to be paid a large sum of money. His reply, tempered with laughter, made an unforgettable impression. "Childs, you surely know that there has never been an honest history written of any war. Why do you think I should start now?"

In the basement of the Capitol, which in the tourist season is a bit like Coney Island with a touch of Gimbel's, I spotted McCarthy as I got off one of the trains from the Senate office building. A lieutenant had brought him a copy of the Washington *Star*, opened to a picture of the Senator with the wife of the Nationalist Chinese ambassador. He had been the center of attention at a British embassy reception for Queen Elizabeth and Prince Philip, the curious swarming around him in that starchy setting. He was exclaiming with pleasure over this cachet as I came up; the slugger from the cutover country wanted to be "in." This was one of the weaknesses of the antihero, the need for an image, always self-admiring, and the television image was his triumph until he began to fall, the Senate at last censuring him for having broken every rule. With the antihero, as with the hero the public creates, image is often the reality. But, with the genuine hero like Marshall, created by his own strength, the image is not all, and power grows in the memory of history.

IV

The Conquered
and the Conquerors

Under the full moon the silent city seemed emptied of human life. Madrid was under siege. At bright noon, from one of the top floors of Telefonika, the city's only tall building, I could see the artillery emplacements of Franco's forces in the nearby suburbs. There was a puff of smoke and seconds later the silence was broken by the sound of the firing. I watched with fascination.

Even this early in the siege, autumn 1937, the suffering and hardship had begun to close in. Taken to an improvised hospital where several German pilots who had been shot down were recovering from their injuries, I talked to partisans who had no doubt of the outcome. These blond young men spoke, with only slightly subdued arrogance, of certain victory. They were the wave of the future. This was the boast of the Nazis and the Fascists who sent, with little or no concealment, all possible help to Franco. The noose was tightening around the city, food was increasingly scarce, a cold winter was in prospect. I left after five weeks, convinced that unless the democracies countered at least in some degree the help from the totalitarian bloc Franco would win and Spain would be an adjunct of Hitler and Mussolini.

Back in Washington, I joined one of those wistfully hopeful organizations, Friends of Loyalist Spain it may have been, formed to propagandize against the Roosevelt policy of untouchability and the arms embargo. In the perspective of the tough-minded we were the innocents. Certainly we were unaware until much later that Moscow was providing just enough arms to keep the war going, not enough to tip the balance, and that commissars with the Loyalist forces were acting on orders from the Kremlin to liquidate those suspected of deviating from the Stalinist line. As I learned much later, my name, along with many thousands of others, was listed in the files of the House Committee on Un-American Activities as a comsympo.

During the preceding summer I had several times flown in and out of London from Scandinavia where I was working on a second book. As we came in over the red tile roofs of those square miles of cottage suburbs of London, I thought of what an irresistible target this was for the new engines of war. An air raid in Valencia, with the ack-ack guns going off and the bombs falling, was an example of the power of those engines. As I moved across Europe a decade later I saw the ruin war had caused. The democracies had not known what to do about their earlier defeat in Spain—and it was their defeat. Now the question recurred to me whether they knew what to do with victory.

Outside what remained of the offices of Krupp in Essen in 1947, a decade later, I stood in the brilliant sun talking with Alfried Krupp. It was a surrealist setting of jagged steel girders against the sky, proof of the efficiency of American bombing. Interpreting for Krupp was his brilliant young lieutenant, Berthold Beitz, the smiling, confident front of the new Germany. Krupp barely concealed his antagonism toward this American who presumed to question him; his answers were guarded, almost sullen. Perhaps to goad him I asked, "Herr Krupp, when will you come to America?"

For a moment he hesitated, his thin grey face a mask of the frustration of the conquered spurning this interrogator for the conqueror.

"I shall never come to America. You put me in jail and you have only recently released me."

Beitz was anxious to give a better look to this hostility. You see, he explained, Krupp had not expected to be put in jail; it was a great shock to him. There seemed little more to say. I next saw Beitz in Peking in 1973. He had become the head not only of the Krupp complex but the Krupp Foundation and as such he was the leader of a group of German industrialists seeking contracts in China. The Germans had made considerable advances in the People's Republic with ready-built petrochemical plants. I thought of what I had said with such bland confidence when, on the day after the fall of Cologne, I had written from that devastated city that it would be twenty-five years or more before any revival of German industry was possible. It was a grave misjudgment shared by many. A large infusion of dollars, a total of perhaps $4 billion, along with the capacity of the German people to labor, produced the German miracle.

No one could accuse the Krupps of lack of nerve. Outside ruined Essen in the British zone of occupation, the North German Coal Commission had offices in Villa Hugel, which had been the seat of the Krupps. One of the most remarkable private houses in the world, this palace of 450 rooms could hardly be called a home. Frau Bertha's two-story bathroom could hold a hippopotamus. A documentary film unearthed by the occupation forces and used at the Nürnberg trials showed Hitler being received at the entrance of the mansion by Alfried's father, Gustav. In 1947, Frau Bertha wrote to the British government in London asking that Villa Hugel be returned to her. The request was ignored and the officers of the Coal Commission continued to occupy the villa, which had come through the bombing more or less unscathed, the magnificent Gobelin tapestries still in place and the family retainers serving the new masters. A Krupp daughter had returned to inspect Villa Hugel and, as the British observed, the servants almost groveled in homage to one of the clan who, as a sardonic Britisher remarked, considered themselves rather above royalty and slightly below the Deity.

In the mass of rubble of flattened Berlin, death seemed almost palpable. The American proconsul in the western sector was Gen. Lucius D. Clay, a thin-lipped regular army man whose proconsulship was the springboard to the hierarchy of finance in New York. He spoke with feeling of the visitors from Washington, congressmen for the most part, who made his task even harder than it would otherwise have been. They wanted to be wined and dined in conquered Germany, but each wanted to have a personal exposition by the general on what he was trying to make of the German people. He had been struggling to keep the national diet at an average of 1100 to 1500 calories a day, and in the dark winter just past it had fallen below even that subsistence level, despite shipments of $600 million in supplies, mostly from the United States. Only Clay's stern discipline kept him from boiling over. He told me of one woman member of Congress who interrupted a conference in his office dealing with a serious aspect of the occupation to say, "I want to know how much you spent on those draperies and this rug. As a representative of the American taxpayer, that is what I want to know." The General explained that the draperies and the rug had been requisitioned from the Germans. They had cost the taxpayer nothing.

In a glass and stucco building on the outskirts of the ruined city, the American viceroy kept a low profile. One MP was stationed at the gate of the courtyard before the main entrance, to inspect credentials; another at the main door. Clay had the symbols of prestige: a

private plane and a private train equipped with living
and office quarters in which he could shuttle between
Berlin and Frankfurt, the principal headquarters of the
American zone. He complained of the difficulty of getting decisions out of Washington. Finally, on his own,
he ordered a stop to reparatory shipments of machinery
from the American sector to Soviet Russia. It was impossible to escape the sense that the enemy stood beyond
the dividing line. There were two Germanys, one
anchored to the West, the other bound to the Communist
East. Yet Clay, the diplomat and tactician, maintained a
personal friendship with his Russian counterpart in
Berlin, Gen. Vasily Sokolovsky. They met three times a
month in the sessions of the Allied Control Council.

Men like Clay could govern with resources that
were constantly being cut back by Congress. The junke-
teers quickly learned how to trade coffee and cigarettes
from the PX for antique Meissen and other treasures in
the commission shops where the Germans took their
prized possessions. Ernst Reuter, the first mayor of
West Berlin after the occupation forces had withdrawn,
told me the Americans wanted to make over Germany
in its own image but it would be impossible. His comment came when he had jousted with a Senator who
preached a free economy. A sensitive, highly intelligent
man, Reuter knew only too well how difficult it was to
impose American-style free enterprise on Germany.
Reuter's successor, Willy Brandt, also learned, during
his own transition from exile in Norway, where he had
escaped the Nazi executioners, to the tough politics of
Social-Democratic Berlin, that the image of an America
dedicated to free enterprise could never be transposed.
With the Marshall Plan and the rebuilding of German
industry, the forces that had dominated the economy
before the war assumed new and, for the conquerors,
acceptable shapes. I remember calling on the director
of a leading chemical company on the eighteenth floor
of a new building in restored Düsseldorf. I congratu-
lated him on his spacious headquarters. Yes, he said

with a rather roguish smile, thank you very much. You gave it to us.

From Germany I traveled to Warsaw. The destruction of Poland's capital, largely the work of the German invading force, was complete. At night, in my room in the surviving wing of the only hotel open for foreigners, I could hear rats gnawing in the walls. One of the few officials available to visiting correspondents was Jakub Berman, believed by many to be the most powerful figure in the government. His official title was Under-Secretary of State of the Council of Ministers. An intellectual and historian, profoundly schooled in Marxism, he had escaped to Moscow in 1939 and returned with the Red Army. Berman received me in his office in the building that housed the Council of Ministers; it was one of the few structures in the center of Warsaw that had not been deliberately destroyed. The office was a piece of the past; in one corner stood the figure of a Polish saint in dark wood, on one wall hung a large painting of a winter scene with a Polish peasant walking down a desolate, rutted road. His white hair receding from a high-domed forehead, his eyes impenetrable, Berman spoke calmly even when I put to him the most provocative of questions: "Will Poland one day be the seventeenth republic of the Soviet Union?"

Berman replied, "Poland will always be an independent state, Poland will always be a Catholic state."

Much of what he said was rationalization for the decrees enforcing dictatorship over every phase of the economy, the press and all aspects of intellectual life. It went like this: "These are only temporary measures. Our country is just now in a very troubled condition. There are elements seeking to create chaos and confusion. They must not be allowed to cause further dissension."

The question at that moment was how far the government meant to push the political trials—reprisals, really, against those who stood for the old order. Among the courageous figures out of the past was Stanislaw Mikolajczyk. Although his Peasant Party had been robbed of position, prestige and funds, he stayed on, defying the threat of prison or worse. Survivors of the Poland of the great landed feudal estates were artifacts that had come through war and occupation. I lunched one day with a Prince Radziwill, an authentic Radziwill who would have scorned the thought of trading on his ancient name. A small cheerful man with a quick wit, he told me of a visit he had recently paid to his former estate. The guest of his one-time gatekeeper in the gate house, he had been pleased that they had been able to reestablish their friendship despite the radical change. Radziwill was one of the leaders of the Democrat Party, a splinter tolerated by the regime because it lent the illusion of democracy to a state ruled by the Communist Party. Radziwill had talked to an American journalist in Warsaw not long before, and with characteristic frankness he spoke about his own position and his attitude toward the government. Thinking it was a private conversation he was dismayed to discover that his remarks had been reported in a magazine of wide circulation. It could hardly have contributed to the delicate balance he maintained between freedom and dependence on the goodwill of the regime.

I left feeling that the only power the Polish people had was their independence, their pride, their courage. They had learned the lesson of survival which was not equivalent to submission. When I returned to Warsaw in 1949 I was impressed by the pace of reconstruction. The old city had been restored with exactitude, through the use of drawings and plans in the archives. It made a handsome center, and the Poles could point with derision to the contrast it offered to the Stalinesque skyscraper that had been a gift of the Soviet Union. On a warm Sunday the cathedral was crowded, many of the worshipers soldiers in uniform.

If the meaning of victory in the shambles of Germany was uncertain, it was more elusive in the Greek microcosm where, under the Truman doctrine of aid to Greece and Turkey, American missions, both economic and military, had moved in. When I arrived in Athens in September 1947, Dwight Griswold, a former governor of Nebraska, had been head of the aid mission for three months. A down-to-earth midwesterner, Griswold frankly talked about his problems in helping to rebuild a country that had been, perhaps more than any other, ravaged by war and revolution. One of his principal complaints was of the almost total irresponsibility of the upper-class Greeks who had survived the holocaust, many with their fortunes, if not intact, in at least reasonable shape. He spoke sardonically of the visit of Madame Papastratos, who had come from her handsome house on Kolonaki Square to implore him to save her country. The chief owner of the cigarette monopoly, she had so many diamonds on her hands, Griswold said, that he was dazzled for a moment. I wanted to tell her that if she'd sell some of those diamonds she could help her own people, but I didn't say that. I just said I'd do the best I could with what Congress had given me. And that was little enough—$350 million to be spent before the following June 30, when Congress might or might not come through with a new appropriation. Used to restore ruined roads and rebuild the port of Piraeus, it fell short of the urgent need to revive industry and provide jobs for the mass of jobless.

Reports of troop movements in the north, where constant Communist replenishments were coming across the Yugoslav and Albanian borders, coupled with rumors of an armed uprising in Athens had during the summer just past sent the rich scurrying to the waterfront to buy their way out. They paid 50 gold sovereigns, $1500 in American money at the legal rate, for an option on a seat in a sailing vessel. They agreed, if they took up the option, to pay an additional 150 sovereigns, this for merely a place to sit in a small boat that might make it to Turkey or Egypt. More serious, as Griswold noted, was the flight of capital. Estimating that more than a billion dollars had found safe haven abroad, he was frank to admit he was not sure a way could be found to compel the wealthy Greeks to bring it back and invest it in their own country. We had rushed to the rescue like a team of amateur fire fighters when the British had put down their burden in the eastern Mediterranean, but we had imposed no requirements in return for our help; we had no plan for the day after tomorrow when the Greek people would again have enough to eat and perhaps even enough to wear.

The dilemma was complicated by a sharp, widely aired difference between two American authorities in Athens who looked at Greece from quite opposite perspectives. Griswold wanted to build roads and docks, and get back to Nebraska as soon as he could. Lincoln MacVeagh, the American ambassador for fourteen years with an interval out for the war, from the same Groton, upper-class background as his friend, Franklin Roosevelt, spoke for the past, the Parthenon, the glories of Greece. He expressed his strong opposition to meddling in Greek politics. The glories of Greece were a precious heritage, he asserted, but the Greeks of the day were a primitive people. Even in their dress, the two Americans were opposites. In the sticky, humid heat of Athens, Griswold wore baggy seersucker pants and a rayon sport shirt. MacVeagh was starchy in his sartorial rectitude, heat or no heat. The basic dispute was over the conviction of Griswold and the members of his aid mission that a broad-based government was essential if the confidence of the Greek people was to be revived. Attached to Constantine Tsaldaris, the stubborn leader of the Populists, MacVeagh was opposed to a coalition that would include the eighty-six-year-old leader of the Liberal Party, Themistocles Sophoulis. Sophoulis, MacVeagh let me know, was a fellow traveler on the Communist line. For a year and a half since his return to Athens, the ambassador had not seen the venerable and revered Sophoulis.

The steady trend was toward authoritarianism with the familiar figures of the past assuming old roles. King

Paul and Queen Frederika, whom we helped to put back on the throne, were of little use. The Hohenzollern queen stopped me in a receiving line when I returned in 1951, fixed me with a sharp eye, and said, "You were the one who wrote those untrue things about my country." In that troubled earlier time when a Communist triumph could not be ruled out, Archbishop Damaskinos was a symbol of faith and more than that. With his long silver beard, his high black headdress, his flowing gown, he spoke with gratitude for American help, and expressed the simple belief that in the end truth and right must triumph. It was like that in Epirus in the north. In an ancient jeep I traveled to the line near the town of Ioannina where a Greek artillery unit fired shells into the blue haze of the mountains. Perhaps ten miles away was the Albanian border and, I was told, the guerrillas were lurking in the valleys from which they came to murder, burn and pillage. At a crossroads village shepherds in blue and white homespun, leaning on their long crooks, told of being captured by a guerrilla band. Most of their 5,000 sheep had been slaughtered, and they were told to tend the rest. The tale of their escape had an epic simplicity. The two senior shepherds were frequently interrupted by corrections from their younger fellows. If it were not for the war they would have been in the mountains with their flocks, but that was far too risky and so sheep and goats were grazing in valleys already overgrazed. Thus the war was cutting further into the meager and primitive economy. And it would go on until Tito, defying Stalin and setting his own independent policy, closed the border with Greece and stopped the influx of Communist-trained guerrillas.

In France and Italy the threat of communism took a different form. In Rome one heard rumors of an armed uprising. After a winter of hunger and hardship, the power of the Communist-dominated trade unions and the organization of the party itself, claiming 5 million members, made a takeover by ostensibly legitimate means a probability in the coming spring. Careful ob-

servers believed that there were as many as 3 million
dues-paying members, and the General Confederation
of Labor, with its 6.7 million members was nearly 60
percent Communist and 20 percent Socialist.

Moscow-trained and conditioned men were in place
and hard at work. The number one Communist was
Palmiro Togliatti, schooled in the Soviet Union for
fifteen years, who would not see an American correspondent or, for that matter, any foreign journalist. Number two was Giuseppe di Vittori, head of the Confederation of Labor, a big man with thick shoulders and a large
head with a shock of black hair. He consented to receive
me. During the early days of fascism he had been in and
out of jail and then in exile. For four years during the
civil war in Spain, di Vittori was a political commissar in
the International Brigade. If any toughening process had
been required, that was it—killing and dying on orders
from Moscow. Even when Nazism had been triumphant
in all of Europe he had traveled through the Communist
underground with forged documents. He spoke of the
agricultural laborers in the north: They had been slaves,
now they were organized. In his comment was no emotion. The sternest response came when I suggested that
he must be very tough to have come through so much.
Not at all, he said. That was a distortion by the American
press where the Communists were made out to be barbarians. "I believe in legal methods," said di Vittori.
"We want to avoid a civil war. There has been too much
bloodshed. We shall not force a resort to arms. I myself
am a humanitarian." But he uttered a warning. If help
came, no matter from what source, to restore those who
had been in power before the war, then he and his followers would fight force with force. This I had no
trouble in believing.

A little later I talked with Pietro Nenni, the head of
the Socialist Party. He looked like Foxy Grandpa, a
figure from my early comic strip days. In my supreme
naiveté I said, "But look, if you join with the Communists and force the Christian Democrats out of the

government then the United States will withdraw its military support for Italy." He laughed uproariously. That is just what we want, he said.

In the soft October weather, Rome was beautiful, despite the menace that lay beneath the surface. The broad piazzas were almost empty, the streets uncluttered, the locust plague of the motor car had not yet descended. Bread and pasta and oil were the only thought of the governed and of those trying uncertainly to govern a people highly resistant to authority. The Eternal City—that ancient tag had an ironic sound in the atomic age. I went out to Castel Gandolfo for a private audience with Pope Pius, arranged by the young seminarians of the North American College. They lived in luxury in the villa of a wealthy American woman who had willed it to the American Church with a generous endowment. At Gandolfo, flourishing my notice of *audenzio solo*, I was ushered through one vast chamber after another filled with nuns, priests, and the devout laity. At last I was alone with only one other occupant. From beyond a screen and through an open door came the sound of two voices. One I thought was that of the Pope. After a few minutes he appeared, dressed entirely in white. I had wanted to ask him about the state of the Church in Poland and Hungary. Apparently puzzled by my questions, he answered with a few words of compassion about our brothers and their suffering in Poland. After another question and another brief answer he said, "Now whom do you want me to bless?" I had come with a supply of rosaries but I ran out of names. After giving me his blessing, he moved on and I followed him through the audience chambers where the nuns, the priests and the devout laity bowed down like grain before a wind. With a sense of guilt I felt I had wasted the time of a man concerned with the plight of mankind but who had not been given the slightest inkling of what my purpose had been by the seminarians who recommended that he see me.

The beauty of Paris was like that of Rome, faded yet

with the grace of the past. Contrasts were startling. Here
was a poorly paid worker in a big hotel kitchen, stealing
fats with which he made soap to be sold on the black
market. The luxury restaurants were crowded with
French for the most part, paying exorbitant prices for
food. In one restaurant a sign behind the bar said, "Did
you ever see a safe deposit box following a funeral
procession?" The big hotels on the Riviera were said to
be still crowded although the "season" had long since
ended. And you heard talk of white yachts in a blue sea.
Paris was crowded with members of Congress who had
come from Washington to see for themselves the condition of Europe before they voted on the Marshall plan.
Without massive help, another winter, the third since
the liberation, would bring hunger and disease. Soap
was scarce in the shops, and that scarcity was a certain
indicator on the disease graph. But in what quantity and
how rapidly should the dollars be dispensed? The six-
teen nations under the umbrella of the Marshall Plan
were drawing up shopping lists to cover their most
urgent needs from 1948 to 1951. The first list added up
to $29 billion. To Americans working with the Euro-
peans that was a shocker. A more reasonable total was
$22 billion, and yet even that figure seemed beyond the
scope of Congress.

Many of the congressmen brought their prejudices
with them and returned with them intact. Others were
seriously concerned with getting at the truth of the situation. One of these was Rep. Christian Herter of Massachusetts, a Republican bent on leading his party out of
the wasteland of isolationism. The members of the
House he had organized spent a month of intensive
effort talking with a wide range of officials in each
country and looking at the life of ordinary people. I
think we really understand the need, Herter said. One of
his group was Everett Dirksen, the sage of Peoria in the
heart of isolationist Illinois, who allowed that he, too,
had been converted. It was to prove a wavering conver-
sion, the temperature of his faith depending on the

politics of the day. Richard Nixon, another of the Herter group, was more cautious in his pronouncements.

Central to all discussion in France was Jean Monnet. I had known this small, slender Frenchman with his indomitable energy in Washington where he had been head of the French purchasing mission. Now in Paris he was the dedicated apostle of a unified Europe. It was intellect he radiated, a clear distillation of the Gallic mind. The initial step was a recovery plan for France which would exercise an attraction on all of Europe. The plan was the work of Monnet and the brilliant young men he had gathered around him in the General Commission. Monnet reported with pride that French coal mines were producing more coal than in 1938. Yes, there were tremendous obstacles—inflation with a runaway currency and the peasants hoarding their gold, the bitter polarization in politics between Left and Right with a feeble centrist government—but nothing could daunt Monnet's optimism. It was so logical, it must come. He insisted in a long talk with me that the Communists could not be excluded. That was an American fixation which, if it were written into the Marshall Plan legislation, would make it impossible for France to cooperate. Of course, the ultimate goal of the Communists was a dictatorship of the Left with Russia as the guiding force, but the Communist leaders of the General Confederation of Workers were Frenchmen, and they had actually urged harder work to hasten recovery. The Monnet logic went like this: France is a very old and complex civilization with a subtle and profound culture. Communism of the dogmatic Marxist-Stalinist type is bound to be modified in such a civilization. By working with the Communists over the years France might be able to achieve a synthesis in which Communist doctrine would undergo a drastic change.

No government that shut out the Communists could hope to succeed since they had polled more than 5 million votes at the last election. He urged me to talk with one or two of the leaders of the workers' confederation to find out their views; I would see for myself that they were reasonable men. To talk with Monnet, as I did over the years in his apartment office on the Avenue Foch, was to be impressed with the clear vigor of his mind. If I make him sound didactic or pontifical, I am in error. French to the core, he was master of the practical arrangements of living: the right wine, the proper dishes, the quiet elegance of a livingroom that was a place of comfort and ease. But even then he was moving on a collision course with the soldier who was the embodiment of *la gloire,* Charles de Gaulle, a man bent on reviving the greatness of France, inspiring his people with the splendors of the past and the promise of an heroic future. Speaking around the country to huge crowds, de Gaulle was denouncing the French Communists as agents of the Soviet Union out to destroy France. Against a resounding appeal to patriotism—for, in its highly refined literary form, it was essentially that—the logic of a Monnet was outdistanced. Monnet never lost his optimism even when de Gaulle came to triumphant power. He continued to believe in a united Europe that would show the way to a new order of life. There were painful disappointments. I remember meeting him outside the National Assembly in 1954 just after the Assembly had voted down the European Defense Community. It was a defeat for those, including many Americans, who had believed this could be the start of a true union. Coming out of the dank Assembly chamber where a melancholy Premier Pierre Mendès-France had presided over the rout was like crawling out of a cellar into blinding daylight. I approached Monnet as he was hurrying away. How serious is this? I asked. It was only temporary; he could bring himself to say nothing more.

So many of the best and brightest had responded to de Gaulle's clarion call. A lunch was arranged by Elizabeth de Mirabelle, a charming young woman who had served in Washington during the war. An ardent Gaullist, she had for a time, overcome with chagrin at the failure of the French to recognize the true stature of her hero, entered a Carmelite nunnery. The legend was that contrary to the stern rules of the order she had had a telephone in her cell and in this way kept in close touch with the world of politics. Among her guests were André Malraux, already the worshipful disciple who would light the candles of culture at the de Gaulle shrine, and Isaiah Berlin, the Oxford scholar. Malraux spoke with nervous rapidity, accentuated by a tic, while Berlin's French proved to be at the same express-train speed as his English, which was virtually unintelligible by reason of a broad Oxonian accent. They became involved in a heated argument over an obscure Russian poet, or so Elizabeth informed us, since she alone seemed able to understand both these dazzlers. The only intrusion came when I made a reference to my impression that Malraux had been a Communist at the time he was flying for the Loyalists in the Spanish Civil War. He showed his annoyance. No, I was never a member of the Communist party, never a Communist; I was simply exercising my conviction of the peril of fascism in the Iberian peninsula and the puerile weakness of the democracies.

An hour away by flying time, London was another world. It was austere, for the socialists in power—men out of the mines, out of trade union offices, out of sooty lower middle-class environs—were attempting the transition against impossible odds. The nation's cupboard had been stripped bare and a people who had been led to believe that the war's end would bring more of the good things of life faced a new pinch. A bitterness that rarely came to the surface emerged as President Truman abruptly cut off lend-lease after, or so they believed, President Roosevelt had pledged it would go on for a year or a year-and-a-half after the end of the war.

Foremost among these men of labor was Ernest Bevin, presiding as Foreign Secretary over the lofty halls of the Foreign Office. As much as any single individual on the other side of the Atlantic, he had brought the Marshall Plan to the threshold of life. With a pleased

grin on his round face, he told the story of the first conference in Paris to make ready for the plan when it was
finally approved. In that initial stage, representatives of
the Communist powers in the East were present; the
American proprosal had not discriminated between
East and West. Molotov, smoking one cigarette after
the other, his expression imperturbable, listened as
Bevin put forward the role of Europe in the plan. As
Bevin told it, Molotov seemed to agree that the Soviet
Union and the satellites would participate. Then halfway through the conference he left the room to make a
telephone call. When he returned he reversed his position. Moscow, and it went without saying the satellites
as well, would have no part in this imperialist plot.
Sure, said Bevin with his rumbling chuckle, you could
be certain of one thing: That call had been to Stalin.
The adoption of the program, and with it the billions
to be appropriated by Congress, had been made immeasurably easier. Bevin understood this, too, as he had
known that what might have appeared as an American
effort to force Europe to choose between Moscow and
Washington would have been rejected by London and
Paris.

Representative Herter was an invaluable catalyst.
Foreseeing that nationalization would be a hurdle with
conservatives in Congress, he called on three Tory
leaders and put the same question to each. Lord Woolton, chairman of the Conservative party; Anthony Eden,
a former Foreign Secretary; and R. A. Butler, the author
of the party's official program that was so far-reaching
in social responsibility that it scared the daylights out
of hidebound American conservatives, were asked what
they thought would be the result in the Conservative
party of a provision written into the Marshall Plan for-
bidding further nationalization. They all gave the same
reply: It would be absolutely fatal; the party could not
support the plan if it contained that provision even
though the Conservatives were implacably opposed to
further nationalization. Coal had been nationalized on
the initiative of the Labour party, and the long-term con-

sequences were already dubious, but such a prohibition, imposed by the United States, would be taken as an affront to the right of free British subjects.

On the stage at this moment were two figures larger than life. One was Aneurin Bevan, the Minister of Health, who at the age of thirteen had gone down into a Welsh coal pit to begin his working career. For many years he had worked at the coal face; it was grueling labor in darkness and fetid air. Solid, thick, with a heavy thatch of iron grey hair, he looked with defiance out of eyes the color of blue ice. Bevan talked about the coal crisis although it was not in his province. Labor in the mines, he said, with his Welsh burr, was slave labor; to go down into the pits each day was to face eight hours of death, eight hours of burial. You in America, he said with half admiration, half contempt, would have had your own problem in persuading men to go down into the mines if you had not converted so much of industry and home heating to oil. And with a prophetic sweep he went on to say that this had created an oil problem not only in the United States, but all over the world. "And you will discover that in the future."

In the Conservative press Bevan was the villain of the piece. He was charged with persuading the Cabinet to carry through the proposed restrictions on the House of Lords as a preliminary to the nationalization of iron and steel. Bevan had more of the militant spirit of the Labour party of the past. The senior Cabinet members had been part of the wartime coalition and, overawed by the enormity of the economic crisis, they were tamed. Out of party loyalty Bevan stopped just short of saying that, but he had not altered his conviction of the unworkability of the capitalist system. Too many IOUs, he put it, were in the hands of the rich. He resented it when I suggested that his government was putting too many IOUs in the pay envelopes of the workers in the form of money that would buy little or nothing and therefore was contributing to Britain's inflation. Not so, not so, what would you have us do?

The other figure was the hero rejected. With the

war ended and his meeting with Truman and Stalin at
Potsdam in the past, Winston Churchill had been turned
out of office by the British voter. It was a stunning
reversal for the man who had been hailed as the savior
of Britain and the West. He and Bevan were poles apart
politically, and when they clashed in the House of Commons, every seat in the gallery was filled. At the Conservative party conference at Brighton, Churchill had
just delivered a savage attack on the Labour government with Bevan as one of his targets. The militant
socialists would be the ruin of the nation, he asserted.
His pursuit of power was unabated. Trying to snatch a
word with him in the lobby of the House or at some
public gathering in London or Washington was, to use
that fine bureaucratic password, counterproductive.

A large share of the burden of meting out the aus-
terities fell on John Strachey, the somber intellectual
who was Minister of Food. Rations were being chipped
away as a consequence of far-distant events over which
he had no control. Because of a strike of Canadian meat
packers, Strachey had to announce that the bacon ra-
tion was to be cut from two ounces to one. This meant
that the working man's "bit of bacon," on which he
put such a high value, would be a mere tantalizing bite.
Strachey's task was to comb the empire, where sterling
still counted, to find foods to replace those unobtain-
able for lack of dollars. One such was whale steak. The
ministry insisted that it could be made palatable if
sufficiently marinated to remove the oily taste. Strachey
himself had come to the defense of snoek. Canned snoek,
the British word for barracuda, was expected to arrive
in quantities from South Africa. This produced a rash of
cartoons and jokes, many of them at Strachey's expense.
Solemnly the minister announced that he had been
informed that snoek was tasty and nutritious.

The Prime Minister in this congeries of intellectuals
was Clement Attlee. I went to Downing Street determined to get his opinion on nationalization, since his
cabinet and his party seemed of two minds. Among a

wide range of such encounters in various parts of the world that one was perhaps my most frustrating. I had noted in the morning papers that the Prime Minister and his wife had attended the previous night the premier of an American film based on the *Forsyte Saga*. As an opening gambit I mentioned the film. Twenty-five minutes later Attlee was still talking about Galsworthy and the injustice the picture had done to a great work. Walter Pidgeon was not Soames Forsyte. Impossible! He had a reverential admiration for Galsworthy, and I could not get him off the track. When the exposition finally came to an end my time had just about run out. A fussy aide had come into the room and put a chit in front of him, obviously to inform him that his next appointment was waiting. A few highly generalized remarks about the problems Britain faced concluded this absurdity.

Although obscured by the tradition of "carrying on," the stiff upper lip, and the habits of caste and class, the facade of the past had been broken. Chaperoned by the National Coal Board, I went down a coal mine. By any standard the equipment seemed primitive, out of the nineteenth century. It seemed a paradox of the conquered and conqueror. The Krupp steel works would be rebuilt with plants far more efficient than those of Britain or, for that matter, the United States. So would the steel plants in Japan, destroyed by American bombers; the advanced oxygen process as high as 90 percent against 30 percent at home. With tamed unions, or no unions at all, and a drive to overcome the shame of defeat, the conquered powers were soon to move into world markets to outsell the British and to invade America with Japanese steel at prices so competitive that "voluntary" quotas were created to fix limits not written into tariff laws. Conquered and conqueror—the terms seemed as remote as the triumphal procession of a Roman emperor with the conquered in chains and the captured gold and treasure held up for the cheering populace to see.

I left London with regret and a foreboding similar to the one I had felt as I flew low over those red roofs years before. They were such a patient people, the British. Civility, the practice of courtesy, had made existence on an overcrowded island a gift. Would it all go as the empire was going, and with it the intangibles, the rewards of money and position that had underwritten the civility? If it was to go the world would be immeasurably the poorer.

Winners
and Losers

He was new to the governor's residence in Springfield, but on that day Adlai Stevenson was enjoying an apolitical role as he invariably did. In the late afternoon he had taken two of his visitors from the East in the governor's official limousine on a tour of the reconstructed village of New Salem, where Abraham Lincoln had come of age. Twice, when we had made some political comment, Stevenson had whispered a word of caution. The chauffeur, a state trooper, had been in the service of his Republican predecessor, and the suspicion was that he reported back whatever this Democrat or his companions might have to say. He would be transferred soon but for the time being, discretion was the rule. Even though the capital on the prairie bore some outward resemblance to that earlier time, it was not the Springfield of Lincoln.

Back in Springfield, we were talking of his inauguration, of the friends who had come from near and far for that ceremony. Stevenson was enjoying himself. As the host—his wife had left him a short time before—he brought life to the stiff officialdom of the big sitting room in the "mansion." From the downstairs office came word that the governor's able administrative assistant, William McCormick Blair, Jr., was wanted. Returning after a quarter of an hour, Blair said, "Sorry, Governor, that is Botchy Conners and he says he has to see you." William J. Conners was one of Chicago Mayor Richard Daley's henchmen, who served in the legislature with formidable clout. There, said Stevenson, turning to us as he rose, you can stay and enjoy yourselves while I have to deal with the Botchy Conners of this world.

I was to recall that remark many times in the years that followed. It had been spoken by the ambivalent Stevenson, never sure which course he wanted to follow: whether to play the game with Botchy Conners, the bosses, the power brokers, or to be one of the happy few absolved from mean care. Good fortune had blessed him; but the choices had been too easy. This was one reason he lacked the instinct for the jugular, the ultimate test of the drive for power.

In the euphoric years after the war I saw many men who had that instinct. There were those, like Bernard Baruch, obsessed with power yet so disciplined that the obsession was rarely evident in the smooth surface. Only the snapping turtle mouth now and then gave it away. For Harry Truman, the name of the game was winning. He scorned any player who failed to give his all. Averell Harriman, putting his considerable intellect in public service, pursued high office with a concentration of aim and some success. Eisenhower, another child of fortune, rode the long climb to the top in the hands of others, counting on his persona, the role he had early adopted, to see him safely through. The fifties were a fascinating period when Americans could still believe they could make over the world in the American image.

Harry Truman had been tapped by one of the last

of the bosses to serve as United States Senator. It was as elemental as that when Tom Pendergast ruled over Missouri. Precipitated into the Presidency wholly unprepared, Truman was what he had always been, the blunt, plain-speaking man from Independence. I had gone to see him early in his Presidency, with a special mission. Agnes Meyer had created the Wendell Willkie Awards for Negro Journalism to encourage higher standards in the Negro press. We were to make the first awards at a banquet in Washington. Who would be the speaker? I suggested the President. At Mrs. Meyer's request I called on him. Well, it's a good thing she sent you instead of coming herself, Truman said. Hardly a day goes by that I don't get a letter from that woman or from Eleanor Roosevelt telling me how to handle this job. I get along pretty well with the burr heads, he went on, until sooner or later I say nigger. I don't see why I shouldn't do it. And he did. As an indication of the state of the capital at that time, segregation was so tight that the only place the banquet with the award winners could be held was in the ballroom of the National Press Club.

Truman never repudiated his origins. He never turned his back on Pendergast nor did he forgive those, of whom I was one, who had helped bring about the boss's downfall and prison sentence. Gambling, prostitution, every form of corruption had given Kansas City at least a family resemblance to Port Said. But when he intervened to fix an insurance deal for a large bribe, or so it was reported, the boss had overreached himself.

The *Post-Dispatch* had begun to dig deep into the scandal. I was assigned to go to New York to try to interview Pendergast, about to sail for Europe on the maiden eastward crossing of the gaudy French liner *Normandie*. It seemed to me a futile exercise, yet any clue from Pendergast would be useful. I braced him outside the door of his suite in the Waldorf Towers just as his and Mrs. Pendergast's matching rawhide luggage was being moved out. He was a short, thick, bullet-headed man, scowling and uncommunicative; she, a weary, willowy blonde, looked at me with elegant disdain. He gave a noncommittal grunt when I said I would try to see him again on the ship. A chance came that I had not anticipated. Making the round trip on the *Normandie* was a friend from Paris, Bertrand de Jouvenel, a journalist and, later in his career, a political philosopher. He was bringing on board half a trunkful of books about current American political trends. Forget it, I said. Cultivate Tom Pendergast on the crossing and you'll get more knowledge about the practice of politics than is in any book. We went up to the Pendergasts' suite on the boat deck, three rooms filled with flowers, orchids, lilies of the valley. It was nothing at all, Mrs. Pendergast said, dismissing the display; there were twice as many down in the cooler, all from the boys back home. I introduced Bertrand, handsome, radiating Gallic charm, as Count de Jouvenel, a fellow passenger. Mrs. Pendergast was impressed. We talked a bit about politics and finally de Jouvenel said, "I must ask you, Mr. Pendergast, how you rule Missouri."

In an expansive mood the boss responded, "Well, I'll tell you how it is. I'm in my office all day long and people come to see me. They want something. Maybe it's half a load of coal or maybe it's a job or maybe some relative is in trouble. I try to help them That's the way it is."

I managed to get in a question about the insurance deal. Yes, I did that, he said, and what're you going to do about it? As the ship was about to sail I disembarked to find the nearest Western Union office. I wrote a long story with the insurance deal as the centerpiece but with a lot about the boat deck suite, the flowers and the magnificence of the Pendergasts' departure. When de Jouvenel returned to America a few months later the first thing he asked me was, "What did you do to that little man? I was in the barbershop the next morning and he rushed at me waving a sheaf of wireless telegrams and shouting." My whole story had been wirelessed to him, and he blamed de Jouvenel for what, as it turned out later, was a major break in the insurance investigation.

No President would ever again come to the office by way of the boss. A case could be made for the broker's role of the bosses. They served a purpose—the load of coal, the job, the handout for the hospital bill or the funeral—but even as Truman entered the White House the bosses had begun to recede. With welfare institutionalized and aid flowing from a wide variety of benefactors, public and private, the bosses had lost a principal excuse for being. As in the example of Pendergast, their power had been grossly abused. Racing stables, sable coats, boat deck suites, all went beyond what New Jersey's Frank Hague had called honest graft. They were replaced by money and the media, the two, because of the fantastic cost of television, inextricably linked. No one can contend that the ratio of corruption to political power has diminished. In the Nixon campaign of 1972 it was enormously inflated.

Given his background, his whole conditioning, Truman could never understand the ambivalent Stevenson. His reluctance, his hesitation, his doubts were beyond the President's comprehension. The party tie was not enough to bridge the gap between them. It was a gap that helped to bring Stevenson to disaster in the years ahead. Truman was familiar with the drive for power in the jungle that was Washington, the power drive in, say, a Bernard Baruch, a pure example of the rewards to the ego, if not in public office then in the guidance and control of men holding high office.

Truman gave Baruch one of the most important assignments of his early tenure as President at a time when Baruch's close friend, James F. Byrnes, was Secretary of State. That was to negotiate an agreement giving the United Nations Atomic Energy Commission sole control over all atomic material and atomic weapons. This put the Chief, as many of Baruch's associates called him, front and center on the world stage. Prior to the assignment, which was thought to have originated with Byrnes, a lengthy report had been prepared by Dean Acheson, then Under-Secretary of State, and David Lilienthal, chairman of the Tennessee Valley Authority, with the help of consultants thoroughly versed in the field. The report was a masterful work with a conceptual and practical approach to the problems of international control of a force that could bring an end to all civilization. Baruch was irritated that the report drew so much attention and detracted from the stage on which he was to perform. Policy differences developed when Baruch incorporated a clause calling for "swift and sure" punishment for any government violating the provisions of the treaty for international control. Nor would any member of the Security Council be allowed to veto a call for such punishment. Acheson and Lilienthal believed this clause would certainly doom the plan since it would appear to the Soviet Union as an American plot to stop its work on the bomb and thereby preserve the American atomic monopoly. Baruch played to the galleries magnificently with a speech intended to ring down the ages. The proposal died in the UN, as it would probably have died in any event, with a maneuver by Molotov before the General Assembly calling for general and total disarmament. Nevertheless, there was among some observers a lingering belief that a more flexible negotiator might have been able to salvage the beginnings of control and the genie still in its infancy might have been kept in the bottle. In a bitter note in his memoirs, Acheson tells how Baruch planted the suspicion that the Under-Secretary, soon to become Secretary of State, might be "soft on communism."

Of Baruch's power there could be no doubt. Byrnes, his fellow South Carolinian, told me that without much trouble he could name 100 members of Congress who had been beneficiaries of Baruch's largesse. A Senator was in a tight reelection campaign; Baruch was on the phone. The typical exchange went like this:

"How is it going?"

"Not too well."

"And money?"

"Well, you know it's the last week and I could commit more radio or television time if I had the money."

"There'll be a check in the mail this afternoon."

It might be for $10,000 or for a friend in a committee chairmanship $25,000, perhaps more. This was capital in the bank of the Baruch political holding company. His capital was enhanced by powerful and worldly friends. He had given substantial help to Winston Churchill when Churchill was out of office, a lonely figure in appeasement Britain.

The range of his friendships was remarkable. One that developed in his later years was with Eleanor Roosevelt. In his study in the five-story brownstone on upper Fifth Avenue, he told me that she had a short time before come to see him in great distress. She was sitting right there where you are. It was the first time I had ever seen her cry. I went over to the desk and wrote out what was the largest personal check I had ever written. She took it and went away. What was the trouble? I asked. You don't think I'd tell you, do you, he said with his good natured smile.

An implacable foe, he kept a surface calm and detachment toward friend and enemy alike. He told me once about a habit he had learned early in life. When he felt he was about to lose his temper he would shut himself up alone for fifteen minutes or half an hour until the seizure passed. One man whom he despised was John Maynard Keynes. For Baruch, a sufficient reason was Keynes' book, *The Economic Consequences of the Peace*, a devastating analysis of Woodrow Wilson's failure at Versailles to understand that a second World War was inevitable, given the accords he had been persuaded to sanction. Wilson had been instrumental in promoting Baruch from speculator to statesman and adviser to Presidents when he made him head of the War Production Board in the First World War. He had thereby won Baruch's undying gratitude. He urged caution, both at the Treasury and the White House, when Keynes came to Washington, in an infirm condition because of an earlier heart attack. When British lend-lease was rudely terminated it was believed Baruch had used his influence to that end. As Britain's continuing economic regression over the years was to show with doomsday certainty, the loan of $3.75 billion was, if not too late, surely too little.

He had used his influence to obtain for his brother, Herman, two ambassadorial posts—to Portugal and the Netherlands. Herman was a caricature of Bernard; he sported a splendid waxed moustache, a pure white goatee and a head of silky white hair. He was a skilled talker who could have made his own fortune selling patent medicine from the tail of a cart. The theatrical strain in the family (another brother, Sailing, was on the professional stage) was strong in Herman. It was apparent in a more restrained form in the Chief when he appeared before congressional committees to dispense in resounding, magisterial fashion the conventional wisdom on the economy and a balanced budget. The performance enchanted senators like Harry Byrd of Virginia, who saw their own views given impressive form. He rarely failed to stress his own Americanism, his origins in the Confederate South, spurning the Zionism which he, a Jew, saw as double loyalty.

As lord of the manor at Hobcaw Barony, his 50,000-acre estate in South Carolina, he lived the dream come true of the impoverished son of a doctor father who had served with the Confederate troops and been ruined by the war. He was an entertaining mimic and often did set pieces out of his past. One was of Sen. Ollie James of Kentucky, six-foot-three or four inches tall and weighing at least 300 pounds, climbing into an upper berth on a fast moving train. He re-created the Senator's struggles, his groans and complaints, the solicitude of the pullman porter and the protests of the man occupying the lower berth. In the evening we played low-stakes roulette with Baruch the croupier calling out, *"Faites vos jeux, monsieur et madame."* In the morning, sitting in the bright spring sun in the garden, he would now and then receive four or five venerable blacks from the nearby town. They would tell him their problems and he would give them sage advice together with modest contributions to their good works. Counseling his faithful retainers and surrounded by the wild unspoiled beauty of Hobcaw, he enjoyed the perfect dénouement.

For Truman, the touchstone of the politics in which he had come to power was loyalty. As he saw it, he had given generously to Baruch. As the difficult campaign of 1948 approached, and the Republicans were beginning to attack the evils of mink coats, deep freezes and other favors, the President asked Baruch for help. The answer was no. This shrewd operator was not putting his money on a number that would never come up. Truman wrote a characteristically Trumanesque letter, giving Baruch what for and adding for good measure, "as for that brother of yours, I can't tell you the trouble I've had with him." Two kinds of power had come into violent collision.

A similar collision was soon to occur with Stevenson. As his first full term in office wore on with the Democrats in increasing trouble, Truman found it hard to understand why the brilliant young Governor out in Illinois did not respond to the call of duty. Determined to find a candidate who could win in 1952, he had summoned Stevenson to the White House to tell him he was the choice. In Springfield not long afterward, I talked with Stevenson at the same time that a friendly emissary had come from Washington to underscore the President's conviction that Stevenson was the only one who could carry the party to victory. At dinner the first evening he was vexed, complaining, Why me? Why should it have to be me? Having carried the state by 480,000 in 1948, and bringing in Truman, who had won Illinois by only 20,000, he was confident he could be reelected to a second term. That was what he wanted; he was convinced that the reforms he had introduced were only in a beginning phase. I want to stay here. I'm not ready for the other. It was in franker form what he had said to the President when he had been summoned to the White House. Implied in his demurral was that after twenty years of Democratic rule in Washington perhaps the time had come for a change.

It was the beginning of a long ordeal for Stevenson. There was every likelihood that Ike, the hero, the savior of Europe, would be the Republican candidate. A Robert Taft might just possibly have been beatable. Of Taft's bitterness and the division within his party there was no doubt. I had dinner with him at Charlottesville, Virginia, just before I moderated a forum at the University of Virginia in which he was opposed by one of his trade union adversaries. This was on the eve of the Republican convention in Chicago. In his high-pitched, rasping voice, the Senator fumed at the press for having built up Eisenhower to such absurd heights, at the flabby opportunists in his own party who cared not a damn for principle and wanted only to win, at the labor unions for their arrogance and their political spending. It was a tirade coming from one who foresaw the fate that was to come a few days later.

In a curious and muted fashion Stevenson's mood bore a resemblance to that of Taft. Nominated by the Democratic convention with the customary brouhaha, he responded with that unhappy reference, "if this cup shall not pass," putting himself in the martyr's role. I was sitting in the press section with a wise woman deeply devoted to him. She was torn by conflicting emotions, the fear he would be lost to the political wars, concern for the coming trial, anguish at his own anguish in accepting a decision he had resisted. The martyr's role was hardly one calculated to send him out ready to take on all comers and give 'em hell. Following him about the country from time to time, I developed a great admiration for his gallantry in the face of every indication that he was running far behind, and even greater admiration for the speeches in which he discussed the issues facing the nation. They were superb political documents, received in city after city with the enthusiasm—adulation, really—he generated in a dedicated following.

Those speeches cost the candidate and members of his staff no little aging. An important text dealing with a vital issue was to be ready several hours in advance of delivery. At the appointed time the assembled press clamored for the release. An hour passed, two hours; where the hell was the speech? Clayton Fritchey, Stevenson's press aide, took much of the buffeting for these unhappy delays. He would shake his head philosophically and say, Well, that's just the way he is and I can't get him to do anything about it. He wants it to be perfect and there it is.

Toughies in the party gave Stevenson short shrift, and this was particularly true in Texas. On the extreme right, nominal Democrats were in open opposition, while smooth customers like John Connally and Lyndon Johnson gave him ostensible support in public and contempt in private. In no country in the world is there anything like the trial by fire of a Presidential campaign. Though heavily taxing the pocketbook, television has eased the strain on the feet, the lungs and the digestion, but only a little. Even for a man loving battle as did Truman and Wendell Willkie, it is an endurance test. For Stevenson, the reluctant dragon, it was purgatory. And to have to run the course twice! That was the ultimate curse which befell this most intelligent and compassionate man.

In September 1955, after several weeks in Europe, I went out to Denver, where Eisenhower was having what was euphemistically called a working vacation. I had been in Geneva for the summit conference at which he had put forth the "open skies" proposal calling for mutual aerial inspection of the armaments on each side. In Geneva, of course, he had been so closely surrounded by his security force that we glimpsed him only in passing and at second hand in the formal sessions of the summit. I had wanted to have a look at him and perhaps even a private background talk, the last unlikely but worth trying. He spent an hour or two each morning at Lowry Air Force base, where he had an office, and the rest of the day was golf. He took his real vacation when he went fishing in the high Rockies with a few cronies, leading the simple life, oblivious to the cares of the world.

On the second or third day I went out to Lowry to learn from the press office that the President was indisposed and would not be in. What was it? Nothing serious, really, a cold. On the way back to the Brown Palace Hotel I drove past the home of Mrs. Min Doud, Mrs. Eisenhower's mother, where the President and his wife were staying. I stopped the car and surveyed this modest dwelling on a modest street, with crop-headed Secret Service agents on the porch and on the walk in front. With a curious feeling that something more than a cold was involved, I nevertheless prepared to drive to Colorado Springs for a weekend with friends. Just as I was about to leave the hotel, a call came from the press office telling all reporters to return to Lowry. There Murray Schneider, acting press secretary in the absence of James Hagerty, announced that the President had suffered a mild heart attack and was already in the hospital. The twenty or so reporters ran madly for the telephones. It was tremendous news. As it ricocheted around the world, the first reaction was that, though Eisenhower might finish out the remaining year and a half of his term at the age of sixty-five, he would surely not run for reelection.

That was my own opinion as I left Denver two or three days after Hagerty arrived to orchestrate the publicity blitz promoting the President's recovery. What a blitz it was! I stopped in Chicago to see Stevenson at the law office where he was a partner. I told him I thought it would be impossible for Eisenhower to run for reelection although it appeared probable that, short of another attack, he would finish his term and Nixon as Vice-President would not inherit the office. Stevenson was greatly interested in all I had to report on the illness and the outlook for the future. I sensed this gave him a new perspective on 1956. Taft was dead and the Republicans would find it difficult to come together on another candidate. At least he would not have to run a second time against an invincible hero. That was a nightmare memory.

The conventions of the following summer revived the nightmare. For the Republicans meeting in San Francisco, the only time their convention came to life was when Harold Stassen tried to dislodge Nixon as Vice-President for the second term. This failed even before it got started; Stassen's name was the talisman of failure. Ike was restored, resurrected. The delegates went wild at the prospect of their hero presiding for another four years over the nation's destiny. That was taken for granted in San Francisco, and, as the Democrats assembled in Chicago, the pros spoke in private as though the Republicans were almost certain to be proved right. It was Adlai again. In a brief encounter with me he had asked wistfully why it could not be someone else. Why not Estes Kefauver, who wanted the nomination? It was in vain. He had a large following among the delegates, who raised their passionate cries of "We want Adlai!" Here was the sacrificial lamb led to a second slaughter, and he must have known it from the first moment.

Truman had turned against him with characteristic bluntness. That fellow knows nothing about politics. He just goes around blowing out a lot of stuff. In an attempt to save the party from a second debacle, the former President picked W. Averell Harriman, who had been elected governor of New York, as a replacement. Harriman, who had had a distinguished diplomatic career in London and Moscow, was willing. After all, it doesn't hurt to run for President even though you are pulled down just beyond the starting line. He set himself up, or was set up, in the Arizona suite of the Palmer House, receiving visitors in an air-conditioned, two-story imitation of a ranch house, complete with an artificial fire in the fireplace and boots and saddles hanging on the walls. It did not seem the appropriate setting for a stellar diplomat. Nor did Truman's political acumen measure up to the delegate count. He had said to a close associate from his administration, working with him at Chicago, that he was sure Idaho would go for Harriman because, look, there was the Union Pacific Railroad and there was Sun Valley. No, Mr. President, his lieutenant said gently, Idaho will not go for Harriman. The Harriman boomlet died a quiet death.

I followed Stevenson through a modest day of campaigning by motor caravan in Pennsylvania. The countryside looked green and peaceful. People turned out, though whether from curiosity, courtesy or admiration it was hard to say. In a park where the organization had produced a crowd or in the town square, he spoke with his familiar warmth and eloquence touched often with humor, sometimes at his own expense. We ended in the late afternoon in Jersey City with a rally that had all the trappings: a parade, marching bands, fireworks bursting overhead, and strutting drum majorettes. But it was an empty charade. Frank Hague's successor, John V. Kenny, was not interested in the national ticket. A feeble imitation of the flamboyant Hague, he was concerned solely with getting local and statewide candidates elected. Evidence of this was the way in which the big meeting that night was mismanaged; by design or indifference, the result was devastating. Instead of coming on stage as the climax, Stevenson sat in full view for a long succession of dreary speeches. Upon being introduced, Robert Meyner, the governor, pranced back and forth in front of the floodlights like a prize bull while the women screamed out their love. By the time the candidate for President rose to speak, the audience in the packed hall was tired and bored and so was the candidate.

I went to the train on which we were to leave shortly after midnight for another leg of the campaign. Finding that the bed in my stateroom had been made up leaving no place to type, I picked up my portable, walked back half a dozen cars and set up shop in what appeared to be an empty work car. I had only begun to write a column when someone opened the rear door. It was Stevenson. His private car adjoined the one I had appropriated, which was used by the staff for turning out releases and for herding in the pols and the adulators who got on at each stop. He drew up a chair and, in an earnest voice that seemed almost at the breaking point, said, May I talk to you? I've got to talk to someone. The question answered itself. He had come through a humiliating experience at the hands of a sleazy boss who was living proof that the day of the effective power brokers at the ward and precinct level was over. Can you imagine, he said, repeating it several times, can you imagine any man going through this twice? He talked about the lack of money, the willing and eager but inexperienced staff, the power of the Republicans to mobilize television and the press. I tried to make the case that with four weeks of the campaign still to run one could not rule out an accident. Remember, after all, the gaffe, "rum, Romanism and rebellion," and how it had turned a campaign around even though the blooper had come not from a candidate but from a lieutenant fairly far down the line. No, he shook his head sadly, they were too carefully staffed, too watchful over Eisenhower, for an accident of any real moment to happen. What I felt then, and what I tried to express to him in that dreary middle of the night as the train began to clank forward, was that by speaking about the issues he had brought informed opinion to a level of awareness Eisenhower could not ignore if he were to have a second term. Above all, this was true about the issue of nuclear testing and the deadly poisoning of the atmosphere with nuclear fall-out as atmospheric tests continued. In one eloquent speech after another, Stevenson had condemned this reckless practice and the failure of the Eisenhower administration to try to get agreement with the Soviet Union to stop it. I think I had not deceived myself. In

cold blood it seemed impossible that he could win, yet
with the lift of the spirit that accompanied almost every
speech, it seemed impossible that the American people
could reject him. He left, and I turned back to my type-
writer. In November, his vote in the electoral college
was 73; it had been 90 in 1952. He received 26 million
votes, 10 million fewer than had been cast for Eisenhower.

By his own measure Truman was right about Stevenson. Stevenson did not understand the game of power
politics. Or it might be more charitable to say that,
though he had a theoretical knowledge, he chose not
to play. In 1960 he was to prove, to put it charitably
again, his indifference; his incompetence, his failure
to perceive where his own best interests were, the
scorners said. Throughout the spring, envoys from John
F. Kennedy had called on him. Their not too subtle
argument was that Kennedy had the nomination all but
in his grasp. A word from Stevenson addressed to the
liberals would put it over. And the reward? It might be
the post for which he was best equipped, better than
any man in the country: Secretary of State. No one said
it in so many words, but it hovered in the air. Several
of his loyal associates made the same case, but he would
not be budged. This is ascribed, again by scornful critics,
to the influence of Eleanor Roosevelt, whose close
friend he was. Mrs. Roosevelt and Mrs. Agnes Meyer,
each in her own way a mover and shaker, were determined to stop Kennedy. They shared many likes and
dislikes, one being a deep-seated skepticism about
Roman Catholics in high office.

While the delegates in Los Angeles were still passing on the platform, Stevenson committed the unfor-
givable political sin. Uninvited and without prior
notice, he entered the sports arena. It took a dozen
police to get him through the crowd. Only his bald head
was visible, bobbing like a cork in the sea of humanity.
When he was identified as he took his seat with the
Illinois delegation, a frenzied demonstration began.

Whether the galleries were packed, as the Kennedy strategists claimed, or whether this was a spontaneous tribute to one who had endured much for the party, mattered little. In any event, he was not an announced candidate, and this was pure Walter Mitty. The Kennedys were outraged. They were fearful that it might demolish their plans so long and carefully laid. From their closely guarded hotel suites frantic telephoning began. What did it mean? Why couldn't it be stopped? The permanent chairman, Gov. Leroy Collins of Florida, was enraged. He repeatedly pounded the gavel and called for silence. Not until he called the demonstrators hoodlums did the shouting and the cheering subside. When Stevenson left after two hours he was caught up in a crowd of several thousand admirers who had been marching around the arena chanting his praises and waving Stevenson banners throughout the day. They were using an ancient double-decker bus as their headquarters and, pushing and pulling, they got him onto the upper deck. Through an inadequate loudspeaker he made one of his wittiest speeches, competing with the cheers that came repeatedly from the crowd. It was his last hurrah, in the light of a gold sunset.

I spent some time with him in his apartment at the Sheraton-West Hotel when he was still of two minds about the Kennedy nomination. It was an oasis of quiet in the frantic convention city. They were still after him, the Kennedy crowd. Should he or shouldn't he? A declaration of support was one thing, but they were suggesting that he might put their man in nomination. What about those who had been loyal to him all through the difficult years? And anyone who had seen what happened in the arena and on the outside could not doubt the loyalty, the enthusiasm, the dedication. Would they understand, these dedicated followers, if he now came out for Kennedy? Would he violate something deep in his own conscience? This was the Hamlet the power brokers ridiculed, the sensitive man unwilling to compromise with the gritty business of who got what and

why. Two or three of us sat with him as he watched the
Kennedy triumph on television, showing no emotion
except, perhaps, a philosophic resignation to the turn
fate had taken. He received 79½ votes to the 760 that
meant nomination for the youngest man ever to run for
President.

Stevenson was to stump the country for the ticket
to little avail. The Kennedys could not forgive that bad
two hours when the structure of the delegate count, put
together with so much effort and so much money, had
been threatened; a mosaic of wards, precincts, congressional districts and states might have been shattered.
His reward for campaigning across the country was one
of the showiest and at the same time one of the emptiest
offices at the command of the new President: ambassador to the United Nations. For Stevenson it meant
one embarrassment—humiliation really—after another,
beginning with the Bay of Pigs when, not having been
informed of the truth, he made a speech denying cul-
pability which was soon proved false. Whether he might
have been a great, or, let's say, a distinguished Secretary of State is questionable. Kennedy was to be his own
Secretary of State, playing the power game with the
zeal of that driving ambition bequeathed by his father,
along with the fortune that made his children independent of the cares plaguing most ambitious office seekers.
Dean Rusk would do for Kennedy, a Secretary of State
prepared always to take orders.

After the assassination and that great state funeral,
Stevenson sat down in the oval office opposite the new
President, Lyndon Johnson. As Stevenson was to tell
me later, Johnson had said, "You should be sitting here
in this chair where I'm sitting." Stevenson wanted to
believe it, and by what presumption could I tell him that
this was still another instance of the great master of
persuasion. Johnson wanted the Kennedy crowd—the
think men, the Schlesingers, the Bundys—around him,
for a time anyway. He wanted Stevenson to stay at his
post like a good soldier, and Stevenson would stay.

Under Kennedy it had been tolerable. One of the rewards was squiring Jackie around New York. The President, it was said, had assigned Arthur Schlesinger to keep Stevenson happy. Under Johnson, as the terrible pressures of the Vietnam tragedy built up, it was intolerable, yet the good soldier Stevenson stayed at his post.

From time to time I was his guest in the apartment on the forty-second floor of the Waldorf Towers that was the American Embassy. I had begun to sense that his role was increasingly difficult, hardly to be endured. I said to him one morning at breakfast, Adlai, you have a debt to pay to my children and grandchildren. That is to write the book that only you can write. Not solely a memoir, an account of your life, it will be infused with your political philosophy. It can be one of the great root documents of a past so rapidly disappearing from view. Theodore Roosevelt's autobiography or *The Education of Henry Adams*, that is the kind of greatness you can achieve; with your style, your magic with words, it can be more than that. This is the only immortality we can know; far more than the brief term in office of a passing President. But you must dedicate yourself completely to writing that book. You must give up all this, the office such as it is, the parties, the social adulation. So you want me to be a hermit, an anchorite. No, St. Simeon Stylites on a pillar with a ball-point pen. His sister, Mrs. Irving Ives, was at the breakfast table and she spoke up. That is just what I've been telling Adlai, she said. He must do it.

Not long afterward I stayed with him again. He returned from a late session of the Security Council and we had dinner alone. With a frankness rare for him, he spoke of the pressures from the White House to support the growing intervention in Vietnam. This made his position almost untenable. Also, his personal life was dust and ashes. When he separated from his wife he had settled on her a half million dollars, virtually his entire resources, including his partial ownership in the family newspaper, the Bloomington *Pantagraph*. Now this was gone and she was trying to borrow money from his sons. He had to talk with someone, and I was glad that I was there. We sat late as he descended into a pit close to despair. Yet such was his temperament, the claim of habit, that on the following evening he could entertain two charming and intelligent women at dinner. His anecdotes sparkled, his laughter rang out. We were in the company of one of the most engaging human beings of this century.

He was the thinking man's candidate. As such he had been twice overwhelmingly rejected. The rejection was evidence of more than the alienation between a President, the head of his party, and a politician who talked sense to the American people. Far more than a difference of style, it was a reflection of the deep dichotomy of our political life. Increasingly the power brokers, using the techniques of television, trading on charisma real or simulated by skilled publicists, were to dominate. From this perspective a Baruch seemed almost an innocent, generating with his own ingenuity, his own skills, not to mention his personal fortune, the aura of power that gave him leverage on the public men of his time. I could not see how, with merely the weapon of naked power, we were to resolve the terrible dilemmas of our day.

The shadow image of television was to rule. Stevenson televised badly. In Chicago, during the second campaign, he was to walk on stage on camera and read a brief speech. Twice the director made him walk on. He had a comic, almost duck-like waddle. Asked to do it once again he rebelled. An actor schooled before the red eye of the cameras was the ideal candidate, and he could always be wired for sound. For anyone who believed in representative government it was not a happy prospect.

VI

Europe
Full Circle

John Foster Dulles wore his humility like a good cloth coat, a Republican coat. It concealed an extraordinary intellect, the pursuit of righteousness and, with it, a pride that hardly distinguished his personal ambition from the fate of America. A sign of his humility was his choice, during two diplomatic sieges in Geneva, to stay at the Hôtel du Rhone, a modest commercial hotel. Other foreign ministers would use luxurious private villas. The du Rhone had little to recommend it other than the terrace, which looked out on the swiftly flowing, dark brown river.

I saw Dulles many times duck into the small, boxlike automatic elevator on his way up to his suite or to the conference rooms. No, there was nothing new, he would invariably say if he encountered press in the lobby, and then move quickly on. In the first siege it made little difference where he stayed since he had come from Washington with the stern resolve to leave as quickly as possible. In sanctioning with his presence the Indochina conference of 1954, for however brief a time, he was in jeopardy; he would be constantly looking back over his shoulder to try to insure that the Asia-firsters in the Senate were convinced of the purity of his intention. He had taken a great risk since he would have to sit at the conference table with a man and a symbol whom the Asia-firsters looked upon as evil incarnate.

Prime Minister and Foreign Minister Chou En-lai had come from Peking for his first encounter with the West. He was a mysterious man, a legend from the civil war that had overturned the old order. The Chinese had leased Villa Grand Mont Flori, the most luxurious private residence in Geneva. There Chou received a few callers, usually heads of delegations, who were impressed by the splendid, museum quality porcelains that had been brought either from Peking or from the Chinese embassy in Berne. Chou, at the outset, was determined to be the center of continuing confrontation. Twenty years later he was to tell me in a long discussion in Peking that he had failed at Geneva through his own lack of knowledge of the nature of the American Secretary of State. I felt that the presence of Chou En-lai and his impressive delegation signaled a desire to end the war with the French in Vietnam, that would save susceptibilities all around. That was also the view shared by the British and Canadians. This first venture outside his own terrain could mean that Chou wanted to end the diplomatic and military isolation of the new China that had been imposed by Dulles' containment policy. He would confront the West with a pride masked by his own reserve. If this had been the purpose, it was quickly thwarted by an incident that occurred during a recess of the first formal session of the conference.

In a tape recorded interview long afterward, U. Alexis Johnson, who had been a witness, gave a precise description of what happened. Dulles had summoned Johnson to Washington from Prague, where he was then ambassador, to help assemble the delegation and to serve as a member during the conference. The delegates were gathered in small groups in a reception room outside the Geneva conference chamber like rival school boys in the playground when class is recessed. In one group were the Communists — Chou, Molotov, the Vietminh representatives and others. In a second group were the British and the Commonwealth countries — Australia, New Zealand, Canada — gathered around Anthony Eden. A third, almost a separate conference, as events were to prove, was clustered around Dulles — the South Koreans and other friends of the "free world." Refreshments were being served. Soon after Dulles came in, Chou started across the room to greet him and shake hands. Just before Chou, ready to extend his hand, reached the Secretary of State, Dulles abruptly turned his back. Photographers were present, and Dulles knew a picture of him shaking hands with a leader of the Communist revolution in China and the head of the delegation of the People's Republic would have been a ten strike. He had promised the Knowlands and the Jenners that he would in no way recognize the presence of Chou, a nonperson, just as the People's Republic was a noncountry. Everyone in the room witnessed the rebuff; for Chou it was a deliberate insult, not only a loss of face but, as Johnson saw it, a deep wound from which the Premier never really recovered. He talked about it long afterward. Dulles' faithful flack, Carl McCardle, hurried down to the Hôtel du Rhone to inform American correspondents there how the Secretary had turned his back on the agent of Peking.

One who was immediately aware of how much the incident signified was Chester Ronning, an adviser to Lester Pearson, Canada's Minister of External Affairs and head of the Canadian delegation. Ronning had grown up in China with a missionary background and spoke Mandarin fluently. As the first shock subsided, he walked over to shake hands with Chou, then brought Pearson over to introduce him and join in the conversation. Chou invited Pearson to lunch on the following day and Pearson accepted. Word of this soon reached the American delegation. That evening Walter Robertson, the Assistant Secretary for Far Eastern affairs, got Pearson on the phone and asked him not to keep the engagement. A very proper Virginian, Robertson was a passionate proponent of Chiang Kai-shek. As Pearson told me later, he had understood from Robertson that the request came from Dulles. Pearson's answer was that he had no intention of breaking the engagement.

Pearson's pleasant, unassuming manner was reminiscent of an earlier and simpler America, an America before the weight of imperial power had come with the vast accretion of strength in the Second World War. Without the burden of representing a superpower he could take positions that corresponded with the independence and the free spirit of a day that had passed for the colossus south of Canada's border. As an academic, then a young foreign service officer when Canada had only a rudimentary service, as Foreign Minister and, in 1963, Prime Minister, he had learned what it meant to live next door to an often careless and unneighborly neighbor. He had come to Geneva to help find a compromise settlement that would end the fighting in Vietnam. This meant working closely with Eden; he was his own man, nevertheless.

I arranged a lunch for Pearson with half a dozen American correspondents. He expounded his view of a compromise peace with the development of two Vietnams, each independent. Two correspondents challenged him. Why don't you support the position of Washington and try to get a united front that will prevent the Communists from taking over any part of Vietnam? Aren't you playing the Communist game? "But are you Americans willing to put in troops to stand up to the Vietminh, since the word we get is that the French cannot hold out much longer?"

Neither correspondent answered that one. It was to be answered a decade later with the sacrifice of blood and treasure and the ruin of Indochina. My two colleagues had used harsh language, as players on the Dulles team, and I apologized to Pearson. "Don't pay it any mind," he said, "I'll hear the same thing from Dulles and I might as well get used to it."

In the well-ordered city of Geneva, with the Palais des Nations of the old League a monument to the past, the fighting and the dying, the jungle heat, the desperate plight of the French garrison in a far-off place called Dien Bien Phu seemed strangely unreal. The belief that a nation-state could be established in a part of the world still ruled on a feudal, tribal basis was a fiction of the Dulles illusion that order could be restored to Southeast Asia by drawing lines on a map. Yet there were those with a passionate, if troubled, belief in those same nation-states. In Washington I had come to know Nong Kimny, the Cambodian ambassador. He had survived the Japanese occupation of his country with his health seriously impaired, his right arm useless from prolonged torture, but he had stood up with courage to the invader. As head of his delegation he was to stand up to the great powers when, in the final settlement, Cambodia's rights were obscured by big-power rhetoric. I went to see him to say: "Nong, I feel I must tell you as a friend that you will succeed only in alienating both sides in this controversy."

"Yes, that may be true." He was his smiling, urbane self, showing no resentment of my presumption. "But I must do what I can to try to preserve the independence of my country and my people." I thought often of Nong Kimny as the headlines later told of the almost total destruction of the beautiful, unspoiled Cambodia he had known.

As the first week of the conference went by, the prospect for Dulles was far from happy. It was surely one of the most trying periods in his career. He was living up to his commitment to the Knowlands and the Jenners that he would not recognize the presence of Chou in the formal and sterile sessions of the conference, even by the raising of an eyebrow. Holding the

line of the Asia-firsters on Korea as well as Vietnam, he
rejected all efforts at a settlement that would anger the
watchdogs in the Senate. The impression in Geneva
was that people back home were paying scant attention
to what the nattering of diplomats and so-called states-
men might signify for a remote and alien part of the
world. Newspapers flown daily from New York and
Washington were filled with reports of the Army-
McCarthy hearings and only glancing references were
made to the Indochina conference.

Suddenly came a totally unexpected blow. President Eisenhower had chosen to give one of his spontaneous and unrehearsed press conferences. He expressed the hope for an accommodation with the
Communists in Asia like that which had been achieved
in Europe, a position diametrically opposed to the one
Dulles was taking in Geneva. Calling for a security
pact short of direct intervention in Vietnam, Dulles
had argued, in one private session after another, that
any accommodation, even an informal arrangement,
would result in a takeover by communism in Southeast Asia. The Eisenhower pronouncement expressed
typically vague goodwill, no specific plan, a course
between two extremes, the unacceptable and the un-
attainable. The effect on the American delegation was
like an electric shock. I managed for a brief time to
get a foot in the door at delegation headquarters. The
delegates were clucking like a flock of hens abruptly
assailed in the barnyard. Their consternation was almost
comic as they bent over the teletype to read the full
text of the press conference just coming in. What could
he have meant? How could he have done this? Certainly it put an end to any hope of intervention by immediate military action to save the French or by a pact
put together in dire urgency. Had the President intended
to disavow or discredit his Secretary of State? Whatever it meant the reaction was not long in coming. Newspapers in the United States and in Britain predicted
that Dulles would have no alternative but to resign

since he had been publicly repudiated in the midst of a difficult diplomatic negotiation. This view grossly underestimated the Secretary's powers of response and recovery.

In the middle of the night, twenty-four hours after the blow had fallen, we were summoned to the briefing room in the du Rhone. It was to be one of those non-attribution sessions that have so bastardized the process of reporting. We were to be propagandists for the Secretary, who confronted us in the dimly lighted conference room. The mutual loyalty between the President and his Secretary of State was unshaken. He had received a warm, personal letter from Eisenhower expressing amazement that anyone could construe his press conference remarks as undermining Dulles, whom he described as the greatest Secretary in his memory. The President conveyed his complete and continuing confidence in the Dulles foreign policy. As Dulles departed for Washington, never having intended to stay beyond a week or ten days, his associates, now revived, ridiculed the idea that he had given any thought to resigning. On his return he was to be received as though he had come from a great triumph. Vice President Nixon and eight Presidential assistants were sent out to greet him at the airport.

The atmosphere within the conference as Dulles took wing was hardly one of triumph. On the following day, my wife and I lunched with Anthony Eden at the apartment of David Morse, the American delegate to the International Labor Organization. Eden looked tired, his thin, almost ascetic face drawn. I asked him if he had any hope that a compromise settlement could be arrived at with the French so close to capitulation. The chances were dim, he felt, making it clear that it would be thanks to his own efforts that catastrophe would be averted if indeed it was. "I pleaded with Foster," he said in his slightly adenoidal, upper-class speech, "to stay for only two or three more days. 'If only you stay things will look entirely different.' But it was of no use.

He would not be persuaded." This marked the beginning
of the sharp difference between Dulles, the Presbyterian
elder, and the hard-pressed legatee of Winston Churchill and representative of what had once been known
as the British ruling class. They were to have another
and more ominous confrontation two years thence, a
confrontation disastrous for both and, far more important, for the "special relationship" that linked their two
countries.

As the days went by, the conference seemed hope-
lessly stalemated. Dien Bien Phu fell, and what remained of the French garrison—grim, half-starved survivors of a military blunder—were prisoners of the
Vietminh. It was not really a setback at all, Dulles said
in Washington. Eden's patience had worn thin but he
persisted with Mendès-France in trying to find a solu-
tion before the deadline the French premier had set for
an end to all resistance. Dulles sent his Under-Secretary,
Walter Bedell Smith, to Geneva with a watching brief.
The irascible Bedell was plagued by a constant flow of
cautionary instructions from the Secretary, underscoring
the need to keep a safe distance from the actual negotiation. Finally, after two months that had seemed interminable, the conference ended with two separate and independent Vietnams, North and South, that were to be
free of any connection with either side in the cold war.
As Eden was about to leave for his plane for London, he
received a call from Bedell, asking if he might ride to the
airport with him. They could have a last informal conversation about the outcome. On the drive out Eden
said, "You know I never was sure where Foster really
stood and I suppose this was one of my greatest difficulties."

With his sardonic expression—half scorn, half grim
humor at the follies of mankind—as Eden was to tell it
later, Bedell said, "Well, what the hell do you think my
problem was?" A sigh of relief went up from Europe. It
was peace, but a short and fragile peace.

The second siege at the Hôtel du Rhone was under

happier circumstances. It was a classic illustration of a split in American foreign policy somewhere east of Suez. Europe, yes, this we could manage. We could restore the past as we had known it or at least we could give new life to the illusion of the old order, an illusion that was not to endure for long. But Asia was a mystification. The men at the top, and this meant Dean Acheson as well as Dulles, never understood the revolution that was shaking people of color. And failing to understand, they compounded past mistakes. Once again Dulles was to come to Geneva, this time as a reluctant bridesmaid attending his principal, the President. The occasion was the summit conference of 1955, promoted by Eden to prove to the voters that their new Prime Minister was a man of peace and not a spear carrier in the Dulles cold war. The British argument had not a little logic: We have followed your lead time and again and now you must give us our inning. If I had heard Dulles say it once I had heard him say a half dozen times that summits were dangerous. The whole world is looking on, and when the Russians utter some nice words, the United States falls for it. There we are, we've given away everything we've struggled for. He never quite said, to the best of my recollection, that it was his President who would succumb to the charms of a mountaintop shared with the wily Russians, but that was what he meant.

The Secretary's reluctance over the summit was underscored by the presence in the White House of a rival who presumed to advise the President on foreign policy. The word rival may exaggerate the role Nelson Rockefeller was to play for a few months until Dulles succeeded in dislodging him, but certainly he did advise Eisenhower on policy and he was a stout advocate of the summit. Not only that, he had engineered a proposal and had convinced the President over the Secretary's frowning disapproval to introduce it at Geneva. It was the "open skies" plan, under which the territory of each side would be free for unrestricted aerial inspection. "It won't work," Dulles said when I met him shortly before the Geneva summit, "even if they agree to it. They'll find a way to get around it. The only thing that could work is on-site inspection and we know they'll never take that." His worry was needless. The summit was a television spectacular with Khrushchev and Bulganin catching the public eye by touring the streets of Geneva in an open car, waving to the populace, while Eisenhower rode in a bullet-proof limousine accompanied by running agents whom European journalists called the ballet of the secret service. As for the "open skies" proposal, it was like a brilliant burst of fireworks against the dark, and just about as enduring. The summit ended with the familiar blurred rhetoric of goodwill. The foreign ministers of the four powers were to translate the results into practical recommendations when they met the following fall. That for Dulles was the brass ring of the summit merry-go-round.

When the ministers returned to Geneva, the bone of contention to be gnawed over was Germany, or rather the two Germanys that, in the language of the summit communiqué, were to be united. Dulles had the perfect formula with which to stand off his adversary, Molotov, whom he once described as the most formidable public figure in the postwar world. Dulles proposed free elections in both Germanys to decide who would unite with whom. They'll never take it, he told us with soaring confidence at one of those nighttime briefing sessions. Molotov sits there smoking those cigarettes one after the other with little to say, all of it negative. Dulles had the amiable support of Harold Macmillan, Eden's Foreign Secretary, who gave the whole business an elegant, upper-class flourish.

I found myself feeling something like awe in the face of Dulles' power of concentration. On a fall day of rare beauty he was lunching on the terrace of the Perle du Lac, one of Geneva's finest restaurants. In the distance, through the haze of the trees in their autumnal colors, was the lake. He sat with one or two associates, going over notes and scribbling from time to time on a yellow legal pad. If he saw the view at all it was by chance. I went over to speak to him and he greeted me in a friendly enough way but with the clear suggestion that he had to get on with the work in hand.

Having come through the second siege crowned with success, Dulles could devote himself to the only Germany he acknowledged and to Konrad Adenauer, the apotheosis of that Germany. This was not diplomacy, it was love; love honed by great expectation of military and industrial strength. For Dulles, Adenauer was no mere political expedient. The religiosity of the chancellor, as he was to become, was a deep attraction for the Presbyterian elder. They were two of a kind, each shrewdly calculating, each with an inner life, a private preserve, that kept even their intimates at a distance. Dulles' preserve was more nearly personal; the central core of Adenauer's life was his union with Catholicism. The furnaces of the Ruhr were roaring again, the big chemical plants of Cologne rebuilding, a government being assembled. Adenauer chose as the seat of his government Bonn, the small provincial capital which faintly echoed the time of Beethoven, whose birthplace it was. He would be free of the urbanism he distrusted. And there was the river, the holy river Rhine, with the Drachenfels rising above it as a reminder of the mythic past.

I first talked with Adenauer when he had a temporary office in the dusty Museum of Natural History on the modest main street that runs parallel with the river through the center of the town. The setting was appropriate; it was as though the old gentleman had just been released from one of the display cases containing rather more ancient history of the Rhineland's origins. Our interpreter was Herbert Blankenhorn of the Foreign Office. You know, he said with that singular pomposity which often marks the upper-class German, I am not an interpreter. Oh, I know that very well, Herr Doktor Blankenhorn, I remember you first as consul general in St. Louis and then in the German embassy in Washington shortly before the United States entered the war against Germany. He was to hold several of the most important posts in the German service. Adenauer's face, with the heavy-lidded eyes, was carved out of a tough, resistant wood. So self-contained that rarely was an expression visible. He talked about the desire of Germany to become part of a united Europe. There would be no atomic weapons or missiles; that prohibition was written into the basic law. What he said, the conventional wisdom of the postwar reconstruction, was less than the weight of his presence, that of a survivor of the Götterdämmerung of the day before yesterday.

It was remarkable how little he changed over the years, as I saw him on successive occasions: the same muted exterior with its sense of an impenetrable inner life. He was installed in the Palais Schamburg, the new office of the Chancellor and his immediate staff, refurbished in Berlin modern. The government was being reconstructed with men from the Nazi past. Occasionally they made news, as when the Trizonal Bank of the German states named as chairman of the board and president two financiers who had been among Hitler's most useful servants. Herman J. Abs and August Schniedwind had put their brains and their skills at the service of the directors of the Nazi economy, the former, in particular, to pillage the occupied countries. I once asked Adenauer why it was necessary to bring back these servants of the holocaust. It is so difficult to find men with sufficient knowledge and experience, he replied. And besides, is not forgiveness the center of the Christian faith?

Any concern over the restoration of at least the outwardly respectable elements of the Nazi past was obscured by the tensions in a Germany divided between the West and the Communist East. The British and the French were troubled over the American push for a centralized German government and a constituent assembly. The French were certain that would mean the centralization of industry and with it the danger that the

old forces behind the revival of a Germany would out-
produce and outsell the rest of Europe. A strong suspicion in France was that American banking interests
meant to have a highly profitable slice of Germany's
restored plant. The phoenix had risen out of the ashes
of 1945 to be heralded as a protector against the Communist East.

To Adenauer, the old fox of the Rhineland, the summer of 1955 gave an unparalleled advantage. Just before
the Geneva summit, Moscow had invited him for a full
dress visit to the Soviet Union. He had waited shrewdly
for the four powers to complete their summit exercise
before responding. Dulles had gone to Bonn to assure
him he need have no worry about what might come out
of Geneva; there was a lingering fear for all the loving
trust that Dulles put in his Chancellor. In the interval
after the stalemate in the West and before his own
mission to Moscow, he would have his own private summit in the Swiss resort of Mürren. For *Der Alte,* as he
was affectionately known in West Germany—he was
nearly eighty—it was rest and contemplation. Walking
along the single street of the mile-high resort where
there were no motorcars, the spry, elderly gentleman
wearing a white straw hat might have been any summer
visitor seeking quiet. When the sun had driven the
clouds away he could look across at the Jungfrau. The
atmosphere was one of calm and peace, remote from the
intrigues of Bonn and the roar of traffic past the Palais
Schamburg. Yet from day to day his ministers came up
the funicular to tell him all that was happening in
Geneva, Moscow and Washington.

Some seventy reporters sought him out at the end
of the Geneva summit. *Der Alte* was composed, un-
ruffled, careful not to be drawn into controversy. I asked
him whether, in light of Premier Bulganin's final speech
at Geneva making clear the Soviet desire to put off
reunification as long as possible, he saw any purpose in
going to Moscow. Without hesitation and with a dry
smile, he replied, "When you have had only the hors

d'oeuvres you don't judge a dinner, even though you may not like the hors d'oeuvres." On his right was his foreign minister, Heinrich von Brentano, and nearly twelve of the younger men in his government. But he had no need of them. When the conference was ended, he paused outside the Hotel Regina to let the tourists snap his picture, then walked jauntily back to the modest villa he had leased for his five-week vacation, under the Jungfrau and the blazing noon sun. The old gentleman exercised power with ageless authority.

He went to Moscow. He played his cards carefully, gaining the release of up to 100,000 German prisoners held since the end of the war, contributing to his image of the father, the shepherd who keeps watch over his people. As the elections of 1961 neared, he seemed impregnable. For Americans in Germany, Adenauer was the symbol, the presiding genius, of the great humming industry. Long lines of truck traffic on the *autobahns* that Hitler had built, the Rhine and the inter-connecting canals carrying an endless flow of barges—this was the new Germany. A high-speed steel mill, larger and more efficient than anything that existed before the war, had just been opened in the Ruhr. West Germany in 1960 became the second largest automobile producer in Europe; despite a planned expansion of 200,000 cars a year, Britain was being pushed hard for the number one position.

But there was discontent inside Germany that reflected a restless sense that restoration of the past was not enough. Symbol of that discontent was Willy Brandt. The Socialist mayor of Berlin was saying, in effect, that more bratwurst, more beer, a Volkswagen, were not enough. I was on a "Meet the Press" panel with Brandt in Berlin when he pleaded for understanding for his city immured 120 miles inside the border of Communist Germany. Brandt had returned to Berlin in 1947 from Norway, to which he had fled for his life from the Nazi executioners. With Ernst Reuter, the first mayor, he fought for the independence and freedom of his city.

His plea now was for patience and perseverance in approaching the problem of the two Germanys. It was a subtle warning to those Americans who would argue for shooting as a way to end Communist harassment on rail and road and relieve the isolated city.

Then, on August 13, with apparently no warning, an event occurred after which, as Brandt was to say, nothing in Germany would ever be the same. The 120-mile border from the West through the Communist East was so carefully patrolled that escape was nearly impossible, but to slip over from East Berlin to West Berlin was comparatively easy. For many weeks a hemorrhage had gone on; thousands of families had crossed into the West to find a ready place in the booming industry of the other Germany. That August night a wall went up, sealing off access to free Berlin. Houses on the dividing line were chopped in two. The *vopos*, the folk police, were stationed with Bren guns at the ready to shoot down anyone trying to climb the barrier. I assumed that this would be a unifying force in West Germany, but the opposite was true. The election campaign then in progress was further embittered by what appeared to put an end to Adenauer's promise of a united Germany.

Three days after the wall went up, I was in Bonn, invited to go with Adenauer on his private plane for a political rally in Regensburg, Bavaria. Of all the campaigns I have covered this was one of the strangest. After an hour-long flight we drove in a cavalcade to the park where the speaker's stand had been set up. A cold rain was falling. Those of us on the stand were protected by a covering, but a crowd of possibly 20,000 stood for an hour and a half in drenching rain to hear the Chancellor deliver an angry, impassioned speech. Farthest from his thoughts was the need for unity of the German people in the face of the outrage of the wall. Twice he called Brandt a bastard. He did this by calling his rival "Herbert Frahm, alias Willy Brandt." As all Germans knew, his Socialist rival was the illegitimate child of a Lübeck waitress named Frahm, his father unknown.

Returning to Bonn late in the night, *Der Alte* was as brisk, as cheerful as ever, encouraged by the repeated cheers and applause the Bavarians had given him. This was the Bavaria of Franz Joseph Strauss, leader of his own faction of the Christian Democrats, who gave me a stern lecture when I met him at breakfast in the restaurant of the *Bundestag* for, so he said, characterizing him as opposed to any compromise to unite divided Germany.

Adenauer won reelection without too much difficulty from a people still profoundly insecure. *Der Alte* and the continuing presence of more than 250,000 American troops were vital if the specters of the past were to be exorcised.

In 1966, the Social Democrats agreed to a coalition with the Christian Democrats, and Brandt became Foreign Minister in the Cabinet of Kurt Georg Kiessinger. He began to create the base for the structure of his foreign policy as it evolved when he became Chancellor three years later, in a coalition government of Social Democrats and the splinter of Free Democrats. I had a long talk with Brandt just after he had come through a hairbreadth escape from what might well have been the ruin of the structure of East-West understanding he and his associates had put together with such patient effort. I sensed, as I had before, his solid quality. Passing him on the street, if you had noticed him at all, you would have taken him for a professional man, perhaps, or even for a tradesman, middle class or lower middle class. With the fright over, he was confident the treaties for which he had labored would open the way to formal recognition of the two Germanys and a stable Berlin. As Chancellor he had constantly spoken out for the reality of the present as against the delusion that the past could be restored. To pretend otherwise was to live in a cloud-cuckoo-land of deception. In the quiet of the Palais Schamburg, the reward was an achievement that promised to put an end to one phase, probably the most important, of the cold war. Although it was necessary to add, given the recent alarm and the feisty nature of the Germans, that this was provisional.

As we were preparing to leave Paris for Bonn, my wife Jane and I received a telegram inviting us to a dinner to be given the following night, a Sunday, by the German foreign minister, Walter Scheele, for Secretary of State William P. Rogers, who was making a stop *en route* to the summit conference to open in Moscow in early May. Arriving in Bonn around noon, I called the American embassy to ask about details of the dinner. You haven't heard then, I was told, that the Secretary received an urgent summons to return to Washington and he left two hours ago. The dinner was to be held in the Hotel Königshof with a substitute host. No one knew why the President had so abruptly recalled his Secretary. That mystery contributed to the subdued atmosphere of the dinner in the brilliant ballroom. The American ambassador, Martin Hillenbrand, pressed by the Germans for an explanation, could only say that he had no information whatsoever. I believe he was telling the truth. We had not long to wait for the answer. President Nixon had ordered the bombing of Hanoi and the mining of Haiphong harbor. It was certain to put an end to the forthcoming summit. Being a natural-born pessimist, I muttered that this could mean the beginning of a third world war. The Brandt treaties with the East would surely be a casualty. But Nixon won the gamble; the summit which was our destination would go on.

When the treaties came before the *Bundestag* for ratification, the Christian Democrats agreed to stand aside in righteous abnegation. They could have defeated the treaties and brought down the government, but strong pressure from Washington had helped to convince them that Brandt's *Ostpolitik* was highly desirable in abating the tensions of the cold war. To a half empty chamber, Brandt spoke for his opening to the East. With approval assured in the complex process in both Upper and Lower Houses, his performance was flat and anticlimactic. Yet the Chancellor had triumphed

over all obstacles, and in the November election the
Social Democrats won a solid victory that increased the
margin of the coalition from twelve to forty-eight seats
and made it the largest single party.

Against the background of this success was a sad
postscript a year later. It was discovered that a member
of Brandt's own staff, Günter Guillaume, had been acting
as a spy for East Germany for eighteen years, since the
time he had come over to the West, ostensibly as a
refugee. The Chancellor had failed to move swiftly
after this was revealed. The affair was blown up in the
frenzied atmosphere of Bonn politics. It was a grievous
blow to the Brandt government, and what an opportunity
for the Christian Democrats to gloat! Brandt, an honorable man, resigned rather than pass the blame to sub-
ordinates who carried a sizable share of responsibility.
He was succeeded by his defense minister, Helmut
Schmidt, an able, managerial type, free of Brandt's
political encumbrances. The spy affair coincided with a
sharp falling away of support for the Brandt coalition, a
symptom of a deep discontent prevalent not only in
Germany but throughout the West. The past had been
patched up and put together again, but for a great many,
and particularly for the young, it was not good enough.
All the inequities, the evils of the old order were still
there. The tame socialism of the Brandt coalition would
not do. In the left wing of the party young neo-Marxists
were crowding hard. They demonstrated at Social
Democratic rallies, shouting down the centrists. A
steady decline was reflected in one by-election after
another; there was a precipitous drop in the popularity
polls. The gradual trend toward inflation reminded the
Germans of the terrible twenties when the middle class
was decimated and the way opened for Nazism. The nationalism of the old order was rising again, threatening
to defeat persistent efforts to bring about a united
Europe. The Europe of nation-states reborn was an
anachronism in the age of computer technology and instant communication across national boundaries. The

mood in the early seventies was one of cynicism and disillusion. Those who had looked to America for leadership felt betrayed by the Nixon debacle. The film *A Clockwork Orange,* with its celebration of violence to music, was the motif for the young.

That Germany should have been at the center of the stage was somehow fitting. It was the climax of the rise and fall and rise again of a people who had endured much. In the horrors they had inflicted on helpless peoples and on themselves they were ten times life size — like figures on a ghastly carnival float representing death and despair. This was written in the record of Brandt's own life. In his last six months or year as Chancellor, he had been subject to fits of depression close to melancholia. That untranslatable German word *Weltschmerz* was descriptive. The literal translation, world sorrow, falls short of its real meaning to the German: the sorrow of one who has taken onto his conscience, into his soul, the suffering of mankind. That was Brandt. His own ordeal was a microcosm of Europe in the crucible. The words he had used when the wall had gone up, "Nothing in Germany will ever be the same again," might also have been said on the day he resigned as Chancellor, a victim of the obsession of fear and distrust that had persisted in the patched-up past.

VII

After the Kings and the Captains

The first impression was that humans were dwarfed in this grand corridor. With its high vaulted roof, light filtering through the slitted openings, and the silence, it was a setting in 1951 for transition from the imperial past to a still indeterminate present. I was waiting in the anteroom for an appointment with Prime Minister Jawaharlal Nehru. Sir Edwin Lutyens had set this model of imperial grandeur in the heart of New Delhi, within the great block of ministerial offices and the vast residence and gardens of the British viceroy. With the departure of the captains and the kings, little had changed outwardly. The royal crowns topping each pilaster had been pried off. Now Nehru, the heir of Gandhi, saint and martyr, was struggling to form a nation out of the diversity of the Indian subcontinent.

A brigade might have bivouacked in the Prime Minister's office, or so it appeared at first sight. Perhaps because of his surroundings, Nehru looked smaller than he had when I saw him briefly during his recent state visit to Washington. The long, handwoven jacket, the fresh rose in his buttonhole, the beautifully modulated voice—these were the hallmarks of a complex figure who symbolized the imperfect meeting of East and West. That evening, after dinner at his official residence, we talked for four hours. Or rather, he talked and I listened, since little prompting was needed. Before we sat down he had shown me at least eight photographs, portraits, and sketches of Gandhi. None, he said, could do justice to his saint-like quality. But Gandhi, assassinated only two years before, had also been a remarkably shrewd politician who knew how to unite the Indian people as no one had united them for centuries. His hold was in the symbols of the spinning wheel, cottage industries, his own simple way of life. Mrs. Sarojini Naidu, the Indian poet and a friend of the Mahatma, once said Gandhiji will never know what it costs to keep him in poverty. He insisted on riding only in a third-class railway carriage, and security precautions required that a similar carriage precede and follow the one he occupied with his followers. There was, I felt, a curious analogy between Truman and Stevenson and Gandhi and Nehru; not that Gandhi in any other way resembled the American President. But the saint was a practical politician, and Nehru, like Stevenson, was a man of words, a man of thought and intellectual concepts strongly colored by the West.

Nehru believed India had to be industrialized. The Russians were building a large steel plant, and his hope was that the United States would provide a far greater volume of aid to hasten the development of modern industry. His attitude toward the United States was ambivalent. Yes, India had gone along with the United Nations in the resolve to repel the Communist invasion of South Korea; India had sent a medical team with the United Nations force. But why did you ignore the warning sent by Pannikar, my ambassador in Peking, a warning coming directly from Chou En-lai, that if your troops advanced to the Yalu River, China

would respond? How, Nehru asked, could anyone
assume these statements were a bluff? They had to be
taken at face value unless one presumed to know the
inner workings of the minds of the men now governing
China. General MacArthur was the villain. Nehru referred to MacArthur's widely quoted remark, that the
sight of dead North Koreans was good for his old eyes.

China was the preoccupation throughout our long
conversation. First, Nehru believed that, having pushed
the Americans back, the Chinese would not again intervene in Korea. Second, he was convinced that China
and Russia would never form a Communist monolith.
China would remain a peasant economy; the shrewd
virtues of the peasant would restrain the Communists,
the intellectuals, in the cities. In the long run, China
would never become a satellite of Russia or a Communist state in the Russian pattern. In Nehru's view,
the American attempt to isolate China would prove a
tragic error. Illuminating his attitude toward the meeting
of East and West, Nehru spoke with pity of Chiang
Kai-shek. The passionate embrace of Chiang by some
Americans had helped to destroy him and make it impossible for him ever to lead the Chinese again. Chiang
had come to seem more and more like an American
puppet and in this was tragedy.

Tragedy was inherent, too, in what was happening
in Indochina. Nehru told me that Ho Chi Minh, when he
was in Paris in 1946, believed he had an agreement
with the French giving "broad independence" to Vietnam. On his return, Ho had stopped over in India to
meet with a representative of the Indian government
in anticipation of close cooperation with the new
independent state. Nehru did not believe that Ho was
at that point a Communist. He was a nationalist, part of
the great sweep of nationalism throughout Asia. After
all, he had two Roman Catholics in his administration
who were certainly not Communists. Then, as Nehru
told it, the French went back on their word and from
Hanoi came reports of widespread fighting as French

forces, the Foreign Legion for the most part, sought to subdue Ho and the rebels. The French colonials would not surrender the highly profitable rubber plantations and other interests in their colony. White men killing yellow men, said Nehru, this can only end in disaster.

He was haunted by fear of a third world war which would bring barbarism, wiping out any semblance of civilization; tribalism and militarism would hold whatever remained out of the general chaos. India was determined to stay neutral, the Prime Minister said, yet as he spoke a rare smile illuminated his grave face, reflecting his understanding of how difficult neutrality would be for a newly independent country trying desperately to curb inflation and to reconstruct the economy. What about troubles close at hand? What about Tibet? Yes, reports came out of that closed fastness that the Chinese were using force to subdue the religious dissidents in an area that had had ties with British India. What Nehru's India might do about this, I gathered, was very little, even with a will to intervene.

In his beautiful voice, he read a quotation from his own book, *The Discovery of India.* The quotation is from a stone inscription left behind by Asoka, an Indian conqueror of the third century B.C. After a victory costing 300,000 lives, Asoka repented and sought thenceforward the conquest of men's hearts. The conclusion of the inscription was: "For his majesty desires that all animate beings should have the security of self-control, peace of mind and joyousness." As he talked on through the Indian night, only the occasional howling of Delhi jackals in the darkness beyond the open windows broke the spell.

I was to find myself embarrassed by a misunderstanding over what I had, or had not, repeated of a conversation I'd had shortly before leaving Washington. During our first talk in his office, Nehru told me, I had expected to have little in common with your President, Mr. Truman, and a great deal in common with your Secretary of State, Mr. Acheson; I found just the op-

posite to be true. The conversation before my departure
was with Acheson. Knowing I was going to India, he
discussed his relations with the Indian Prime Minister.
He talked about how he had taken Nehru out of the
hubbub of a large dinner party during the Prime Minister's state visit and into the privacy of his study.
Acheson hoped he had convinced Nehru of the right-
ness of American policy in Asia and the generosity of
American intentions toward India. For all his sophisticated wisdom, there was in this, it seemed to me, a
certain condescension toward Nehru. It was a reflection of the Europeanist confronting the East. Later, as
his memoirs revealed, Acheson was to realize that this
essay in persuasiveness had been in vain. Now I had
Nehru's version of their encounter. He obviously felt
Acheson was trying to put something over on him. He
sensed the condescension, and he was not persuaded.
I was charged by Acheson with having repeated to
Nehru Acheson's belief that it was impossible to come
to terms with an Asian who had spent eighteen years in
white men's jails. I have no recollection of having
heard this and certainly not of having repeated it. But
Acheson, who, in any event, regarded newspaper men
as a lower species, never forgave me for what he considered a serious indiscretion.

Of Nehru's sensitivity there could be no question.
Despite his roots deep in the past of India, his allegiance
to the Gandhian nonviolence that had overthrown the
British Raj, Nehru nevertheless had a British upper-class
education. Harrow and Cambridge were an important
element in his approach to the world. The snobbism
of a wealthy Brahmin combined with the intellectual
snobbery of the ivied halls gave him a sense of superiority toward things American. With wry humor he could
describe the state arrival of his friends, the Earl and
Viscountess Mountbatten, and how the wife of the
American ambassador had pushed beyond the barrier
to welcome the noble visitors to "my country." Acheson
and Nehru were destined to misunderstand one another.

Believing in the rapid industrialization of India, Nehru and the members of his government talked a great deal about steel plants, American aid and the conflict between private enterprise, which in India meant the complex holdings of the Birlas, the great industrialists, and socialism. The industrial structure Nehru fostered was to be superimposed on an agricultural economy that suffered from the uncertainty of the monsoons, the rapacity of the moneylenders and the domination of the landlords. Nehru's confidence, his arrogance the critics called it, reflected the freedom of the new India. Yes, of course, the caste system was a problem, but he meant to have an Untouchable in his cabinet. These remnants of the past would soon disappear.

The size of the mortgage that the past held on the present and the future was a matter no foreigner could judge, although I tended to discount Nehru's optimism. By good fortune I had a look at one part of the past rapidly receding from view. Thanks to a wire from my cousin, George Merrell, who had been acting head of the United States mission to New Delhi during the war, I was invited to spend the festival weekend of *Dussehara* with the Maharaja and Maharani of Jaipur.

An aide-de-camp who met me at the Jaipur airport in an aged Daimler gave me a mimeographed schedule of the events over the weekend. There was just time to go to the palace and freshen up and then, with the other palace guests, I would be taken to the procession. A dozen or more guests whose names I never learned, all Indians, including the Minister of Defense of the central government, were in suites in the Maharaja's palace a short way out of town. We were whisked off to be seated on a small stand on a rooftop looking down a narrow street. Very smart soldiery, a band of bagpipers blowing as noisily as if they were on a Scottish moor, and cheering crowds on either side. Then came elephants with brilliant scarlet and gold cloths, each with a triangular design painted in color on its head. "Isn't it sad," the Indian lady seated next to me said. "His Highness has only twelve elephants now." More and more smart soldiers followed, and finally, toward the end, came a cart fitted out in cut velvet and pulled by four white bullocks. A figure seated cross-legged was resplendent in a long, glittering coat and a jeweled turban. I turned to my Indian lady to ask who this was. With something like reproach she said, "Why, that is your host." This was the Maharaja in the panoply of princely rule.

Back at the palace I consulted the schedule, which said that after one hour for rest and change guests were to assemble on the terrace. My bearer lurking outside my door had pressed and laid out dinner jacket, shirt and tie. He drew my bath, and brought me a whiskey soda. The guests on the terrace in the soft Indian night were a brave array of a vanishing style. With her great beauty, the Maharani, Aischa, was a familiar figure in the smart life of London, Paris, Rome, the Riviera. Rumor had it that an older wife was isolated somewhere in the palace and never seen. As we were having our drinks on the terrace, a Rolls Royce convertible whirled up the private road and stopped at the steps below. Out sprang the Maharaja. He tore off his turban with its great clutch of diamonds and his ceremonial sword with its diamond and encrusted hilt. "For God's sake, give me some champagne." This was quickly taken care of. He had been meeting with relatives and councillors, a boring proceeding required on this festival day.

On a nearby hill was the treasure house, decorated with strings of light for the occasion. The custom was that each new inheritor was blindfolded and allowed to make one visit to the treasure trove. He could take away whichever piece he put his hands on. The Maharaja's prize was a solid gold bird, the wings set with rubies, sapphires and emeralds. I asked to see this fabulous bird, and the chamberlain said he would try to arrange it. But, I was told, His Highness kept it in his dressing room and was rather superstitious about anyone seeing it.

The climax of the weekend was a reception in the gardens of the pink palace in town; the trees hung with colored lights, and the company, for the most part Indian, in brilliant dress on a lawn said to be the most carefully tended in the world. At the proper moment, the Maharaja's band played the official Jaipur air as Their Highnesses appeared on a lighted terrace and slowly, hand in hand, descended the steps to greet the company. The Maharani was wearing a soft pink sari sewn with diamonds; loops of diamonds hung around her neck.

The weekend was over. I was one of the last remaining for Sunday lunch before flying back to New Delhi. One guest had been a charming older woman who spoke of how much she liked America; but I am happy to come back to India, since even when I am far out from the shore I hear those thousands of prayers rising into the air. I repeated this conversation to the Maharaja. Oh, yes, he said, that was auntie; she's crackers. Having done his duty by *Dussehara*, he was going duck shooting with his chamberlain and two gun bearers.

The Maharani was to enter politics and become a leader of a hard line party opposing Nehru's socialism. It was curious to see in later photographs that this beautiful woman had been transformed into a rather severe member of the League of Women Voters. But her party was to remain a splinter. The power was Nehru's, the power of a father figure who had been blessed by Saint Gandhi. When he spoke in the Lok Sabha, his voice carried to the farthest reaches of the vast land with its castes, tribes, strange religions, strange tongues. He was the chieftain and it was his authority over the second most populous nation in the world that the power brokers courted.

I returned to New Delhi in 1955 at the time of the visit by Khrushchev and Bulganin. They were like pilgrims from another planet. With their clumsily cut suits, the pants so wide they could have been used as sails, and their floppy felt hats, they were as alien as the familiar caricatures of the little men with green heads

from outer space. I was staying with Escott and Ruth
Reid, Escott being the Canadian High Commissioner,
one of the idealistic foreign service officers nurtured
by Lester Pearson. We went to the initial welcome in the
Moghul Gardens of what had been the viceregal palace
and was now the residence of the President of India.
Nehru, with whom Escott had established a warm friendship, met us at the entrance. The Prime Minister was in
an exalted mood. Now, he said, taking me by the hand,
I want to show you how we do this. As the throng re-
treated before us we proceeded to a small rise that looked
across a grassy expanse with flowering borders. The
band began to play the national anthem, and at this
signal the President, the Prime Minister and their
respective suites started forward. Khrushchev and Bulganin advanced at the same signal and the two groups
met halfway with an exchange of ceremonial greetings.
Nehru took over and with obvious pride escorted his
guests about the gardens, introducing them to officials
of his government and to high ranking members of the
diplomatic corps.

It was a personal triumph and he was enjoying it to
the full. What it meant beyond that was less clear at
the moment. The hope was for a further flow of economic and military aid and, more important, the pledge
of an ally against Pakistan in the long dispute over
Kashmir and in the larger conflict that erupted later over
Bangladesh. Large numbers turned out to hear the
Russians speak at the Gandhi Grounds, the huge rally-
ing place for all political events. The closely packed
crowd could have had only the vaguest notion of whom
they had been called on to honor, but there they were
and they sat with characteristic passivity. They could
share with their Prime Minister pride that these important visitors had come from that other planet to do them
honor.

In his attitude toward the West and toward change,
this complex and brilliant man was curiously ambivalent.
Western friends who accompanied him on a speaking

tour told this anecdote: Sitting at the rear of the platform in the dusty, intense premonsoon heat they drank Coca-Cola. Nehru interrupted the flow of his oratory to turn and give them a look of sharp disapproval. This was directed particularly at his charming sister, Madame Pandit, who had been ambassador to Washington. But his disapproval was not confined to a scorching look. He turned to his audience and spoke of those who were foolish enough to drink that terrible black stuff. By choosing "civilized" Coca-Cola over the hazards of the local water supply the Westerners had incurred Nehru's wrath.

The visitor who arrived in 1959 was a fitting and eminent exemplar of that "civilized" world. President Eisenhower's tour of Western Europe and Asia was a strange interlude in his Presidency and one of the oddest episodes in American diplomatic history. It had been undertaken to fill in a gap that had been created when the plan for a four-power summit and the President's mission to Moscow in the late fall had been scuttled by General de Gaulle. In September Khrushchev had spent three days with President Eisenhower out of which had come something called the Spirit of Camp David. Then the Soviet Premier had toured the United States. De Gaulle insisted that he must have his own inning with Khrushchev before there could be any summit. So a visit to France was arranged for early the next spring, and the summit and Eisenhower's mission to the Soviet Union postponed until June. During this fateful interval the American U-2 spy plane was shot down with the end of what had been intended as a winding down of the cold war and the beginning of a new relationship between East and West. Eisenhower's boldest essay in world politics after John Foster Dulles' death was aborted by the mischance of a piece of espionage disastrously ill timed.

In early December he started his grand tour of eleven nations. America's place in the world was unchallenged, the President hailed as an apostle of goodwill.

Arches across his route in at least one capital welcomed the Prince of Peace. The highway from the airport at Teheran to the residence of the Shah was paved with Persian carpets. Each country outdid itself in acclaiming the head of state of a nation that had done so much to restore a shattered world and keep the peace. While India may not have been intended as the climax of the pilgrimage, high priority was given to the courtship of Nehru. Eisenhower spent four days in the capital and even took a quick look at the Taj Mahal.

We in the press plane were relaxed and cheerful. Demanding as was the schedule, with predawn departures and late night ceremonial dinners, the content of the exchanges at stop after stop was far from taxing. The similarity of the President's speeches required those writing straight news to do little more than insert the name of the capital and the response of the ruler. We went first to Pakistan. In Karachi like met like. The ruler was Gen. Mohammed Ayub Khan, an undiluted type out of the past—Sandhurst, the British military tradition, the polo field, the officers' mess, *pukka sahib*. He and our own general understood each other. At a press conference granted by the two generals the locals put one or two rather far-out questions about the government of Pakistan. Ayub Khan spoke up with a frown to say there should be no more of that nonsense. Peace prevailed and the questioning thereafter was devoted to the happy relations between the two nations.

We left Karachi before dawn. As we flew toward the east and Afghanistan, the sky was red against the dark Hindu Kush mountains. At Kabul, a lonely outpost, there was a king, a ruler. What was his name? we asked. How do you spell it? He gave the President a lunch. They got on very well, we were told. The ruler was grateful for the economic aid that had come from America. So we were told. Four hours were spent in Kabul and then the long and tiresome drive was made through empty countryside to the military airport built by the Russians, where the planes were waiting. We arrived in New Delhi, Palam airport, in the late afternoon. For all the great crowds Eisenhower had seen in the course of his extraordinary career, this was beyond doubt the supreme of supremes. The airport was a sea of humanity and all the way into the city the mass along the route was unbroken. Under Nehru's orders, between 2 and 3 million people had been brought into the capital. They had been given free tickets on buses and commuter trains. They had come in government trucks. They had tramped the dusty roads. Many came from outlying districts in bullock carts. As with the visitors from the other planet they had only the sketchiest notion of who this personage might be. Questions put at random drew the response that he must be an emperor, a prince, a ruler in some far country. But they were happy, celebrating. A journey to the capital was a rare experience.

Order was soon engulfed by the mass. Our press bus was stalled at least a mile behind the head of the procession where Nehru and Eisenhower rode in an open car. Night had fallen and torches fitfully lit the way. The more energetic among the crowd at the point where we were stalled clambered over the press bus. They danced on the roof, which loudly reverberated their shouts of joy. What, we asked ourselves, if something should happen to one of the principals? What if Eisenhower should be shot? Nehru? We might as well be in the desert somewhere. Nothing like that happens here, someone said consolingly. Oh no! They shot Gandhi. We learned later that all security had broken down. Going around Connaught Circle in the center of the city, the procession came to a complete standstill. Intensely annoyed, Nehru himself jumped out of the car to try to break the jam.

This was the pattern for the three days of the President's stay in Delhi. When Eisenhower went with Nehru to the Gandhi Grounds the crowd was said to be nearly twice as large as the one which had sat patiently to receive Khrushchev and Bulganin. Here was the Prime Minister's pride. He was showing the men of power who came from afar that his people were with him. They would do his bidding.

Thanks to one of his aides, I had a private talk with Nehru. It was early in the evening before a mass reception. In the garden of his private residence all was serene. I remember a night-blooming plant with a penetrating scent. It might have been jasmine, although it was somehow stronger than that; it seemed to me that underlying the sweetness were all the rank smells of people and animals that are India. Nehru was in the same high key as when he had taken me by the hand to show me the ceremonial meeting with the Russians. Exalted may be too strong a word but it was something like that.

He spoke of how well the meeting with Eisenhower was going, what rapport they had established although they were utterly different. I raised the question of China and the Chinese threat to the border of the Northeast Frontier Agency that had been recurring in the news. This was the McMahon line, and Peking claimed territory in this far north down to the border of the plain of Assam. That would be a line impossible to defend. At the end of August of that year the Chinese had crossed the line and captured an Indian outpost in the south of Longju. It was as though I had touched a hidden spring. He himself had gone to the Assam Himalayas. One could scarcely describe how remote, how strange, how beautiful it was. To talk of war, an attack, at that altitude in that difficult terrain was absurd. Surely the Chinese knew this. And why should they attack to try to gain an almost uninhabited bit of territory? The sun on the snowy crest of the mountains was impossible to describe. The crystal air defied distance. The peaks might have been twenty miles off, a hundred miles. Unless one had a map and a government authority, one would never know. This was spun out of the deep strain of poetry in Nehru's temperament.

I saw Nehru only once again. That was at the Commonwealth Conference in London in 1963. The Chinese had attacked across the McMahon line in force in October of the previous year. They had swept everything before them until it appeared the plain of Assam was wide open with nothing to check their incursion. New Delhi was close to panic. The American ambassador, John Kenneth Galbraith, called up a flotilla of planes to bring military aid. Abruptly the attack stopped; later the Chinese agreed to pull back approximately to the McMahon line. For Nehru it was more deeply disillusioning than anything in his entire career. He had staked so much on Peking and his friendship with Chou En-lai. Because his schedule in London was crowded, my wife and I were invited to have breakfast with him at the residence of the Indian High Commissioner. He was withdrawn, a totally different man. I doubt if he spoke more than a dozen words during the course of the meal, even when he was directly addressed. His daughter, Mrs. Indira Gandhi, kept the conversation going when, as he looked down at his plate, his long silences seemed interminable. As we left my wife said to me, "Was that little old man Nehru? Are you sure?" Yes, it was Nehru. His actual physical stature seemed to have been reduced. When he died, the outpouring at his funeral rivaled that for Gandhi. Wave after wave of emotion swept the great crowd as the lighting of the funeral pyre went forward. The son, who had become the father, was gone.

Although the accident of her name in marriage had nothing to do with the Mahatma, Mrs. Gandhi was more nearly like him than her father, Nehru, had been; she was a shrewd, calculating politician who repeatedly held off the political opposition. To her people and the world she showed a sterner, more resolute face. Her square jaw, the severe line of her mouth, were evidence of her tough approach to the incalculable problems of her country. I saw her in Washington in 1973 on the eve of India's war with Pakistan. She had come hoping to receive a pledge of help or, failing that, at least of neutrality in the conflict soon to break out. She failed, but in her encounter with Nixon she scarcely troubled to conceal her failure with any idle rhetoric. It was the same stern, unemotional face with which she confronted her enemies at home.

Returning to New Delhi, Mrs. Gandhi won widespread popularity as Indian troops triumphed and Bangladesh became an independent state. But the guns could not triumph over hunger, rioting, and the breakdown of order in several provinces, where many were killed by police and the military seeking to maintain order. It was hard to escape the conclusion that the central government could not contain the fragmentation. That was the verdict I heard in China: India is breaking up. The differences between the two countries were great. The Chinese had ruthlessly swept away the encumbrances of the past, but, in India, the moneylenders, the landlords, the hoarders and the speculators were still in place despite the oil price squeeze and the shortfall of food, fertilizer, electric power. Yet a distinguished Indian diplomat could also say, having seen at first hand the devastation of the cultural revolution, China is breaking up.

This was the Asia the West still looked on as an enigma. I went back to India in late 1964 to give a series of lectures to editors and to journalism seminars in the universities. The image of America was tarnished by the Kennedy assassination and the use of American troops in Vietnam. Though my audiences pressed their provocative questions, they were nonetheless friendly. I remember one editor saying, I wonder if you realize that the *New York Times* in a Sunday edition two weeks before Christmas uses more newsprint than we have available for all newspapers in all of India for a year. This was a measure of the contrast in wealth between our two countries. A decade later there was a sterner measure as India looked to the United States for help in alleviating the great famine.

For the first time I went to Trivandrum, the capital of the state of Travancore, at the extreme southern tip of the subcontinent, more densely populated than any other region. The streets were like a river in flood with people of every size, age, color. It was good to find an able young USIA officer, Thomas Dove, with his wife Marguerite, manning a lonely outpost and showing and telling what was hopeful in America. They took me into their rambling house, a survival of the missionary era, with both a cobra and a mongoose in the garden, and quickly cured me of a threatening dysentery. Late one afternoon we went to a temple with a pool beside it where each evening worshippers came to bathe. The stillness, the peace, were far removed from the noise and confusion of the streets. Here was the paradox of India: the inheritance of the spirit to which troubled Westerners increasingly turned in a retreat from materialism. Often self-deceived, with a fakery by teachers far removed from their professed contemplation, the seekers after solace were in vain pursuit of passage to an India that would forever elude them. All the time, a materialism as harsh as any anywhere in the world was bearing down on a helpless people.

VIII

East
of Suez

The Egyptian ambassador to Washington in the summer of 1956 was Ahmed Hussein, a corpulent, amiable man. On July 19 he was summoned to the presence of John Foster Dulles to be informed that the United States had withdrawn its offer of help for the Aswan high dam on the Upper Nile. Hussein was to tell me a day or two later that it was not so much the pronouncement that offended him as the brutal manner in which it was delivered. The many months of preparation that had gone into the initial offer by Britain, the United States and the World Bank were thus erased in an hour.

Egypt was to become a theater of war, with Britain and France the defeated and the United States theoretically the moral victor, and with fragmentation of the Western alliance the spoils of war. I had heard Dulles expatiate a half dozen times on a favorite theme: Because our origins were revolutionary we were not handicapped by the taint of colonialism. He could feel justified, therefore, in prodding the British to take their troops, a hopeless vestige of the colonial past, out of Egypt. A comic opera dispute arose within the Tory party: Should the technicians remaining behind to operate the machines continue to wear Her Majesty's uniform or not? When Gamal Abdel Nasser, eleven days after the Dulles pronouncement, took over the Suez Canal, it came as a nasty surprise, evidence that the West was living in a dream. The Secretary of State was on the road. In Lima to represent President Eisenhower at the installation of a new Peruvian president, he was in a flap over whether to skip the ceremony and proceed at once to Washington to direct this new crisis. But he stuck it out for twenty-four hours, not a little of that time spent on the telephone with his lieutenants in the State Department, then flying back for an instant conference at his home. Word had come from Robert Murphy, whom he had sent to London as his emissary, that the use of force could not be ruled out; Anthony Eden was determined Nasser would not get away with this brigandage.

Egypt was a figment of the political imagination; the mass of *fellahin* existing in age-old poverty on the narrow strip of arable land along the Nile could not have been more remote from Cairo's pseudorevolution if they were on the moon. Nasser ruled by the word; he believed his own fabrications. In a talk I had with him much later, in the interval between 1956, when he was saved by Washington joining hands with Moscow, and the catastrophic defeat of 1967, he was the masterful polemicist. In the study of his modest suburban home, I listened to the swift flow of words and watched the flashing eyes. The reproaches to the West were familiar, but the ardor was new. I managed to get in a question about Egypt's rate of population increase, one of the highest in the world. He brushed this aside with an obvious fiction. That's all solved. The pill . . . we manufacture the pill. A week's supply costs. . . . Well, it was thirty-five cents or fifty cents and within the reach of every woman. He made no mention of the discipline of a calendar and a pill-a-day and the problem of education in the mud huts. The wisdom of the leader could not be challenged. He was a little sensitive about the burning down of the handsome United States Information Agency library. It was the work of foreigners who had eluded his police, he said, a fiction for the benefit of the ignorant American.

But he sat athwart the canal, and Dulles had to use his magical powers of persuasion to dislodge him without war. Dulles was propelled on a venture in shuttle diplomacy, setting a precedent Kissinger found useful later, spanning the Atlantic three times to convince the British and the French that Nasser would in the end behave when he learned he would lose dollars and pounds if he denied the ships of the world the right of passage.

The Presidential campaign was heating up. The Republican slogan to reelect Ike was peace and prosperity. On and off the campaign trail I saw reason to believe that the President would be returned for a second term with a large majority. A small war in the Middle East would not matter much to the voters. Once or twice when I had a chance to sound out Stevenson, I found this was his view, too. Ike was a famous general who had won the greatest of all wars. Who could better steer a course through a small war?

Before Dulles left on the first lap between Washington and London he called together a group of reporters for one of those intimate "background" sessions that had become a journalistic habit since the Second World War when, impressed by the confidence, we wrote under the rule of compulsory plagiarism. We might refer to "government sources" or to "high officials," but even these euphemisms were barred in the more sensitive "deep background" talks. Holding forth in the study of the home of Herbert Elliston, editorial page editor for the Washington *Post*, Dulles expressed his conviction that all would be well. It could be taken for granted that the Egyptians would not be able to oper-

ate the canal. (I remembered the comforting fiction circulated after Pearl Harbor that the Japanese had eye
defects and therefore would be unable to fly planes and
the war would be over in six weeks.) When the contracts
with Western pilots ran out or were abrogated, the flow
of traffic would stop and so would the flow of tolls into
the Egyptian treasury. When Nasser realized his folly
he would come to an agreement with the maritime nations of the world. The answer was international supervision; Dulles was going to London to persuade the
British and the French to accept the plan he had evolved
for the user powers. But what if Nasser balked? Surely
he could be made to understand that he could not seize
a property, regardless of its geographic location, that
existed because of a treaty signed by Egypt in 1888
recognizing the right of all nations to free access. This
view conveniently ignored the fact that Israeli ships
had been kept out with little or no protest from anyone connected with the ownership—the shareholders in
Paris and London—and the operation of the canal. With
a brief, tight smile, Dulles left for his overnight flight
to London.

He was to be proved entirely wrong. A training program for maritime pilots—Egyptians, Yugoslavs and
others from Third World countries—provided a ready
transition. The Western ships were speeded on their
way, the canal was operated without a hitch. But
Dulles' powerful persuasiveness overrode any doubts
Eden and the French Foreign Minister, Antoine Pinay,
may have had about Nasser's willingness to conform.
Twenty-four maritime nations were invited to a full-
dress conference. Two weeks later Dulles returned on
the second lap of the shuttle and, his aides agreed, made
one of the most impressive speeches of his career.

The election campaign was moving on and the
Dulles sleight of hand would hopefully delay until
after that all-important November date any rash action.
Back home he was making "nonpolitical" speeches
hailing Ike as the savior of mankind. But while he

might quiet the doubts at home, delaying tactics to postpone any drastic action until after the election could only exacerbate opinion in Britain and make Eden's position intolerable. The division between the Tory government and the Labour party was a reflection of the hostility in the Third World toward the empire loyalists clinging to the old order. For Eden it was do or die. In a remarkably frank statement Eden had said he would rather see the whole structure of empire fall in one crash than be nibbled away. In the House of Commons, the Prime Minister was challenged to say whether force would ultimately be used to open the canal, since Nasser had already said no to any scheme of international supervision. And when would Her Majesty's government take the whole matter before the United Nations Security Council? The unhappy Eden was caught between an American Secretary of State intent upon delay and the angry demands of his own opposition.

Perched on a narrow seat in the gallery of the House, the mother of parliaments, I have often followed the drama of debate and division with a profound sense that I was watching living history: half-light of the chamber, the bewigged speaker, the gleam of the mace; the benches at first empty, then rapidly filling as the question hour goes forward; the rippling murmurs of approval or disapproval as a cabinet minister stands before the box. There are no written speeches, no notes really; each member must know and speak from his experience and knowledge. The men and women down below may be as second-rate or as third-rate as any members of Congress I have observed over the years, but they are in the thrall of tradition and even the most radical and antiestablishmentarian among them has a sense of that. What is more, they are there when a great issue is before the House, and the benches of government and opposition are crowded, for part of the tradition is a jealous refusal to enlarge the House or add modern improvements. And, unlike our Congress, the members are not indulged in elaborate private offices to which they can retreat when not hurrying onto the floor for a vote.

Sometimes the House is torn by a division that goes to the very roots of England's past and future. It was one of those deeply moving occasions when Eden stood before the House to justify a resort to the Canal Users Association, Dulles' third strategy to hold off a showdown. "Resign!" broke from the Labour benches. Was he talking of going to war if all else failed? Although he managed to hold his temper, this finely drawn aristocrat was beginning to show the strain of the long frustration. On the following day, September 13, Selwyn Lloyd, the foreign secretary, bore the initial attack until Eden was compelled to take the floor to face the leader of the Opposition. I had known Hugh Gaitskell just after the war when he was minister of fuel and power in the Attlee cabinet and in that position required to make painful decisions limiting heating and light in cold, dark Britain. In this confrontation in the House he got a dramatic assist from the American Secretary of State, who at that very time was holding a press conference in Washington. At a climactic moment in the debate, someone handed Gaitskell a piece of teletype tape with Dulles' declaration: "We do not intend to shoot our way through." That brought jeers and howls from the Labourites. Would the government give the same pledge? Why would not the government say when the issue was to be taken before the United Nations? The Prime Minister spoke deliberately, silencing the angry House: "If such a pledge [not to use force] or guarantee is to be absolute, then neither I nor any other Minister standing at this box could give it. . . . If circumstances allow, or in other words, except in an emergency, to refer a matter of that kind to the Security Council. . . . the government must be the judge of the circumstances . . . something no government, no executive, can share with anybody else. . . ."

The interlude that followed is surely one of the

strangest in America's diplomatic history. To those of us following Dulles from press conference to speech to press conference, he was the prophet of peace. But for all his outward confidence he was troubled. Shortly after mid-October, he called his close personal assistant, William Macomber, into his small inner office at the end of a crowded day to ask if he had been aware that no communication had come from any high-level source in either London or Paris. Macomber had noticed this strange silence. A message dispatched to the American ambassadors in the two capitals brought no satisfactory explanation. They were puzzled. Troops and planes of the two Atlantic powers were massing on Cyprus. David Ben-Gurion had made a secret trip to Paris to arrange coordination of the three forces. According to their plan, the Israelis were to attack through the Sinai. London and Paris would then call on both Egypt and Israel for a cease-fire. The Egyptians were expected to refuse. Allied paratroops would then occupy principal points along the canal to insure its continued operation.

On the eve of the American election, Eisenhower sent a stern message to Ben-Gurion warning that if the attack went forward all military and economic aid to Israel would cease. When Israel's forces moved into the Sinai the president was enraged, we were told, by the perfidy of the allies, and Dulles was furious. After a morning of feverish conferences at the White House, a decision was reached that Dulles would go to the United Nations and put before the General Assembly a uniting-for-peace resolution. This would circumvent the Security Council, where the British had already presented a resolution condemning Egypt for seizing the Canal. But every airport on the Eastern seaboard was weathered in. The next forty-eight hours were described by Carl McCardle in an unpublished taped narrative found among the Dulles papers in the Princeton University Library. The Secretary and his party set out in an Air Force plane, and for more than an hour hovered over

Philadelphia waiting for a break in the dense cloud mass. Word came at last that Newark was open, and the plane slid down to a landing. Limousines had been kept waiting at all the airports, and the Secretary sped to the great glass beehive on the East River. He was the central figure in an extraordinary drama as he strode down the aisle of the Assembly; never the image of the suave diplomat, he looked weather-worn, stooped. His greeting to Pierson Dixon, the British delegate, was noticeably cool. The silence as he mounted the rostrum was charged with a sense of how much turned on one man's words. He began by saying he was sure no one had ever spoken from this place with so heavy a heart. Then he proceeded to condemn those who had broken the peace. Since there had been no time to type a text he spoke extemporaneously. Written words could hardly have improved the magisterial tone of the condemnation.

Afterward he asked McCardle and Macomber if he could at last go to his apartment in the Waldorf Towers. He was tired. They said no, he must wait for the vote. When it came it was sixty-four to five, with Britain, France and Israel in opposition. Then, after the vote, they urged him to stay until the Italian delegate, Manlio Brosio, had presented a resolution condemning the Soviet invasion of Hungary. It was five o'clock in the morning before he reached the Waldorf and could relax, stirring his rye on the rocks as he always did with his index finger, sucking his finger, then sipping slowly. Chaffing about how early departure should be, Dulles finally conceded nine-thirty in deference to mere sissies who seemed to want to sleep the hours away. The return trip ended with a landing in Washington at ceiling zero.

Dulles spent most of the day dictating and conferring. That night, awakened with intense pain, he managed to sleep again until the pain returned. He called Macomber and asked him to come. An ambulance had been summoned. To take the big man down the stairs of his house on a stretcher proved an almost impossible task; Dulles resolved the problem by sliding down on his rear, a step at a time. Before Dulles was taken to the operating room he told Macomber that on the second day, the doctors permitting, he could discuss departmental affairs for twenty minutes; on the third day, for an hour; and then progressively longer depending on the seriousness of the operation and the rate of his recovery. All routine matters were to be handled by Herbert Hoover, Jr., the Under-Secretary, while everything on Suez was to be brought to him. It was cancer of the intestine, a major operation, yet Dulles kept to the schedule he had set for himself.

An incident that went unreported may have contributed as much as anything else to the alienation that was to have dire, long-term effects on the alliance. Eden telephoned Eisenhower to discuss certain aspects of the crisis with, it can be assumed, although no record of the conversation is yet available, a half-expressed hope that the break might be mended. On a typically generous impulse the President invited Eden to fly over that night and bring with him the French Premier, Guy Mollet. Eden was elated at the prospect and began hurried preparation for the journey. When word reached Dulles, he called the President and asked him to rescind the invitation. It was too early; it would seem no punishment at all if forgiveness came only a few days after the crime. Reluctantly Eisenhower agreed. An embarrassed President got Eden back and explained lamely that on second thought he believed it was better to postpone the visit.

Britain was short of oil, and so was compelled to pay for shipments around the Cape of Good Hope. An offer had come from the American side to finance such shipments, as well as those of oil from American sources in the Western Hemisphere, through Export-Import Bank loans. But as the British well knew, these loans would have to be repaid with interest, and the pound was already under heavy pressure in the world money markets. In mid-November I flew to London. I called the Prime Minister's press secretary at No. 10 to tell him I wanted to see Eden for a background talk. He would inquire. Within a short time he phoned to ask when I wanted to see the Prime Minister. But when is it convenient for him to see me? You are to set the time. Those of us in the business of scuttling back and forth around the periphery of the political sickrooms of the world know the surest sign that the great man is in trouble is his readiness to receive the reporter. But this was precipitous. I set the following morning at eleven o'clock. I was arranging at the same time to see Harold Macmillan, who was then Chancellor of the Exchequer. I was told I could go there at once, shortly before noon.

Macmillan launched into an astonishing disquisition. He had hoped throughout the balance of his life to serve his country. That had been his ambition. Truly it was not a personal ambition but one that would best serve his people. But now it was over. My bewilderment must have been in my face. Yes, the social order of which he had been a part was rapidly coming to an end. This was a great actor pronouncing a requiem. That, I am sure, was one of the reasons for his survival and subsequent success. He was given to set pieces, as I suspect this was, rehearsed with others not once but several times. I had seen him when he was Foreign Secretary after the signing of the Austrian treaty in Vienna in 1954. He had talked then about Molotov, whom he had encountered for the first time. Molotov was like a head gardener who had been invited into the drawing room to meet the company. You understand, of course, the head gardener of a very important garden. Dressed in sober black, he stood there turning his hat in his hands, not at all sure of the propriety of his place. I remember thinking at the time that this greatly underrated Molotov. I was amused to discover later that Macmillan had put the same account in his memoirs.

A more impressive set piece came later when Macmillan was prime minister. While Downing Street, which had been shaken by the bombs, was being restored his offices were in the Admiralty. In the course of an account of the visit of Charles de Gaulle to the Macmillan country place, Macmillan interjected into the piece his Scottish gamekeeper.

"We were in a serious discussion when a note came to me from my gamekeeper. If he could not see me at once he would not be responsible for what would happen. I sent back word that a very important conference with the President of France was going forward. But again a message came that he had to see me. I stepped out of the room for a moment. In his thick Scottish burr he told me that all those people tramping about would put an end to the best shoot unless they were stopped. He was speaking, of course, of the French security men who were all through the grounds. I did my best to quiet him," Macmillan said, "and returned to the discussion with General de Gaulle."

But now Macmillan was Horatius at the bridge. It was a moving performance. I found myself saying, and how ridiculous it sounds in retrospect, that I wondered if there were anything I could do to help. I wish you could, I wish you could, he said. I'm a friend, I heard myself saying, of George Humphrey, and I might send him a message telling him how urgent this financial crisis is. With Humphrey, then Secretary of the Treasury, I had a friendship of sorts. Quite apart from his views, which were those of an Ohio conservative, an isolationist even, Humphrey was the most personally sympathetic man in the Eisenhower administration. He had a natural warmth and charm. I told Macmillan I would go back to Claridge's and send a telegram to Humphrey. He was grateful, far more grateful than he had any reason to be. A telegram to Humphrey at that juncture — a telegram from me, that is—was like a puff of wind.

No. 10 had a sooty, plain exterior, no pretentious security, no armed guards, just two London bobbies. Now and then a knot of provincials would gather across the narrow street to stare at the door and the comings and goings. The heart of No. 10 was the Cabinet room, furnished with a long, green baize table with chairs with name plates ranged on each side and at the head. The windows at the end looked out on the Horse Guards' parade ground. During the war I had talked there with Churchill, who was dressed in his blue-grey siren suit. After I waited a few minutes, Eden came in. The adjectives so often applied—debonair, jaunty—seemed to fit. He sat relaxed, his feet, in what I would have called dancing pumps, thrust up on another chair. He uttered the familiar, rather throaty laugh. He spoke of Foster more in sorrow than in anger and of his admiration for his friend Ike in a forgiving spirit, since Ike was said to have addressed him, as the crisis was about to break, in brutal cavalryman's language. Yet as we talked I sensed a difference. He seemed to grow subdued, one might almost have said watchful. I might have imagined this since I had heard of the serious collapse he had suffered in mid-October when he had gone to visit his wife, Lady Eden, who was ill in London University Hospital. He had fallen suddenly, doctors were summoned, and he was found to have a temperature of 105°. He was put in a room next to that of his wife for a week. On his return his close associates noted a marked change. The temperamental outbursts were no more. He was calm, almost detached, as he took the moves that led to the tragic war. Part of the tragedy was the failure to coordinate British air and naval forces so that they would take over key points along the canal at the same time as Israeli troops moved swiftly in the Sinai. As the Prime Minister spoke there was no bitterness; instead, a poignant, half-expressed hope that matters between the two sides of the Atlantic might be patched up. We had talked for perhaps twenty minutes when Macmillan came into the Cabinet room. "Have you sent the telegram to George?" I had to confess that because of distractions the previous evening I had not sent it. I promised to get it off as soon as I returned to the hotel, which I did. I sent him a copy of the wire and received a discreetly phrased note of thanks. The fol-

lowing morning I was not surprised to find in the newspaper on my doorstep a black headline, "Eden to take
long rest." I felt certain he would never come back to
Downing Street as Prime Minister. American power
had worked its way, with the Secretary of State, the
surrogate for the President, as power broker.

A cold, dark winter had settled down on Paris; the
banks of the Seine were piled with snow and ice and
traffic moved slowly over icy streets. France had perhaps half the normal supply of petroleum. A call had
gone out for voluntary rationing, and in a nation of indi-
vidualists that had meant an immediate rush for the
gas pumps. The price of a gallon of gas had gone up to
$1.60 before a form of rationing had been put into effect.
As industry began to slow, housewives, remembering
the lessons of the war and the occupation, rushed out to
buy and to hoard goods that might become scarce. The
effects of the broken alliance were evident enough. In
the Hotel Matignon, where the French kings looked
down serenely from their portraits, the mild-mannered
former schoolteacher, Guy Mollet, now Socialist Premier, spoke with sadness of the invitation to Washington that had been so abruptly rescinded. Like Eden,
although for quite different reasons, Mollet seemed a
vanishing species; the gentle reformer, the idealist in
the Socialist tradition of Léon Blum.

While the difficulties at home were serious enough,
across the Mediterranean in Algeria, 400,000 French
troops were resisting a fanatical nationalist uprising.
A sizable force had already been withdrawn to take part
in the assault on Suez. I had been in Morocco at the critical moment when independence had become inevitable. In the ancient walled city of Fez the French
Foreign Legion was an occupying force. Yes, said the
colonel in command in a sunny courtyard, you may go
into Fez but you must have an escort. He had ordered
the entire population off the crooked, narrow streets. It
was a strange experience. With six legionnaires with
guns at the ready preceding me and six at the rear, I
toured this beautiful survival of the Moslem past, the

silence broken only by the military step of my escort.
Faces peered out from barred windows.

The ancient dogma that every action has a reaction
was soon apparent in the aftermath of Suez. In France,
de Gaulle came to power with the old nationalism of
la gloire, withdrew from NATO and closed bases that had
cost the United States hundreds of millions of dollars.
Britain limped along trying to shore up the facade of
the past and the "special relationship" with the United
States as the props of the economy wore away. The
reaction in Israel said more about the balance of war
and peace, not only in the Middle East but throughout the world, than what was happening in Western
Europe. The stern demand of the Eisenhower administration that every foot of the Sinai taken by Israeli
forces in the brief war be returned to Egypt was a bitter lesson. The only compensation—a detested compensation—was that a United Nations force be interposed
to keep the peace. The betrayal hardened the resolve
that it should never happen again. Steadily and swiftly,
with American aid after 1960 and the massive infusion of
Zionist dollars, a formidable military force was built up
with the underpinning of a vigorous economy. The end
result was the triumph of the Six-Day War in 1967 and
the occupation of the Sinai, the Golan Heights, and the
West Bank of the Jordan River.

Each time I returned to Israel I found the resolve to
hold fast as ironhard as before. They were building their
own settlements in conquered territory, new kibbutzim
in the Golan Heights. Not one inch could be returned
to Syria. Standing by the gun emplacements, looking
out on the plain that swept away to Damascus, one
understood why. The Syrian guns were visible without binoculars, and the visitor who stood too tall on
the parapet was quickly pulled down. The kibbutzim,
the restored towns—even Tiberias, with its splendid
view of the Sea of Galilee—would be in range if Golan
were to go back to Syria. Along the highway to the
front were the ruined, rusted Russian-made tanks that
had been overwhelmed in the Six-Day War. The vigi-

lant young men and women in uniform on the front had
one thing to say: It must never happen again.

In somewhat more politic language, this was also
the word of Golda Meir in the Prime Minister's office
in Jerusalem. And why, she wanted to know, should
Israel make the concessions? The Arabs were prom-
ising war every day of the year, and the Russians were
giving them the latest equipment to fight another war. I
asked her once why Israel was establishing an Israeli
colony in Hebron, an all-Arab community on the West
Bank. With an edge of indignation she replied that
apparently I did not know that thirty years before the
Arabs in Hebron had massacred the Jewish community
there. The dark fears went so deep. At seventy-six she
was a force of nature, expounding with her twangy,
Milwaukee accent the achievements of her people. A
matriarch in the ancient tradition, a Jewish mama of the
present day, she was in full command of her government; her critics in Israel accused her of arrogating sole
power to the Prime Minister's office. She traveled
around the world, with Washington, New York and
Miami as focal points of her appeal for help but, also a
good Socialist, she turned up at meetings of the Socialist
International with Willy Brandt and Bruno Kreisky of
Austria.

She would invariably say, go out and see what we've
done, go out and look for yourself. They had literally
made the desert bloom. Orange groves extended almost
to the runways of the Lod airport at Tel Aviv, and it
was that way throughout the country—the intensity of
cultivation, the intensity of effort. We flew to Sharm-el-
Sheikh, the point in the extreme tip of the Sinai that
gives onto the Red Sea. Housing, hotels, military instal-
lations—all this had gone up in the desert heat since
the Six-Day War. That this port of entry and exit would
ever be returned was inconceivable. New apartment
buildings were rising in the section of Jerusalem that
had once belonged to Jordan. They were the greatest
propagandists, casting a spell on even the most skeptical visitor. But nothing could erase the tragic truth that

they were three million Jews living in the latter part of the technological twentieth century, surrounded by Arabs, most of whom existed in a primitive past. Eighty or ninety million Arabs were outbreeding the frugal Jews, who planned their lives carefully under high taxation and close living conditions. We were returning one late afternoon from Beersheba, the capital of the Negev, where the government had constructed a new town with first-class, modern housing. A short way from Beersheba we noticed a collection of black tents off the highway. "Bedouins," said our driver, an Iraqui Jew. "Could we visit them?" "Why not!" He drove across the uneven desert to the tent family. An old woman showed us to seats on a bank of carpets in the main tent, and offered us tea. The atmosphere was Biblical. Yet the younger men went into town each day to drive bulldozers and tractors for good wages; change would certainly come. But would it come quickly enough? Palestinian extremists were killing innocent women and children. Israeli reprisals against their refugee camps simply intensified the hatred. For Israel the threat was an unending cycle of war and preparation for war.

The Yom Kippur War in October 1973 was one more turn of the screw. Israeli miscalculations gave the Egyptians an advantage, as did advanced weapons provided by Moscow. Arab pride rose with military success. Secretary of State Henry Kissinger's month of intensive shuttle diplomacy between Jerusalem, Cairo and Damascus ended with a fragile disengagement of the military forces of each side monitored by United Nations peace-keeping troops. With an avowed fear of an imminent Syrian attack, Israel called up reservists to carry out maneuvers. A new Prime Minister, Yitzhak Rabin, the general who manned Israeli forces in the Six-Day War, faced pressures at home and abroad to enter peace negotiations to strengthen the tenuous truce. With a small margin in the Knesset, Rabin confronted a hard line opposition determined that none of the occupied territory should be returned.

The West emerged gradually from the trap of Suez having learned nothing of what the flow of Arab oil meant. No long-term steps had been taken to counter that dependence. Again it was a nasty surprise when first the oil embargo was applied and then petroleum prices quadrupled. The Europeans and Japan were wholly dependent on the Shah of Iran, King Faisal and a handful of sheiks in the Persian Gulf, with the United States, thanks to production at home, in slightly less of a bind. Nor were lectures by President Ford and Secretary Kissinger of any use. They merely brought the threat of even higher prices and a possible slowdown of production. If you want a price war, Saudi Arabia's oil boss, Sheik Yamani, was saying, we will show you how it is done. As intolerable as the humiliation was there seemed to be no way out.

With every month that passed the shadow of still another war in the Middle East grew darker. The Israelis had held off from negotiation with King Hussein over occupied Jordan for seven years. They had launched a building campaign in occupied Jerusalem. At this juncture, with the Third World and the Communist powers having a majority in the General Assembly of the United Nations, Yasir Arafat of the Palestinian Liberation Organization was invited to present his case before that body. Received with wild acclaim, he called for a secular state in which Palestinians and Jews would live side by side. This profoundly shocked not only Israel but Israel's friends throughout the world. The Israelis would never negotiate with Arafat, whose followers were terrorists and murderers bent on driving the Jews into the sea. Kissinger, the peacemaker, who had worked so tirelessly to achieve the first step of disengagement, was confronted with a new and perhaps impossible challenge. One thing was certain: Advanced weapons on both sides promised a far more destructive war. And there was no assurance that it could be confined to the cockpit where four times before bloody conflict had endangered the young state.

Triumph and Tragedy:
The Kennedys

Washington is a closed city. The only industry is government, with politics a wholly owned subsidiary — or perhaps it should be put the other way. Get out in the country, find out what's happening, find out what people are thinking. This is well-worn advice to those of us who live year after year by the journalist's trade in the capital. It had particular merit when the Kennedys consolidated their hold. They had created an ambience that was engaging, fresh, exciting. To me it seemed to come as close as anything I had observed to the first years of FDR; it was young, yeasty, ready to experiment with the new and the untried. But it was like that question put long ago about New York: Was it America? Certainly the froth — such antics as pushing people into swimming pools with their clothes on at large showy parties — did not sound like the heartland.

In October 1963 I was in the South and the Southwest. At Jackson, Mississippi, a dreary city if ever I saw one, I rented a car and drove across the delta with the fields of cotton stretching out to the horizon, to keep an appointment with Sen. James Eastland at Sunflower. He received me in his spanking new bank building with the solemn dignity of a master who had so long presided over the Senate Judiciary Committee with its long reach over the Department of Justice. I spoke of how empty the countryside was. "Do you know how many people I used to have on my place? About three hundred and twenty. Do you know how many I have now? Thirty-five and I don't really need them" Where had the three hundred gone? "I wouldn't know." I knew and so did he. They had gone to Chicago or St. Louis or New York; the field hands in a great migration, replaced by the mechanical cotton picker. In the ghettos of the North, Sunflower was only a lingering memory. Though each of us had spent much of our lives in Washington, his was altogether a different capital from mine. He was a transient there, and Sunflower was his home.

Talking with people in Mississippi, Texas and Oklahoma, I was startled by their hostility toward the President. "Who the hell does he think he is? He wants to change the things this country stands for." From smug editorial writers to filling station attendants I heard hatred. Whether it was hatred of the man as President or hatred of the times, of the threat to what had once been taken for granted as a stable order with America secure and alone, it was hard to tell. "What about the Communists? He's never stood up to them. They're getting their own way." "That crowd up in Washington. . . . They think they can do whatever they want to and we'll have to take it. Well, we won't." There was much more of this hard talk about that young upstart in the White House and that smart-aleck crowd around him. Part of it was hatred of forced integration. It had a familiar sound. It reminded me of the hatred of another President, FDR; the rich and the privileged were again excoriating that son of a bitch in Washington and not only the rich and the privileged this time. It was for me a deeply disturbing phenomenon.

When I returned to Washington I made an appointment through Kenny O'Donnell to see the President. The White House glistened in the late afternoon sun. The branches of the big, old trees were cluttered with noisy starlings. I told the President what I had heard in the South and the Southwest. I said this had suggested a short book like the one I had written in 1936, *They Hate Roosevelt,* which had caused some stir in the Presidential campaign that year. "I don't believe it," he said. "I just don't believe that's true." I cited chapter and verse. "I don't think they feel toward me the way they felt toward Roosevelt. I can't believe that." He seemed more tense than I had ever known him to be, impatient. There was no use pursuing what I had come to talk about, so we shifted to politics — the coming Presidential election year. I had been an ambassador bringing unwelcome tidings, and he was curt, barely civil as he hurried away to keep a dinner engagement. I think he had mentioned a possible trip to Texas. Texas would be important for 1964. It was October 31. Dallas came soon after that.

Promise or performance, style or substance — that will be debated endlessly. The promise had been youth, a new generation, a new beginning. I had known him only slightly when he had been a comparatively unknown and indifferent Congressman from Boston. He was looking ahead then, and I could hardly believe that the Presidency was a practical goal. But in 1952, after he had defeated the incumbent, sacrosanct Yankee Senator, Henry Cabot Lodge, the train began to move. The blitz in Massachusetts was a masterful union of old Joe Kennedy's money and new Kennedy skill. The crew already recruited, soon called the Irish Mafia, were new to Washington. Kenneth O'Donnell, who looked like a leprechaun, had a steel-sharp mind. Lawrence O'Brien was a shrewd political operator in Massachusetts, and he was soon at home in the nation. They began at once to put together the structure of precincts, wards, congressional districts, states that was to become the solid base for a Kennedy dynasty.

Jack's office in the Senate Office Building became command headquarters. Phones rang constantly, typewriters clacked, mimeograph machines whirred. Presiding over this ceaseless activity was Mrs. Evelyn Lincoln, the daughter of a Methodist minister, with a good, plain personality, who seemed curiously incongruous amid the vibrant young in that vital center. Neither in the Senate office nor later when she performed the same function in the White House did I ever see her show any sign of perturbation. Seated at her desk outside the inner sanctum, she seemed always to know who was to be admitted and who was to be tactfully put off. That Kennedy had the wit, and also perhaps the good luck, to find such a fitting and, in a sense, out-of-character master of the rolls was a tribute to his judgment.

The flow of personal publicity about the family became a flood. The press had discovered a remarkable tribe, and our curiosity was insatiable. We learned of the discipline, the will to win, enforced by Old Joe; how Kennedys who lost at tennis or failed to come in first in a sailing race felt the fury of the father and retired from the scene weeping. I have wondered to what degree we created the romantic legend that ended sentimentally in Camelot. Jack had influential friends in the press who were eager to further his ambitions. One was Joseph Alsop, a prince of the realm, to whose elegant house and smart dinners the Kennedys were only too anxious to come. Another was Arthur Krock, a paladin of the press, for many years head of the *New York Times* Washington Bureau. Arthur is, I am sure, reporting on some lofty Olympus, looking down with disdain on the incompetents of the contemporary scene. He loved power and the use of power, and to leave the observer's seat to involve himself in the exercise of power caused him little or no concern. During his service on the Pulitzer Prize advisory board his influence was considerable. I would say that Kennedy owed his Pulitzer Prize for *Profiles in Courage* to Krock more than to any other individual. He gave the son of his old friend sage advice and earnest warning of the pitfalls of political Washington.

The Kennedys were a salable product. A gold rush was on to Hyannisport, where this strange tribe had built a pleasure dome. I toyed with the idea of a book about the fabulous Kennedys. Jack was enthusiastic; he would give me all possible help. My daughter, Malissa Redfield, whose Marine Corps husband was in Korea, would do the background research. We went to New York at Jack's suggestion to talk with his father. He gave us lunch at Pavillon, which he is said to have owned, and all went well until I said we would want to describe the origins of his fortune. He flared out in anger. Don't think you're going to tell how I made my first dollar. A little later, more subdued, he said he knew someone who in early September 1929, on the eve of the great stock market crash, had relatively little money. "Do you know how much he had on December 15? Thirteen million dollars!" I knew the legend of his own brilliant success in short-selling as the market fell apart. He said, as luncheon ended, that *he* would decide what went into my book.

We went on to Boston, where Rose Kennedy received us with her iron charm at the Somerset Hotel where she was staying. We stressed the importance of anecdotes if we were to bring the Kennedys to life with Jack at the center. She complied with tales of births, christenings, first communions, rosaries said in childish voices. When I got back to Washington I told Jack what his father had said. Don't worry about that, he assured me. I can take care of it, you can write what you want to. But I was doubtful that he could cope with his father and the idea of the book was abandoned.

The Eisenhowers presided over a solemn, stiffly formal White House; the young Kennedys were the regency—flair and ambition for the succession was held in check in public at least. Occasionally I found myself seated next to Jackie, as she quickly became known in

the headlines, at one of those small Georgetown dinner parties, with candlelight on a terrace overlooking a
garden on a spring evening. She was not an easy dinner
partner. Her close friends described her as shy, reserved; her conversation was her own shorthand of the
hunting field, the ballet, Baudelaire, the people she
had known always in the correct places. With a husband
so self-centered, so ambitious, the center of a jealous
protective clan, she found her role circumscribed. The
two became part of a Washington of future promise
amid the reminders of the past and the glories of other
societies. It was reflected even in the protocol of embassy dinner parties with a controlled sampling from
Congress, "social Washington," the press, the guests of
honor. At one such occasion at the British Embassy for
the Archbishop of York, the ranking lady was Mrs.
Woodrow Wilson, widow of the former President, who
had come out of retirement to honor the distinguished
man of the cloth; the host that engaging scholar and
ambassador, Sir Oliver Franks, who could bring a formidable assemblage to life. The presence of Mrs. Wilson,
seen so infrequently, illustrated the geology of Washington: successive layers of the artifacts of the past
survived into the present. As Sen. Richard Neuberger
was to write, "They never go back to Pocatello."

Nineteen sixty and the primaries were upon us.
The Kennedys were ready; the principal rival was Sen.
Hubert Humphrey of Minnesota, a self-made Midwesterner competing with Harvard, Cape Cod, and
the Court of St. James. Above all, the difference was
money or, as the Kennedys were to charge, it was made
to seem money. I joined Humphrey in Madison, Wisconsin, for a day or two of campaigning. We toured in an
over-age bus, a staff aide was his nineteen-year-old
son-in-law, learning the trade by passing out speech
texts and news releases. Humphrey joked about the
modesty of his campaign. "Sorry boys, if you're going
to travel with Humphrey you'll have to travel poor."
A put-on, the Kennedys said; Hubert is getting a lot of
money.

The Kennedy approach was smooth and professional all the way, with careful cultivation of the press. Kennedy offstage was candid and disarming. He was one of the boys, and this was not entirely disingenuous since the writing and broadcasting trade held a fascination for him apart from his own political fortunes. The money was always there. Only long afterward, when Teddy made his tax returns public, did I realize how massive was the beneficence of the Founding Father. Annual income from two trust funds he established was close to a half million dollars, and each son and daughter had the same. Humphrey lost his neighboring state, Wisconsin, with 44 percent of the vote to 56 for Kennedy.

Then came West Virginia. Stopping at a crossroads village for fifteen minutes on a swift motor foray through mountain country, Kennedy spoke to the several hundred gathered there as though he knew them. The performance was so natural that it was not a performance at all. It had been the same on the Boston Common. For all the intensity of his ambition, that said a great deal about the inner man. In Wisconsin, Catholics were 30 percent of the population and they had turned out for their coreligionist in impressive numbers, nuns out of convents, seminarians to a man. West Virginia was a state with strong, even militant, Protestant roots. The contest there was sharper, meaner. Humphrey came into the state charging that Kennedy was armed with an open-ended checkbook, buying votes in coal mining towns and isolated mountain villages. Kennedy's companion in arms, Franklin Roosevelt, Jr., delivered the low blows. Sure, Humphrey was a good Democrat but where was he when the war was on? Jack's heroic record, the account of the PT boat ordeal so skillfully told by Robert Donovan (commissioned by Old Joe), was an important part of the Kennedy appeal.

The score in West Virginia was roughly 150,000 votes for Kennedy to 100,000 for Humphrey. Jack predicted he would certainly be the Democratic nominee. Humphrey returned to Washington to announce he was out of the race. Those of us writing on politics resorted to that stalest of fallback positions to keep interest in the game alive: A stop-Kennedy movement was sure to develop. The fringe candidates—Lyndon Johnson and Stuart Symington among them—would come together, pool their delegate strength, and stop a first ballot nomination. After that, in a febrile convention, anything might happen.

Inchoate Los Angeles was the perfect setting for the Democratic convention. My room in the Biltmore Hotel was next door to Bobby Kennedy's headquarters, or one of them, a kind of hideout where he was in touch, on a battery of telephones, night and day with delegate counters planted in all the key delegations and with the principal Kennedy lieutenants in their own hideouts. Topmost was the commanding general, Old Joe, at Jack's side. These were the invisible men holding together the power center they had assembled. And these invisible men would have no public word until their count was verified on the public stage of the convention. I found that out after managing a brief encounter with Bobby Kennedy. It's going to work, that's all. We know it's going to work. The contrived excitement of bands, banners, balloons, the national rain dance, was more incongruous than ever that summer of 1960. The summit meeting in Paris had blown up after the U-2 spy plane fiasco, President Eisenhower had been humiliated, his invitation to the Soviet Union cancelled. Riots in Tokyo that threatened the government frustrated the President's desire to visit Japan. The Congo was rebelling against the white colonials. Yet the ritual had to run the five days that had been guaranteed the hotelkeepers.

Tremors, such as Adlai Stevenson's intrusion on the convention floor, only sweetened the Kennedy victory. All that was left was to find a Vice-Presidential candidate. What may well have been the decisive move in that choice came from Philip Graham, brilliant publisher of the Washington *Post*, who had been top of his class at Harvard Law School and had a submerged aggression driving him to the power center. He was close to both Kennedy and Johnson. Graham set out to convince Kennedy that he needed Johnson and to persuade Johnson that he should forget his pride and take second place. As the hardy river men on the lower Mississippi used to say in the early nineteenth century, you had to be half horse, half alligator to win.

Convincing the Kennedys was less difficult than bringing Johnson around. Speaker Sam Rayburn, who had been from the beginning Johnson's counsellor and father confessor, was opposed. I had known Rayburn from my first years in Washington, when he shepherded much of the early New Deal through the Congress, and I had developed a healthy admiration for his stern independence. I was sitting with him in his office in the Capitol one day when he took a call from a television network president inviting him to participate in a panel discussion on some issue or other. Brusquely, with no apology, he refused and put down the phone. He said to me, "I'm not going to help 'em sell their goddamn cornflakes." From the closely guarded Johnson suite in the Biltmore at Los Angeles, Rayburn got John Nance Garner on the phone in Uvalde, Texas, to support his argument of the worthlessness, the inconsequentiality, of the Vice-Presidency. Garner was happy to comply. Lyndon, he said, it ain't worth a bottle of cold piss. But of course, Johnson capitulated at last. Many delegates were unhappy when Kennedy's choice was announced to a final ratifying session of the convention. Boos and shouts of no came from the floor. With the skilled organizers running the show, a vote of acclamation was put, making the choice unanimous, or, well, nearly unanimous. Finally, on a fine sunny evening before the crowd in the Memorial Coliseum, the two candidates accepted the nominations and set their campaign rolling. I have long believed that the choice of Johnson swung the election to the Democrats by an incredibly small margin in the popular vote.

The campaign was sharpened by the contrast in

temperaments of the two candidates. Traveling with Kennedy, I was engulfed in consideration and kindness. On a short run between campaign stops, I was invited aboard the *Caroline,* the Kennedy family plane, for a chat with Jack. I was received with warmth and candor. Part of this, to be sure, was careful calculation, but he liked reporters. With the Nixon entourage all was correct and frigidly formal. Except for set performances, the candidate was rarely visible. Aside from a few friends in the media who had proved their unquestioning loyalty, most reporters found him aloof; he was deeply distrustful of the press. Later, during his presidency, it was to become a monomania. Nixon's people could say that we were biased, that we slanted the news in favor of his rival. They seem never to have understood why.

With the election over, the Kennedys set out to fulfill the worlds of promise. The newly elected President was earnestly searching for the ablest men and women he could find for his new administration. I saw him in New York in the Hotel Carlyle while he was on a recruiting drive. Troubled about a specialist on Latin America, he asked my advice. I urged on him, as Assistant Secretary, Adolf Berle, who had served FDR in this capacity and later, as ambassador to Brazil, had shown his broad understanding of a deeply disturbed domain. No gambit is more flattering for the outsider than to be called on to recommend an individual or a policy, and that applies with far greater force for the reporter-commentator. But I believe he was genuinely interested in finding the best man, since Cuba was a formidable threat to Latin American stability. Eventually chosen for the post, Berle was unhappy, out of phase with the young, onrushing administration, and he soon departed. That should have been a warning to me to stay clear of such matters.

It was inevitably a family operation. Bobby was to be Attorney General. Although Bobby had had an early connection with Joe McCarthy and, as an adjutant of Senator McClellan, the scourge of Arkansas, had

offended elements in labor and the civil rights movement, the new President said he needed his brother at
his side. To direct the Peace Corps, an imaginative and
creative proposal, he named his brother-in-law, Sargent Shriver. Early classmates and friends were enlisted.
The test was loyalty. He brought advisers of exceptional
intellect and ability out of the highest levels of academia
into the White House. McGeorge Bundy, Walt Rostow,
Arthur Schlesinger, Jr., were to serve him with devo-
tion, if without a power base. The members of the President's Cabinet were also creatures of the chief executive. The two principal posts, State to Dean Rusk and
Treasury to Douglas Dillon, went to men whose records
had never been passed on by any segment of the elec-
torate. This is surely one reason for the increasing
concentration of power in the Presidency. A British
Prime Minister would have in his Cabinet men and
women anchored in their respective constituencies and
bringing to the government an independent strength.
Still, with two former Governors and one member of
Congress, the Kennedy Cabinet had more political
experience than the average Cabinet. Both Dillon and
Rusk had extensive experience in foreign policy.

The President took an unflagging interest in every
aspect of how his administration and his family were
reported. No detail was too small to escape his attention. "Why the goddamned hell is so-and-so saying
that?" he would demand of his press secretary, Pierre
Salinger. He was deeply wounded by Drew Pearson's
allegation that his book *Profiles in Courage* had been
ghostwritten. Pearson retracted the charge after Clark
Clifford showed him evidence of Jack's own authorship.
On the eve of one important policy pronouncement he
ordered Ted Clifton to see that Walter Lippmann and
Mark Childs were thoroughly brainwashed.

Even normally starchy state dinners and luncheons
could give a sense of the current of youth. At a lunch
for Japanese Prime Minister Hayato Ikeda I found myself seated next to Mrs. George Meany. In her rich

Brooklyn accent she said, "I tell George, 'Let the boy alone. Can't you let the boy alone?' That's what I tell him." I felt sure that George would never let the boy alone. At the center of the long table of honored guests the President did look remarkably youthful. The toast Kennedy proposed to his guest of honor had characteristic wit and irony.

In April of his first year in office, an initiative Kennedy inherited from the Eisenhower administration led to a disaster. In late January, I learned, along with other reporters, of preparations for an invasion of Cuba designed to overthrow Castro. The CIA planners had convinced themselves that an attack by a small force of Cuban exiles and others would spark an uprising by the disaffected in Castro's own militia, and the dictator would be toppled. At the very least the invaders would succeed in establishing a provisional government in the mountains and that government could then receive recognition and military aid from the United States and the Organization of American States. Relying on sources in the State Department and the Pentagon, I had written a column in late January saying that an invasion on that scale could not possibly succeed. The fatal flaw was the belief that landing on the beaches would generate a revolt. Castro had trained and armed, with Russian matériel, an estimated 450,000 to 500,000 militiamen. Even if one-tenth of this force were loyal, so my sources estimated, the invasion could not possibly succeed. Far more important was the miscalculation, typical of the sort made repeatedly in American intelligence appraisals of revolutionary movements around the world, that the Cubans would turn against the man who had taken the property of foreign owners—factories, farms, resorts— and given them to the people. That was the powerful propaganda line spewed out on the state-owned radio day after day.

The atmosphere in the White House, as the full dimensions of the disaster became apparent thirty-six hours after the landing, was one of unrelieved gloom.

This could not happen to a new, vigorous, bold administration. The pressure on the President to order an air
cover that might salvage the operation was tremendous.
The temptation was great. For the Kennedys to fail
before the world was intolerable. Fortunately, he had as
his military aide, Major General Ted Clifton, a constant
exponent of reason and deliberation. As an aide to Gen.
Omar Bradley when he was Chief of Staff, Clifton had
been an invaluable counsellor in the interservice rivalry
that had broken around Bradley's head. In the White
House, his knowledge of Pentagon politics served the
President well during the Bay of Pigs disaster and, a
year and a half later, in the more menacing crisis over
the Soviet missiles in Cuba, ninety-seven miles off
America's shores. And in all candor I must add that, as a
friend, he was for me an unfailing source of hour-by-
hour information that kept me abreast of what was happening.

    I remember that on the Saturday night when nuclear
war seemed the inevitable outcome of the missile
crisis, I went with my family to a movie. I have no
recollection of what it was about nor whether it provided any relief from the tension we were under. It was
like being at the bottom of a deep well with one's eyes
constantly strained to see whether the dark had closed
in or whether a little light was still visible. I wondered
then, as I have often since, how clearly the fear and the
tension were communicated to the people of the country
outside the closed circle of the capital. There were the
staring headlines that told of American warships quaran-
tining Cuba, Russian ships being stopped and searched.
But who could comprehend that this might lead to
nuclear war and who could conceivably know what such
a war must mean? I have written thousands of words
about the enormity of the weapons of mass annihilation
as they have constantly accumulated on both sides of
the divide, and it has always been with a sense of futility
and even despair of being able to convey what they
mean. One of the wisest things Truman did after the

war's atomic bomb toll was to set off a demonstration
bomb on the Bikini atoll in the Pacific, allowing observers, including foreign representatives, to see at
first hand what it meant to unleash a force like that of
the sun. When he was chairman of the policy planning
staff in the State Department, Gerard Smith tried to
persuade John Foster Dulles, and through him President
Eisenhower, that another such demonstration, this time
with the hydrogen bomb, would help to arouse an understanding of what was talked and written about so
glibly. Dulles was not interested.

On Sunday morning word came over the teletype
of Khrushchev's announcement that he would remove
the missiles. It was a reprieve. Kennedy had behaved
with calm, careful wisdom. He had resisted the selfish,
self-centered counsel of those, including Sen. George
Smathers, Florida's gift to statesmanship, that an American invasion would bring Castro down and restore the
American properties he had seized. On that halcyon day
when the American flag was raised, those who had
enjoyed the privileges, the corruption, of the Batista
dictatorship would return to do business as usual. This
lunatic fantasy was seriously urged upon the President.

Even at the climactic moment, a hairbreadth or so
it seemed from doomsday, Kennedy was concerned
about the press. Those close to him told me they had
never seen him as angry as he was at a story written by
his friend, Rowland Evans, for the New York *Herald
Tribune*. The story said that Khrushchev's message of
capitulation had shown the Soviet leader hysterical
and close to a breakdown. After the President's private
rage had subsided, he instructed Salinger to say there
was no truth whatsoever in the story. He had warned
all those around him against gloating. He wanted the
ordeal to close with the largeness of spirit, the calm
calculation, he had shown from the start. Khrushchev's
opposition in the Kremlin might have taken the Evans
story, particularly since he was known to be a friend
of the President and one close to the sources of news,

as evidence that Kennedy was scoffing at the weakness of a leader who had not only capitulated, but had succumbed to hysteria. I talked with four persons who had read the Khrushchev message. They all agreed that while it was, in part, maundering on the horrors of nuclear war, it showed the Soviet premier in full possession of his faculties in reaching a decision that surely had the most wracking consequences, as we were to learn when he was removed two years later.

In the previous spring the President had had a toe-to-toe encounter with Khrushchev in Vienna. Several hundred of us, massed behind a barrier outside the entrance of the American embassy, waited for what seemed an interminable time for the principals to appear. The pattern was a familiar one. Back at the briefing room in the hotel we were fed small morsels of information, the language vague yet conveying how abrasive the session had been. Gradually, in the course of the next twelve hours, the somber truth emerged. Khrushchev had delivered what sounded like an ultimatum on Berlin: the city could no longer be considered part of the Western Zone; it was to be an independent entity with access determined by the Soviet occupying authority. This caused a tremendous flap: heels dug in, more troops to Germany, ringing declarations of solidarity with Berlin, and one of the most absurd off-shoots, the "gee whiz" of the counter-insurgency program, in the course of which aging foreign service officers spent hours being instructed in how to man the barricades around a beleaguered embassy. This absurdity was ascribed to the zeal of Bobby Kennedy.

On the way to Vienna and the rendezvous with Khrushchev, the President had stopped in Paris to meet with de Gaulle. With Jackie at his side adoring all things French, it was a celebration of *la gloire* and the springtime of youth and beauty. In the splendor of the Elysee Palace and Versailles the young Americans shone brilliantly. At a press luncheon, in his famous response to a question as to why he had come to Paris,

Kennedy said he was there to accompany his wife. At the end of the state dinner at the Elysee some of us in the press, with tailcoats and white ties rented for the occasion, were invited to meet de Gaulle. Kennedy was at his gracious best. Although this invasion may have been rather more overwhelming than de Gaulle had expected, he was impressively dignified, like a dweller on Olympus tolerant toward mortals down below. He used his precise, schoolbook English to convey the grave politesse of a royal host.

The accomplishments of this excursion into summitry were small. Berlin was a holding action, traffic was stopped on the access route from time to time. The Congress, without the old whip-cracking ringmaster, Lyndon Johnson, was recalcitrant and the Kennedy domestic legislative program made only a modest advance. But the President had perfected a style. With all the rough edges honed, it showed to best advantage in his press conferences, virtuoso performances in the large auditorium in the State Department. The Kennedy parties, reported as fully as any diplomatic negotiation between states, were also a brilliant reflection of that style.

Whatever the balance of forces in the larger world of foreign and domestic policy might have been, the President had in his personal life reached a plateau of sorts, an accommodation with his destiny, whatever it might be. For all his competitiveness, and his unfailing concern with his image, a certain fatalism was part of his character: the sense of a man who will try to shape the future if he can but will not deceive himself about the relationship of mortal men to the overpowering forces loose in the world. In a private talk I had with him fairly early on, he did not conceal his pessimism. "The country is all but ungovernable," he told me. In late March 1963, his mood had changed. There were rhythms, cycles, when action was possible. January, February, March, even April, were months in which Congress did nothing. Then came activity, a rush, and one could move. He spoke to me this time with hope about his proposed tax cut.

"I think we're going to get it even though everybody says that this is wrong with it or that is wrong with it. A lot of people don't realize how much of a pioneering undertaking it is — the idea of a deliberate deficit through a tax cut to stimulate the economy. People have talked about it for twenty or thirty years but no one has tried it before.

"Now you get Nelson Rockefeller, the Committee for Economic Development, you get all the conservatives in Congress saying at the same time that you have to cut federal expenditures by anywhere from four to five billion or more; Rockefeller says four to five billion, so does the CED. Well, if you do that you nullify the effect of a tax cut, you take that much money out of the spending stream."

He spoke with a special scorn of a speech that Gerald Ford, the minority leader in the House, had made boasting that Republicans had delayed expenditures on space. "Now what kind of a claim is that?"

The economy was inevitably linked to 1964. The economic indicators were moving up and even conservative economists believed that a period of high prosperity was ahead toward the end of the year and early in '64. "If that is true, then we're all right. If things should go bad, if we go into a recession, then it won't matter who they put up because they can beat us. I think with the showing of the economic indicators in the latter half of this year we would be all right if it weren't for the great new numbers coming into the labor force."

The young adventurer, the activist, moved to the fore when he talked about the Cuban exiles and their daring raids on Russian ships in Cuban waters. The Cubans were operating from an empty key, one of the several hundred Bahamian keys that were uninhabited. They had some American arms but not substantial numbers. In their latest attack they had gotten through the harbor defenses in their small, fast boat. They shot a homemade torpedo into the Russian vessel, and they got away. Here was the PT boat skipper admiring, in spite of his realization of the harm this could do, a skillfully executed operation. The National Security Council had met on the subject of the Cuban raids the day before. "What if we arrested the leader and this was a Robert Emmet [Irish rebel hanged in 1803 for a conspiracy against the crown], and he made a speech from the dock as he was condemned. What would the effect of that be?" Of course the raids were bad, they made everything worse. The Soviets would say that, under the circumstances, it was obviously impossible for both military and political reasons to pull out more of their forces. He had traced an emotional outbreak among conservatives in Congress after the first of the year to a *New York Times* story by Tad Szulc saying the Russians were moving more arms into Cuba. Although the report was false it nevertheless served to touch off a new uproar aimed at the weakness of the Kennedy policy on Cuba. Rocking gently in his chair, as he talked with me, he looked both strong and frail, set resolutely against any weakness. In the unseasonal heat the big French doors to the terrace were wide open, outside on the lawn the early pink magnolias were in bloom, at a distance two little girls were playing.

The Kennedy style was displayed also in his travels, a phenomenon of the late twentieth century. FDR moved around the world during the war but as the commander-in-chief on a secret mission without an army of reporters and camera men. Today the traveling President is a television star. He is seen by the mass audience against a foreign background, meeting foreign dignitaries. The television satellite instantly brings the traveler into 20 million livingrooms across the nation. How much significance this has in actual negotiation on matters of substance is highly questionable. Dean Acheson was one of many who expressed skepticism about summits and the showy meeting of heads of government. But cheering crowds across the world are high drama. So when in doubt, travel. When Eisenhower set out to fill in the time before his mission to Moscow, he was hailed as the Prince of Peace. Kennedy, in his journey through Europe, was the embodiment of young, vigorous America.

I am grateful that I followed him on that journey. Berlin was a demonstration of the trust, the hope, that the beleaguered city put in the President as symbol of American strength. Before the several hundred thousand Berliners massed in the Town Hall Square and the access streets, his repeated *"Ich bin ein Berliner"* drew roar after roar of cheering that could surely have been heard in East Berlin. The contrast with the venerable Adenauer, as the two leaders worshipped together in St. Paul's Kirche in Frankfurt, dramatized young America in partnership with a Europe revived after the horrors of Nazism and war. Whatever the promise for the longer future, with Willy Brandt, the governing mayor, at Kennedy's side in this moment, nothing, even a reunited Germany, was impossible.

In Ireland the Kennedy legend came to life. That pilgrimage to the home of his forebears, the old sod with all its sentimental blather, might have seemed mawkish and distasteful but Kennedy showed himself the mature man by the humor and the irony with which he tempered his speeches at the stations of the sentimental past, including the alleged birthplace of his ancestors, duly tidied up for the occasion. With the ancient de Valera in Dublin, as with Adenauer, it was again youth and age united, this time by ties of consanguinity and sentiment. Putting aside for this interval the burdens of the Presidency, Kennedy was a happy man. The rare Dublin sun was gentle, warming. The last stop before his departure for London and Rome was Galway. He stepped off the plane to confront the serried ranks of a girls' school, the girls dressed in the Irish colors of green, yellow and white. They sang "Galway Bay" and when they had finished he moved among

them shaking hands until they surrounded him. He
spoke from the main square with the ocean in the distance. "Some of us left here as my people did," he said.
"And I think if you look hard you can see the docks in
Boston and you can see men working there who came
from Galway. That is how close we all are."

As though he had gathered strength from the encounter with Europe, he began to move up in the
months that followed. His commencement address at
American University was one of the finest of his career;
his forthright and courageous words expressed the
imperative of peace in the nuclear age. The nuclear test
ban treaty signed in Moscow was a reward long striven
for. So much would happen in the second term, when
1964 and reelection were behind him. He is supposed
to have said, although I have never been able to find a
record of it, that with a substantial majority in a new
term, not just the squeak of 1960, he would be able to
put an end to American participation in the Vietnam
war. Although it was little understood by the public
then, Vietnam was for Kennedy a grave responsibility.
Early in 1961 he had sent Walt Rostow and Gen. Maxwell Taylor on a mission to Saigon. On their recom-
mendation, he had ordered the dispatch of 10,000 troops
empowered to shoot at the enemy. That was the beginning. The catastrophic end would not wait on a second
Kennedy term.

After Dallas, the dynasty prevailed. The wishes of
the Founding Father had been carved on tablets of
stone. The younger brother was next. From his position
as first-term Senator from New York, Bobby was going
to run for President in 1968. He was forty-three years
old. I talked with him in the big livingroom of the house
in McLean, Virginia, on the eve of his swing through
the West. He had always seemed tighter, more con-
stricted than Jack. Yes, he thought he had a good
chance for the nomination. Humphrey had a head start
but that was of small moment since Humphrey would
not go into the primaries. If McCarthy could be shut out

in Oregon and California he would be on his way. You had to show your strength in the primaries. This was something Humphrey didn't understand; there was little that he could or would say. I felt, as I had before, that on anything really serious and important the Kennedys communicated only with each other, with a secret language never written down. It served them well in the intimate transactions out of sight of the public view.

That second assassination was unbearable; a half-mad Palestinian choked with hatred, a thirst for revenge, firing point-blank in the dreary storeroom of the kitchens in a Los Angeles hotel. It had come after the California primary had given Kennedy a margin not large enough to tip the scales to victory following his loss in Oregon. The nation followed the funeral train with consuming sorrow.

The youngest brother was ready. Handsome in a roughhewn way, coarser, he came on harder than either of the other two and yet he had the same appeal and the ability to put it over. Even after the tragedy of Chappaquiddick and the miserable aftermath, with its shabby and fake confessional, he could go before the Democratic convention in Miami Beach and stir that troubled mass to cheers. In almost every poll he topped Republicans and Democrats alike in the guessing game of 1976. He went to Alabama to give George Wallace a gesture of friendship. Surely he meant to run. How could a Kennedy not run? And this would be the foulest campaign of them all. The Republicans had filled whole filing cabinets with Chappaquiddick and the lesser lapses of the Senator from Massachusetts.

I had a quick sandwich lunch with him in his office after his young son had had a leg amputated in an attempt to arrest cancer of the bone. He told me he would not make a commitment until well into 1975. "I have to be thinking always of my son. What if I'd agreed to speak at a big convention that meant staying overnight. Then word came that he was in a bad way, that he wanted me, and I couldn't get back." I discounted this. He could have the nomination for the asking. In Boston, speaking in the busing controversy, he was pelted with tomatoes and not long afterward he announced that under no circumstances would he seek the Presidency in 1976. It seemed to me a wise decision. The tragedy that stalks the Kennedys would hardly have stopped short of this last of the line. No one but the President received the volume of hate mail Teddy received. There was not only his son but his fragile, lovely wife, Joan, suffering from the pressures of politics and the strains within that aggressive family.

So it had run its course, or had it? We could not escape a share of the blame. They had dared too much. They had seen themselves as a dynasty and that went against the grain of *Demos,* the common people, as most Americans like to think of themselves. It went back to what I had heard in the South and the Southwest. "They think they're better than we are." That is a heresy *Demos* will not allow.

Hope
Long Deferred

We boarded a comfortable diesel powered steamer at Rostov-on-Don for a leisurely downstream trip ending at Stalingrad. We were the only foreigners on board. The other passengers were vacationers from Moscow, many going the whole way to Astrakhan. The year was 1955: the cold war, Foster Dulles preaching the doctrine of containment of the wicked Communists, Nikita Khrushchev breathing anathema at the Imperialist West. Our fellow passengers could not have been more courteous and friendly. They were, to be sure, the privileged elite. One family, the father a space scientist, sent their young son to our cabin to give us a bowl of the crayfish salad they had brought on board. It was a generous gesture, but since the temperature was in the nineties and there was no air conditioning and little refrigeration, we thanked them profusely and then, in the middle of the night, disposed of the crayfish salad over the side of the boat. The father told me the approximate date of the next Soviet space shot. When I handed him my card, which identified me as a newsman, he paled and hardly spoke to us again. We were among the few who used the dining saloon since almost everyone else had brought hampers of food on board. There were two kind women attendants, one middle-aged, the other a young girl, who had learned passable English from lessons on the radio. When the dining saloon was intolerably hot because the sun had beaten down on it all day, they would in the early evening move a table out on deck for us.

Nearing the end of our journey we asked our guide-interpreter, Sonia, about tips for the two women. They would, she said, have been deeply offended if we had made any such proffer. We were their guests and they were honored to serve us. Sonia finally agreed that my wife might present two pairs each of nylon stockings, a rarity in the Soviet Union. They accepted the gift with what seemed genuine reluctance and touching gratitude. Stalingrad, to be renamed Volgagrad after Khrushchev had unmasked the tyrant, dominated by the vast, oppressive Stalinist memorial to the dead who had held back the Nazis, offered little and we flew back to Moscow.

Everywhere we went on the 10,000-mile-journey that took us as far as Tashkent and Samarkand we found, with rare exceptions, the same courtesy and kindness. It was in marked contrast to the attitude of officialdom. Although my main objective was to gather material for an article on life in the Soviet Union for the Britannica Yearbook, I had, as a working journalist, along with so many of my kind, another goal. That was to interview Khrushchev. Returning to Moscow a half dozen times after sorties around the country, I prodded and poked at one level of the bureaucracy after another. The highest point I reached was a talk with a deputy foreign minister, Vasily Kuznetsov. It was quite unproductive, consisting as it did of bland replies to questions I hoped would draw a response on the future of Soviet policy toward the West and, in particular, the United States. In

transposing Western journalistic practices we are remarkably naive when we pound on the locked doors of
the Communist wall. They open rarely and then only
when there is a desire at the very top to make some pronouncement with a convenient mouthpiece at hand. I
saw Khrushchev only once during my month's stay.
That was at the reception at the British embassy on the
occasion of the Queen's birthday. The accepted custom
was for the journalists present to press in and hurl provocative questions meant to arouse the bear to anger. On
that day he was in a feisty mood, and it was all his interpreter, Viktor Sukhodrev, the hardy survivor of so many
encounters, could do to keep up with his sputtering.
With Khrushchev's departure, the working press rushed
to filing points to cable to the outside world the glean-
ings from this brush with the No. 1 in the closed fastness
of the Kremlin. Having thus to report the random words
of one of the two or three most powerful men in the world
was a curious reflection on the practice of journalism
behind the Iron Curtain.

Each time we returned to Moscow we stayed at the
National Hotel. The tourist rush and the construction of
such mass shelters as the Intourist and the Rossiya had
not yet begun. Looking out on Red Square, The National
had an aura of the past, with the art nouveau decor in the
diningroom, at the windows and in the stairwells. On
our last stay we were assigned, for some unknown
reason, the royal suite, which included a large livingroom with a great mirror framed in rococo splendor,
slightly frayed furniture of past grandeur, and a long
balcony overlooking Red Square. From that balcony
Lenin was said to have made one of his most passionate
addresses, exhorting a huge crowd to revolutionary fervor.

On our last evening, Sonia tried to exchange our
unused food coupons for caviar which we would take
to Prague where we were to stay with the John Alli-
sons at the American embassy. With the efficiency and
zeal she had shown throughout our journey she managed

to get perhaps a pound. The Americans, she was told, hoard their coupons to get caviar and this is all your Americans may have. Determined not to discard the coupons, which in any event no Russian could use, we ordered up a case of champagne; German champagne, as it turned out, possibly the last of Herr Heikel, the champagne merchant who had made a pact with Molotov in 1940. It was a strange evening. At the suggestion of Llewellyn Thompson, then on his second tour as ambassador, I had had a portrait sketch done by a young artist whom Tommy had befriended. My wife had said she would have nothing to do with portrait sketches until she had a session with a proper hairdresser. The artist was to come by for his fee, roughly eighty dollars in rubles, that evening. The sketch, which made me look like a character out of Dostoevski in a mood of melancholy contemplation, was propped up on a chair in our grand salon. Before the artist arrived we had a farewell visit from an American correspondent and his Russian wife, an acerbic intrigante. Tanya took one look at the sketch, pronounced it a disgrace, and declared that under no circumstances should I pay for it. Telling her to mind her own business, I said that of course I would live up to my bargain no matter what I might think of the portrait. Shortly afterward the artist arrived and Tanya began speaking to him in Russian. To my intense annoyance I could tell that she was deliver-her opinion of his work. With a downcast look he said to me in his soft English that he could not accept payment since I did not like the sketch. I gave Tanya a piece of my mind and began to argue with the young artist. He was adamant. The champagne had circulated freely. Very well, said I, walking out on the balcony, then I will throw my rubles down into the square. This brought an immediate response from the Russians, galvanizing even the disdainful Tanya. No, no, not that. An American had only recently tossed money down from a balcony and the secret police had responded at once. There was a standoff. The artist got in touch with his wife. She would come down and discuss the whole matter. His wife proved to be a charming young woman who looked as though she had stepped out of a Renoir painting. In a quiet corner of the room I explained the unwanted intervention of Tanya. The wife had brought us a present, a fourteenth-century bronze insignia from a priest's hat. She accepted the rubles and we accepted the present. All was well as Herr Heikel's champagne continued to flow. From down below came laughter and song. Students, said Sonia, celebrating the end of the school year. In the soft northern darkness, with the early dawn beginning to break, they were parading across the square. Free, free, free, this brief moment of freedom so rare in a closed, repressive society.

Earlier, on our return to Moscow, I had encountered at the embassy July 4 party one of the bureaucracy whom I had been prodding. With a smug self-satisfaction he asked me if I had enjoyed my stay in the Soviet Union. Yes, I said, I had enjoyed it very much, finding everyone friendly and hospitable except in Moscow, where people like him had put every obstacle in the way of an inquirer seeking information about the operation of government. My childish explosion produced the expected result: a look of cold scorn as he turned away.

Leaving the Soviet Union, the visitor has curiously mixed emotions. There is an enormous relief at departing from a prison where, despite the friendly encounters in one stop after another, the awareness of the controls, the restraints, the barriers, was never far away. At the same time one feels he is deserting a people, in many ways a splendid, even an heroic people. That is the insoluble dilemma in the relationship between the two powers at whatever level; the contradictions in two modes of life intrude in even the most routine exchange, generating an atmosphere of suspicion and distrust. We felt all these emotions as we left on an Ilyushin jet for Prague. Sonia, our guide, had never intruded her political convictions on us as we had not intruded ours on her. She had become our friend, and we said good-bye with great sadness at parting from one whom, in all probability, we would never see again.

The chances have come and gone, hope advanced and hope deferred, that the differences between the two adversaries, the two superpowers, might be reconciled, or if not reconciled then equated, so that the nuclear threat would be confined and the fearful burden of the arms race at least abated. When Nikita Khrushchev came to Washington in the summer of 1959 at President Eisenhower's invitation, I believe both men wanted this outcome. Khrushchev had confronted the terrible consequences of nuclear war. The President, having given his greatly admired Secretary of State, John Foster Dulles, a state funeral, consigned his policy of containment to a quiet diplomatic grave. The opening to the Soviet Union had been the President's initiative.

Arriving at Andrews Air Force base with a full entourage, including the dour Gromyko, the Soviet Premier proved to be as shrewd a grandstander as any American politician. Traveling across the country with him was an assignment full of surprise. This thick, bullet-headed little man was determined that no one should outdo him. In Hollywood, Spyros Skouras gave a great luncheon in his honor on the 20th Century lot with all the emperors and empresses of film present. In a typically vainglorious speech, Skouras told his guest that he had come from a barren Greek island and was now head of this great company. "Just a minute, just a minute," Khrushchev, who had a simultaneous interpreter at his side, broke in. "I was a poor boy on a Ukrainian farm and I am head of the largest country in the world!" From then on the host suffered one interruption after another. The Khrushchevs were escorted to the set of *Can-Can* where the can-can dancers did a high-kicking performance, flaunting their lace underpants. Here was another instance of the impossible meeting of the permissive West and the puritanical, repressive East. Although they did not display it, the Khrushchevs were offended, Mrs. K, a motherly, comfortable type in particular. But the Premier felt that he had his revenge when he told off the mayor of Los Angeles, whom he blamed for frustrating the planned visit to Disneyland on grounds of security. His description of how he had put down the mayor would have done justice to Harry Truman at his barnyard best. Happier in urbane San Francisco, Khrushchev greeted a friendly crowd from a balcony high up on the Mark Hopkins Hotel. Following a stop in the cornfields of Iowa, where K. was dazzled by the production records of Bob Garst's hybrid corn, the trip ended with the Spirit of Camp David.

However evanescent this may have seemed in retrospect, the solid base was the President's return visit. The foremost Kremlinologists, Chip Bohlen and Tommy Thompson, went to work long in advance on the speech Eisenhower would deliver on television and radio networks throughout the Soviet Union. They predicted, these two wise scholar-diplomats, that the President would receive as great a welcome as anyone, whether Russian or foreign, since the days of the czars. After all, he was one of the heroes of the war who, with their own Marshal Zhukov, had triumphed over the Nazis. The return visit was to have come as soon afterward as possible until de Gaulle, asserting the presumption of a great power, insisted on having his own personal inning with Khrushchev. In the interval, Eisenhower went on his eleven-nation goodwill trip and de Gaulle received Khrushchev with all pomp and ceremony. The months slipped by and a date in June was fixed for the journey that was to take the President across much of the vast Soviet land.

I was in Paris on that warm June day when the structure of hopeful reconciliation fell into ruin. That ruin may not have been inevitable when the U-2 spy plane was shot down over Sverdlovsk. An admission by Eisenhower that he had been unaware of the plane's mission might have saved Khrushchev's face. But when the President, with Jim Hagerty at his elbow, took public responsibility for the U-2, the humiliation and anger of the Soviet Premier produced an explosive break. Khrushchev had come to Paris to renounce the invitation and to vent his fury on the President who had betrayed him. Would he participate in the meeting with de Gaulle, Macmillan and Eisenhower? Yes, he would attend for the sole purpose of denouncing his betrayers. The three could do nothing except sit in embarrassed silence. The same fury flared out at his mass press conference in the ramshackle Palais de Chaillot, which was ready for the wreckers and was nearly brought down as the floor of the auditorium trembled and shook under the weight of a thousand "journalists" and Khrushchev's thumping and pounding. Journalists was a misnomer for the audience since a number of emigrés had managed to get in, and their shouted questions sent K. off into new spasms of rage. Like the ancient practice of bear-baiting, it was altogether a shocking performance by both the baiters and the baited. That press conference was a punctuation mark, a full stop, preliminary to years of contention that at times was close to total breakdown over Berlin, Cuba and other festering centers of discord.

Since the end of the Second World War I have written innumerable times about nuclear weapons, always knowing that I was far out on the periphery. This annihilating force was multiplying in a secret life beyond the comprehension of all but a handful of the most advanced physicists. Here was a priesthood dedicated to a religion of death. The outsider, the layman, even, say, a President of the United States or the ruler of the Communist hierarchy in Moscow, can have only the most simplistic knowledge of the mysteries that year after year the priesthood spin out in new and more arcane forms of total and instant obliteration. President Johnson's hope of a meeting with Leonid Brezhnev to work out an arms agreement was thwarted on the eve of his departure by the Soviet invasion of Czechoslovakia. Such coincidences have been the fate of those who would abate the arms race. A few small chips —

the banning of atmospheric tests, the nuclear nonpro-liferation treaty—have been dislodged from the great, ever-growing mass, but they are minuscule and the treaty, as far as it goes, is almost totally ineffectual.

One has to be an idealist, perhaps a naive idealist, to believe that the military powers on both sides of the great divide will ever yield any significant fraction of their right, in the name of national superiority, to push on to ever newer and more devastating weaponry. In Helsinki, toward the end of the first round of the stra-tegic arms limitation (SALT) talks in May 1972, hope was in the air. At the head of the American delegation was Gerard Smith, a dedicated public servant. During three years of labor, alternating between Vienna, Hel-sinki and Washington, Smith had mastered the incredibly complex tangle of nuclear weaponry—which side had what and where might lie the best chance of agreeing on a limited standstill in some areas. He had also learned to read and speak Russian with considerable fluency, an important asset in the friendship he had developed with his opposite number, Vladimir Semenov, the head of the Soviet delegation.

On the second day after our arrival I went out to the headquarters of the American delegation on the edge of the city where, in a remarkably frank talk, Smith gave me a thorough rundown on what could be expected in Moscow a few days later. A lot remained to be done and the delegation—Paul Nitze, representing Secre-tary of Defense Melvin Laird and Gen. John Allison for the Joint Chiefs of Staff—was working twelve to fourteen hours a day. They were to get down to the final dotting of the *i*'s and the crossing of the *t*'s on the plane from Helsinki that was to take the Americans and Semenov and one or two of his lieutenants to Moscow. But something happened on the way to the final ceremony in the Kremlin after the party arrived in Moscow.

Although just what it was has never been entirely clear, the ensuing rancor cast a shadow over a great initial achievement. The opening briefing for American correspondents at the embassy began with Smith. A cautious man, he is hardly a skilled briefer. After perhaps fifteen minutes Henry Kissinger, who had come with the President from Washington, took over. At that time assistant to the President for national security affairs, Kissinger is a highly articulate and superbly organized briefer. He had to leave for the signing ceremony, but he promised to meet with us afterward no matter what the hour and he kept that promise at one-thirty in the morning. Kissinger had not been overwhelmed by modesty when he made sure it was known that approximately a year before he had negotiated a breakthrough with Soviet Ambassador Anatoly Dobrynin at a critical moment in the SALT talks in Washington. Without that breakthrough the limitation on antiballistic missiles, the heart of the agreement, might never have come about. But surely this did not mean that the interminable hours spent by the American delegation in arriving at the details of the agreement were without value. In the confusion of the Moscow climax—staff arrangements covering even the room assignments of the delegation had been mishandled—Smith and the others were left with the feeling they had been dismissed as supernumeraries. I saw this as a sorry note in what was otherwise a hopeful conclusion.

To watch the President take the honors in that last Kremlin reception, held in the splendid gold and white Hall of St. George, was to see the unbelievable: Richard Nixon marching from one end of the room to the other escorted by Brezhnev, the Kremlin hierarchy applauding, the diplomatic corps serving as backdrop. Nixon had built his whole career on anticommunism in one form or another. From his campaign against soft-spoken, gentle Jerry Voorhis through his attacks on fiery Helen Gahagan Douglas, Alger Hiss, Dean Acheson, Adlai Stevenson, and his Cowardly College of Communist Containment, the war on communism was his stock in trade. Fear, suspicion, distrust had carried him to that high moment of personal triumph and, it was possible, an opening to his promised generation of peace. The conventional wisdom was that only a bona fide anti-Communist could have brought off the opening to Peking and Moscow. That view may have some validity. If Hubert Humphrey had won in 1968 by a shift of a few thousand votes in the marginal states it is not hard to imagine Richard Nixon attacking Humphrey as President if he had moved in the same way to write an end to the cold war and the policy of containment. Nixon knew how to exploit the Moscow détente to the fullest with the television spectaculars within the Kremlin and the theatrics of his speech to the Congress immediately upon his return to Washington. And even though Watergate had begun to inundate the White House when Brezhnev came for a payback summit in June 1973, the meeting made the headlines despite its meager substance.

The riddle wrapped in an enigma surrounded by a mystery: this has been a large part of the lure of Russia. After the communiqués, the florid toasts, the high sounding speeches, I have always come away with a sense of how little we knew of what had gone on behind the locked doors of those conference rooms. No more, to be sure, than they, these men of power who supposedly hold the life of mankind in their hands, wanted us to know. I persisted in a foolish conviction that the mystery could be penetrated, that some significant word might be dropped to lift at least a small corner of the curtain. In pursuit of this illusion I collected Soviet ambassadors, which was rather more interesting than collecting, say, butterflies, though equally elusive and variegated. One of the first was Constantine Oumansky. He had a glittering assemblage of gold teeth and the manners of a *maître d'hôtel* serving a restaurant not quite first-class. When he paid a visit to St. Louis I arranged for him to meet my former editor, O. K. Bovard, who had taken on rather late in life a heavy dose of undigested Marxism. Bovard gave him a dinner at his

estate in the country to which he invited the *haute
bourgeoisie* of the city. There was to be a shock effect
on each side. A handsome cherry orchard was one of
the assets of the Bovard property. When Oumansky
returned to Washington he said he could think of nothing but Chekov; you could almost hear those axes and
they were bringing down not just the cherry trees but
the system itself.

Isaiah Berlin arrived in Washington shortly after
the German attack on Russia, intending with his fluent
knowledge of Russian to cross the Pacific and approach
Moscow and the British embassy by way of Siberia.
The Nazi conquest of Europe had made any other
approach difficult. Hoping for help in obtaining a visa,
he went to lunch with Oumansky. Berlin complimented
his host on the fish course. Very rare, said Oumansky,
it is flown in from my country. And what is its name?
Berlin asked. The ambassador turned to the tall, lugu-
brious butler for an answer. Bass was the reply. The
butler, it was thought at the time, was KGB headman.

Poor Oumansky was killed in a plane crash in a
flight out of Mexico City; it was rumored to have been
sabotage.

After Pearl Harbor, the Russians sent Maxim
Litvinov to preside over the big, somewhat shopworn
embassy on Sixteenth Street that had been built by
George Mortimer Pullman, the sleeping car magnate.
The era of red plush and gilt had carried over incon-
gruously into the Communist occupation or, rather, in a
curious way it matched the contemporary Communist
decor that equates conspicuous shine with elegance.
Litvinov was of the old school insofar as the system
tolerated at that time any deviation from iron orthodoxy.
But having been an internationalist, a proponent of the
League of Nations, he was right for Washington at the
moment when we would of dire necessity cooperate
in defeating the Nazis. He was the epitome of caution,
and I soon found that any effort at even the most background of background conversations was futile. He was

taking no chances in his new role. The great wartime collaboration had moments of irony, as when social and official Washington welcomed the Russian sniper, Ludmilla Pavlichenko, at a party in the gardens of Tregaron, the Joseph Davies estate (or, more accurately, the estate of his wife, Marjorie Merriweather Post). Introducing Ludmilla, Jesse Jones, the tight-fisted embodiment of capitalism then head of the Reconstruction Finance Corporation, hailed her for having personally shot 103, or maybe 113, of the enemy. It would have been worth a great deal to have known a little of what went on behind the ambassador's carefully controlled mask when confronted with this scene of baroque contradiction. His life summed up so much history. His British wife, Ivy, was to write pleasant vignettes of Russian life for the *New Yorker* long after he was dead; their son, Pavel, was a dissident who paid the penalty in a Siberian prison camp before he was allowed to emigrate.

A rather ordinary specimen was Mikhail Menshikov, who came as a member of the Politburo. He soon established himself on the party circuit and won notice in the gossip columns as "Smiling Mike." Every five or six weeks I would go to the embassy for lunch. It always began with two or three stiff vodkas. Usually we lunched alone, sometimes one of his counsellors was present. Getting behind the trivia to something substantive was a futile exercise. He had been ambassador to India, and I once remarked that a high Indian official let it be known he had not slept with his wife for twenty-seven years. "What is a wife for?" Smiling Mike growled.

A successor was Vladimir Smirnovsky, who gave every evidence of being a professional diplomat. He was quiet and mannerly, and not infrequently he responded to questions of substance about Soviet policy. We had a friendship of sorts, correct yet pleasant. Once he and his wife came to dinner at our house.

I could not help wondering what purpose these men served or at least I wondered until the arrival of

Anatoly Dobrynin. It quickly became apparent that he exercised far more authority than his predecessors. He was close to Dean Rusk and then to William Rogers, who once remarked in his amiable way, "I call him Toly now." But his relationship with Henry Kissinger was a benchmark in relations between the Soviet Union and the United States. Although their joint negotiation of the breakthrough in the SALT talks was well known, this was only one of their common undertakings. His round face often creased with a genial smile, Dobrynin could make an effort to be amusing with rather corny jokes. But beneath this surface he concentrated always on the business at hand. That business was to knit together the ties between the two superpowers in such a way that nuclear war would be all but impossible and, eventually, the terrible drain in money and resources of the competition in nuclear weaponry could be slowed and even brought to a full stop. He knew a great deal about the internal politics of American foreign policy and I was convinced early on that he used this knowledge to further the hopes of peace on the roller coaster that seemed all too often to be the fastest means of travel between Washington and Moscow.

I have developed, and not entirely as a consequence of my Russian collection, a cynicism about ambassadors. In the era of the transoceanic telephone, the jet plane, the hot line and the summit, they are very often a superfluity. The President picks up the telephone, with the scrambler insuring security, and gets the Premier on the line. If the ambassador and his wife are pleasant and fairly attractive, willing to spend their own money beyond the chintzy foreign service allowance for large formal dinners, receptions, and teas, well and good; they can carry on, inured to the boredom of this life, while the specialists conduct the day-to-day business of the embassy. The trouble is that the big monied men and women who buy their embassies deprive the career officers of the important posts. Considering how new is America's big power role, the foreign service has on the whole performed well. The foolish old clichés about cookie pushers and striped pants deserve oblivion. How many who treasure the title Mr. Ambassador deserve even a footnote in history?

Two exceptions that bear on the difficult and perilous connection between the giants should be noted. Charles Bohlen and Llewellyn Thompson were the indispensable men bridging, often under the most trying circumstances when the roof seemed about to fall in, the enormous distance between the two disparate powers. They had in common a maturity based on long and intimate knowledge of Russian history and, above all, the nature of the Communist regime. With this background they were able to maintain a middle course between the naive fellow travelers, who believed that somehow the good and true must be there, and the cold warriors, determined to exorcise the devil of communism. Often this was a difficult position to sustain. Bohlen came under the gun of Joe McCarthy and his henchman, Scott McLeod, who had been planted in the State Department. He suffered no little humiliation before he was cleared, with John Foster Dulles doing little or nothing to help him out of the quagmire of innuendo and suspicion. Because he had been Franklin Roosevelt's interpreter and counsellor at Yalta he was the subject of the darkest scrutiny. His exposition before a Senate committee of the realities behind the agreements of Yalta, which permitted Soviet troops to occupy virtually all of Poland, was a masterpiece of cool, calm reason. And given the prejudices of his interlocutors, Republicans bent on proving that Yalta was a plot to give Eastern Europe to the Communists, and the nature of the times, it was an act of quiet courage.

The two men could hardly have been more unlike in origin. Chip was St. Paul's and Harvard, he had the U cachet of the Eastern seaboard, and was descended from an aristocratic German family. Born in Las Animas, Colorado, Tommy had a B.A. from the University of Colorado. He had a rugged, unmistakably American look, his manner gentle, understated. Each had a sense of humor that was a saving grace in the often bleak atmosphere of Moscow, where a summons to the foreign office meant a dressing down over the latest incident that threatened to escalate into still another major crisis. Both fluent in Russian, they could talk with Khrushchev in his own earthy idiom. Once when Khrushchev came to the embassy for a reception, Tommy showed him the corn he had planted in the embassy garden. K. promptly ferreted out from the crowd his Minister of Agriculture, dragged him to the garden, and demanded to know why he couldn't grow corn as fine as that.

Appointment to Moscow is, of course, the greatest accolade since it is the most important post in the service. But with it go heavy penalties. Life in Moscow during the long, dark winters, when the sun rises at nine o'clock and sets around three-thirty or four, is dreary indeed. Spasso House, the ambassador's residence, is a large, gloomy relic of the prerevolutionary days of the wealthy sugar merchants who collected Impressionist paintings. Part of the burden is to live knowing that, however zealously and efficiently the American security officers sweep every nook and cranny for concealed bugs, there is always the possibility that the most private and intimate conversations are being taped. Surveillance is constant, including the surveillance of the servants coming by way of the foreign office, the only source available to the diplomatic corps. Dinner parties tend to be stiff, formal and exceptionally dull, the salvation being that, protocol being strictly observed, they end on the stroke of eleven. The embassy office building is inadequate, overcrowded. At this writing an interminable negotiation appears at last to have been concluded with agreement for both parties to build a new office complex. One advantage until the recent onset of détente was that few American visitors came to make demands on the ambassador. That has all changed with an endless procession of businessmen, scientists, heart specialists, astronauts and others covered by the various forms of cooperation under détente trooping through Moscow.

We were more fortunate than we deserved in having had two such accomplished diplomats with the authority of broad knowledge serving at a critical time. Tommy Thompson's willingness to return to Moscow for a second tour of duty was proof, if any proof had been needed, of his readiness to serve his country. This has not always been so. In 1917, at the time of the Bolshevik revolution, the American ambassador was David Francis, a St. Louis banker. His chief distinction in the view of cynical observers in St. Petersburg was his travelling spittoon, which opened with a foot pedal. He took it with him everywhere, including to his box at the opera. In the late thirties, Joseph Davies, a political appointee, was, in his determined innocence, myopic about the purge trials and the terrible calculated famines that took so many millions of lives in the course of Stalin's liquidation of the *kulaks*. Chip Bohlen, who, as a young counsellor of embassy, sat with Davies during the purge trials, told a classic anecdote. In one of the intervals the ambassador approached a foreign correspondent covering the trial to ask what he made of it. The answer was, "I believe everything but the facts." Puzzled, Davies turned to Bohlen as the charade resumed to ask what this could mean.

In the wartime ambassador, the United States was once again exceptionally fortunate. Through his long career of public service Averell Harriman has held many posts but none of greater service to the nation than his four years in Moscow. Cooperation with the Russian ally, as he was to discover, was always difficult and sometimes impossible. The wall of suspicion and distrust was not breached by the desperate need to destroy Hitler's armies. Again it was a matter of balance, this time between the persuasion of Soviet-American propaganda, given wide currency at home through official channels and in the enthusiasm of the one-time fellow travelers who seized the opportunity to proselytize for their cause, and the realities as Harriman knew them in Moscow. Returning to Washington for consultation after the victory in Europe, he met with a half dozen of us to give us the facts as he knew them. Cooperation with Stalin's Russia in peacetime was a vain delusion. His armies occupied Eastern Europe and he meant to rule there by the most ruthless means. Should he consolidate a hold on Iran the whole Middle East would be in peril. The dictator had responded to appeals from Roosevelt at the end of the President's life with blunt rejection, if not contempt. This was strong medicine for those of us who had gone a bit overboard if only in admiration for the extraordinary powers of resistance of the Soviet people as they had withstood the terrible sieges at Leningrad and Stalingrad. This was the word Harriman had given President Truman and he was proved, it is hardly necessary to add, entirely right.

Yet he never hardened into a doctrinaire, professional anti-Communist. To hear him talk nearly thirty years later, at the age of eighty-three, about the vital importance of maintaining détente was to realize that age does not inevitably bring hardening of the mental arteries. Détente was a Nixon policy, one of the President's principal claims to achievement before the Watergate inundation. An unshakable Democrat, Harriman nevertheless argued that the agreements reached with the Soviet Union were of inestimable benefit to all Americans with a hope for the future, and they should not be played off for party advantage. He supported the Kissinger view that to make emigration of the Jews and other minorities a condition of détente was sure to be self-defeating since it was, in effect, a demand that the Soviets abolish their system. And however repugnant that system, it was not to be transformed by fiat laid down by another power.

In the spring of 1974, with his wife, Pamela, and several friends, he returned to the Soviet Union for a three-week stay that ended with a two-hour talk with Leonid Brezhnev. By what he heard at various levels he was convinced the Soviets deeply and genuinely wanted a relaxation of tensions. He spread this view by every means within his reach. It was contrary, of course, to a widely advertised conviction of important figures in his party, notably Sen. Henry Jackson, who was advancing with all the powers at his disposal on the presidential nomination in 1976. To the politics of anticommunism, long a staple in the American mix, Jackson had added another powerful ingredient. That was the plight of the Jews in the Soviet Union seeking to emigrate to Israel. Working with the Zionists, he was given an unfailing succession of instances of repression and cruelty. With these weapons and the continuing pressure of the Zionist lobby, together with the almost instinctive American reaction against injustice, he enlisted more than two-thirds of the Senate against any trade concessions such as Export-Import bank loans to the Soviet Union. At the same time Jackson was a big weapons advocate, repeatedly urging larger defense appropriations. In the midst of the mood of disillusion with the scandals of Washington, Jackson's views seemed to promise a return to the unthinking anticommunism of the cold war. If you couldn't be for something, you could be against something, and in this perspective it might enlist wide support. That was what Jackson, with his rough-hewn rhetoric, was counting on. Yet he finally agreed to a compromise on Soviet emigration in the Trade Reform act which drew a Soviet renunciation of the trade agreement.

A beginning of sorts to the limitation of offensive nuclear weapons came out of the meeting between President Ford and Chairman Brezhnev at Vladivostok late in 1974. Whether it would materialize into an agreement that would be ratified by the Senate no one could say with assurance, least of all Henry Kissinger, who had been the negotiator. One reason for the doubt was the approaching presidential year and the likelihood that any agreement to come before the Senate would become a political issue. Jackson, foremost among the herd of Democratic candidates, made an early start by opposing the tentative arrangement reached at Vladivostok. Moreover, there was no stop in the development of new and ever more fantastic weapons such as the Trident submarine and the new manned bomber. So it was at best hope deferred as within the $100 billion American arms budget these new weapons took form.

XI

The Giant
and the Slave

The cowhand costume was obviously the work of a first-rate tailor, the material the finest sand-colored gabardine. Lyndon Johnson on the ranch was playing his favorite role. He was the self-made President, the bootstrap President, risen like a genie from the sand hills of Texas. Even when theoretically he was relaxing, which in fact he never did, no one was allowed to forget his power. It fed upon itself with strange manifestations which now and then seemed to give him the anointed arrogance of the Sun King.

Long since behind him was the derisory title Land-slide Lyndon, deriving from his first election to the Senate which he won by eighty-seven votes through some rigged counting in a bossed district. Nineteen-sixty-four was a refutation of all the uncertainties of his past; it had been a massive triumph—486 electoral votes, 43 million popular votes; his opponent, Barry Goldwater, with only his native Arizona and four states of the Deep South.

With the disaster of Vietnam still over the horizon, he was riding the crest of the wave and happy enough to have other riders in his triumphal chariot. The chariot was a white Lincoln Continental which he drove himself. We piled in, three or four of us who were Lyndon-watching with exceptional privileges at the ranch. Let's go for a ride. We rode first over the range, rough ups and downs, looking at his cattle through his familial eyes. Before one solid, short-legged bull the President stopped to give his spiel. That one, he said, doesn't know his business. Dutiful end men, we asked why. I could tell you, he said, if Dorothy wasn't with us. Dorothy was Mrs. McCardle, a conscientious reporter for the Washington *Post*, with the gentle civility of a vanishing day. On cue Dorothy said, Don't let that stop you, Mr. President. It didn't. Well, I'll tell you, he gets it in the wrong hole. After a pause to admire one or two more satisfactory performers we drove on, stopping at the ranch house for paper containers of beer from a draft dispenser provided by the Busch Brewing Company, and turned onto the public highway outside the Johnson preserve. The sudden darkness was falling on the Texas hills. Around a curve and down a hill the President speeded, swerving on the left at perhaps sixty or seventy miles an hour, forcing an oncoming car off the road. "Is the Secret Service still with us?" he asked over his shoulder. A colleague in the rear seat with me whispered, "This will be a great story but we won't be alive to write it." Our destination was a hunting lodge where in the season the deer were reported so numerous they could be shot like cows. An attraction in the off-season was watching the deer mating. Darkness deprived us of this legendary spectacle.

In the press room at the Driskell Hotel in Austin the buzz-buzz quickly gave the ride the widest currency. Johnson was deeply hurt by this publicity. In my experience no president, even including John Kennedy, cultivated the press so incessantly and so industriously. All things considered, he got a far better press than he deserved and one reason was this unfailing cultivation. With his fantastic energy he smothered the Washington press corps, reaching out octopus-like to editors and publishers around the country. In the face of adverse criticism he was like a hurt child, unable to understand how anyone could do that to him. During my few days at the ranch, the *Wall Street Journal* was running a series of articles on how he and Mrs. Johnson had amassed their television and radio properties, beginning with a small bequest that had come to his wife, and the use of influence to insure that no intruders were allowed into a domain they held to be their own. Several times he spoke with contempt of the rich man's paper, the *Wall Street Journal.* On his death he left an estate estimated as high as $35 million which, to say the least, was remarkable for one who had spent his entire life on a public payroll. The television properties were the principal part of that estate. Several days after returning from Texas I paid a call on a friend who was a guest in the White House. Walking toward the Rose Garden on my way out I encountered the President. I told him I had not written about the ride nor had I discussed it in the press room. He paused and fixed me with a look of sorrowful disdain. It doesn't matter, he said, a lot of others did. It was a minor incident yet it seemed to me to epitomize the plight of this Gargantua. He had extraordinary ability, a mind second to none, remarkable powers of persuasion and analysis, but his temperament, his ego, constantly betrayed his intellect. Again and again the demands of that ego overwhelmed the carefully calculated structure evolved in his shrewd and, at times, even subtle brain. The war in Vietnam as it escalated on such a monstrous scale was in a sense a projection of the Johnson ego. Shortly after the assassination he had told Henry Cabot Lodge, then the American ambassador in Saigon, after Lodge had given him a foreboding of defeat, "I don't intend to be the first president to lose a war."

One aspect of that ego was a streak of what can only be called sadism. He could not forgive his friends, to say nothing of his foes, for having had the privilege of his friendship. In fact his foes often seemed to fare better since he was under a compulsion to convert them to his allegiance. The Democratic convention in 1964, in the seamy purlieus of Atlantic City, was a stage for his ego. His own renomination had become a kind of coronation. The selection of a Vice-Presidential candidate was all that was left to the submissive delegates, some few of whom had made a gesture of independence by seating a delegation from Mississippi that represented blacks as well as whites. No one had the slightest illusion about how the choice was to be made. At the time of his second Presidential nomination in 1956, Adlai Stevenson had opened the decision to the delegates. Lyndon Johnson would never make that mistake. Picking the Vice President has long been a game of political Russian roulette. President Johnson played the game with the zest of the riverboat gambler, as Philip Geyelin so aptly described him. Whatever private conclusion he may have reached early on, he dangled the prize before one hopeful after another, insuring that each hope was duly ventilated in the press. Some of the potential candidates who were elevated to a moment of headline fame were curious indeed. One was Sen. Thomas Dodd of Connecticut, soon to fall out when his financial machinations were exposed by Drew Pearson. Another was Sen. Eugene McCarthy of Minnesota, destined to play a leading part in Johnson's ultimate downfall. He may, as I have said, have known from the beginning that Hubert Humphrey would be his choice. But, along with the others, Humphrey was kept dangling until a late hour. The night of Humphrey's selection, with appropriate oratorial salvos and the ritualistic polling of the delegates, should have been his moment of glory, but Johnson sat looking down on the convention in what was for him the royal box. His gestures, his greetings to those who approached the throne, were the center of attention as his choice was officially ratified. In that ceremony sanctioned from the royal box was a dark foreboding of the ordeal of the incoming Vice President.

As a public servant Humphrey has demonstrated many virtues over the years. Punctuality is not one of them. Keeping an appointment at his office in the Executive Office Building, I would wait half an hour, forty-five minutes, an hour. Where is the Vice President? He is with the President at the White House. No further explanation was required. Finally he would return, ashen, shaken. Once he went so far as to say to me that he did not know whether he could go on. His loyalty was such that he gave no particulars of what he had endured in the eye of the storm. But particulars were hardly necessary. Gargantua's embrace, whether in rage or exultation, was overwhelming. It could be creative, as it was in the far-reaching civil rights legislation that was Johnson's monumental contribution to American life. Or it could be destructive, as in the hopeless war in Vietnam. Humphrey was the victim of many of the President's sudden impulses, for example, when the Vice President was ordered off on a tour of Southeast Asia where he was to make extravagant claims for America's noble mission in slaying the Communist dragon. His rhetoric, so little related to the truth, was to haunt him in the months to come as the deep wound of the war set Americans one against the other in bitterness and despair.

Survival in the eye of the storm was an unnerving experience. A White House aide who had come from Texas as one of the President's loyal friends was charged with a homosexual incident in the YMCA. It developed that he had driven himself to the breaking point, staying at his desk each night until nine-thirty or ten o'clock to answer the backlog of telephone calls that accumulated during the day. Johnson's response was to send Clark Clifford and Abe Fortas to the newspaper offices with a request from the President that the incident be kept out of print. By chance I had an appointment with the President on the day this painful story broke. He was wrapped in Stygian, almost incommunicable gloom. We were carrying on a desultory conversation when Mrs. Johnson entered with her smiling, imperturbable manner. I see, she said, that I have two fine gentlemen for lunch. Don't want any lunch, came from Johnson in a growl. The First Lady was undeterred. Maybe you'll have some dinner then. This drew no response. She came over and kissed him on the forehead. She might as well have bestowed this mark of affection on a marble president preserved in statuary hall at the Capitol.

Of his powers of persuasion there could be no question. They were exercised in full force on Arthur Goldberg, an associate justice who had been appointed to the Supreme Court by President Kennedy. Johnson held out a dazzling prospect. If he would leave the Court to become ambassador to the United Nations, Johnson is said to have told the Justice, history would write him down as the Prince of Peace. Having at least a normal share of human vanity, Goldberg succumbed, a decision he was to regret thereafter. How he was to bring peace to the world in an office so subservient to the wishes of the executive and his Secretary of State was never made clear. But Goldberg's resignation opened the way for the President to carry out an intention uppermost in his mind. He named Fortas to the vacancy with the prospect that when Chief Justice Warren stepped down, as was fully expected, the President's friend and counsellor would be elevated to that office. Fortas had been a close confidant, giving his old friend unfailing support on Vietnam. The appointment was one of Johnson's great gaffes for it was soon disclosed that the new Justice had privately agreed to accept from Lewis Wolfson, a financier-speculator, an annual payment of $20,000 a year for as long as he lived, the payments to go to his wife after his death for as long as she lived. Wolfson was involved in a case to come before the courts. Fortas resigned with his career as a brilliant lawyer in ruins.

When it became clear that the Democrats would take notable losses in the congressional elections of 1966, with Johnson friends in the Senate among the victims who would pay heavily for the escalation of the war and the fearful casualty lists, the President chose the old, reliable antidote, foreign travel. Southeast Asia was in dire need of his ministering hand. If he were in far parts performing his duty he could not go into states and districts where the axe seemed certain to fall on luckless Democrats. An extensive tour was planned with a summit meeting, one of the most bogus of all summits, in Manila. He would dominate the television screens at the climax of the congressional campaign. By a happy coincidence the Pacific satellite would begin operating just as he arrived in Asia and there would be instant coverage. Three television crews of fourteen or fifteen men each were on the press plane. It was a kind of imperial entourage. Before the soft green of the mountains in Pago Pago, American Samoa, he was greeted by chieftains, wearing the lava lava, naked from the waist, behind them their women in brilliantly flowered mumus. Chief Pele said in his address of welcome: "Not since the time when our ancestors first set out across the seas for your land has such an honor come to us as your visit today." He was referring to the ancient memory of long outriggers and the mysterious vastness of the great ocean. If the American king had any intimation of the significance of the moment spanning the centuries, he gave no sign of it, but after a perfunctory response he read a dull bureaucratic speech reciting the benefits the United States had brought to Samoa. When we crossed the International Dateline and reached New Zealand much later that same merciless day, we were greeted by nearly naked Maoris in a ceremonial dance. It was a puzzlement for the king who had obviously not been briefed about these curious customs.

He wanted to get down to the business of the tour: beads and gewgaws for the natives; promises scattered in every country he visited, which, as it turned out, were no more substantial in value. Speaking at a formal parliamentary lunch in Wellington he said, "I don't want just to have liberty for myself, but I want to be the protector of liberty everywhere." In the shadow of Vietnam, that was a dangerous pledge.

When a President travels he must be protected from the more squalid sights of the capitals he visits. On the route from the airport into Manila, bamboo screens had been put up to conceal some of the most noisome slums in the world. The Philippines was becoming one of the harshest and most corrupt dictatorships in Asia. At a reception honoring the great men gathered for the summit, the Taiwanese ambassador told me, with due caution and in a low voice, that the latest squeeze on the Chinese, who did most of the commercial business in the islands, was close to confiscatory. He did not know how his compatriots could endure it. Similar stories were heard on the periphery of the conference table at which the words democracy and freedom soared into the air with oratorical abandon. A taxi driver, that ubiquitous source, spoke sadly of his eight children (the annual rate of population increase was 3.4 or 3.5 percent) and his struggle to feed them.

From the start of the tour a buzz of rumors circulated about the President's intention to visit Vietnam. He would, he wouldn't, he might, he might not. It was all very secret. Security was at the heart of it. Naturally the Communists would have liked nothing better than staging a raid to destroy the king. We left in great secrecy from the American naval base of Subic Bay, with no official assurance that this was it. Our destination was Cam Ranh Bay. The commander-in-chief was met by Gen. William C. Westmoreland, commander of the then roughly 400,000 American forces, in Vietnam. At a review of American and Vietnamese troops, the President stood on a raised platform with President Nguyen Van Ky and Gen. Nguyen Van Thieu, who was to have his turn as president. A dozen or more Vietnamese in business suits stood by uneasily like hastily invited guests. Midway through his patriotic invocation in the

steamy heat the President stripped off his battle jacket
and drew a cheer from the American ranks. Cam Ranh
Bay was proof positive of America's might and America's
engineering genius; the harbor, barracks, runways, fuel
dumps cost $500 million. This, the skeptical audience
was told by Johnson, the Vietnamese would take over
when the war ended. That the invited guests found it
hard to believe they were one day to come into possession of this vast installation is not surprising.

Later, in the cluster of mess halls, a small combo
played "The Yellow Rose of Texas." On a footpath I
ran smack into the President, his escort having fallen
behind. "Mr. President," I said, "this was a very moving
experience as I'm sure it was for you." Without a word
he looked right through me and passed on. As a critic
of the war, an opponent of what he held best and bravest,
I had no business there. In the mess hall, or so it was
reported, he had said, "Come home, bring the coonskin
and hang it on the door."

I had been in Bangkok when it still retained some
of the simplicity of *The King and I,* the *klongs* with
their diverse peoples, relaxed, laughing, in the water
and out of the water. The motorcar had done it in, the
streets jammed with traffic, exhaust gas a noxious cloud,
the *klongs* roofed over to provide more streets for more
cars that would overflow those same streets. The "progress" that millions in American aid had wrought was
sad to see. One oasis remained. I went to call on James
Thompson, whom I had known in that earlier time. In
six houses and gardens he had created a museum of
Asian art filled with splendid bronzes out of the eighth
and ninth centuries, rare pieces collected in Thailand
following his years as a spook in the war. The silk
business he started had prospered greatly, inspiring the
government to start a rival operation. From the lower
terrace I could see across the *klong* his weavers spinning
in the lamplight. They came after the heat of day and
worked through the evening. He said good-bye to me
in the entrance hall, his big, white macaw on his shoul-

der. A short time later, while visiting friends in Malaysia, he disappeared on a solitary walk, leaving not a trace.

King Phumipol and our king exchanged state dinners. The little king had two advantages, a sense of humor and his artistry on the saxophone (he played in several combos). The King and his queen arrived in the palace gardens in a large, beige Mercedes-Benz that looked as though it were half a block long. Their Majesties, lost in this remarkable vehicle, required a few minutes to be disengaged. It would have better suited our king, and indeed it seemed to me that he looked at it with an envious eye. King Phumipol is said to have remarked that if everyone in his kingdom who was guilty of corrupt practice were to be put in jail no one would be left outside. The Thai joke current at the moment was that the widow of Prime Minister Sarit Thanarat was being forced by the government to disgorge the loot her husband had stowed away in six companies he controlled. It was said to be $30 million, by an interesting coincidence the amount of direct United States economic aid received during his reign. He had engaged, I was told on a previous visit, in the highly profitable business of running opium from the Chinese border to Thai ports. The government had also seized the art treasures in his luxurious beach house and that, the Thais felt, was going a bit too far. And why hadn't he known about Swiss bank accounts? asked the wiser ones. Undeterred by these disclosures, the President talked about washing machines and refrigerators.

The grand climax came in Seoul. All the satellite participants in the Manila summit, with the exception of Malaysia, had contributed something to the Vietnam war. Korea had sent several thousand troops that quickly won a reputation for unrivaled ferocity. The permanent president, Park Chung Hee, had been determined to turn out the biggest crowd of the whole tour to greet "The Giant Texan," as the signs hailed him. Two million, or perhaps three, stood along the route from the airport and in the square in the center of the city; they formed a dense mass primed to cheer as the giant passed in his bubble-top limousine. On the way into the city I spotted a boy of about fourteen or fifteen in a school uniform, holding a large, neatly lettered sign: "Korea Ready for the Take-Off!" It referred to Walt Rostow's thesis that American economic aid applied to local industry would result in economic independence. I cornered Rostow. "Did you plant that boy with that sign out there?" I had meant this humorously. The legend could have had little or no meaning for the child or, indeed, for any Korean below the official propaganda level. Rostow replied rather reproachfully, "But you see they are ready for the take-off." As we were to learn much later, the take-off was to mean young women working virtually as slaves at a subsistence wage, twelve hours a day, seven days a week, turning out ready-to-wear garments to undersell competitors in world markets. At the airport on our departure, massed choirs of Korean girls serenaded the departing king with "Sayonara."

Nothing had been changed. Bill Moyers, the President's press secretary, assured us privately, while we were still on the road, that Johnson would soon begin a vigorous campaign for congressional candidates, taking him into perhaps as many as eighteen states. This proved to be a slight error. Back in Washington the President hunkered down, as he aptly put it, to wait out the election. As it turned out, Democratic losses were scarcely more than what could have been normally expected in an off-year. But as the Vietnam war pulled more and more young Americans into its bloody maw, a change came over the nation. Johnson's rating dropped in the polls. Some persisted in believing we could see it through, stick it out, and lick those Communists, but others were fed up, with Johnson, with his noisy claims, with his buffoonery.

A new and unexpected challenger, at first almost unnoticed, sauntered onto the national stage. Sen. Eugene McCarthy of Minnesota had sensed the mood of the country, though in truth he was not a politician at all; perhaps a poet, a dreamer, a schemer too, a gentle bull smashing a china shop, seemingly in inadvertence, yet with a private amusement. The New Hampshire primary was Lyndon Johnson's china shop. Traveling with McCarthy for a day or two I found it hard to believe that he was a serious candidate. His often pixieish humor, his dry understatement fitted the mood of the country. He offered relief from the Johnsonian bombast and from the improbable claims behind the bombast. With his wife, Abigail, and one or two of his daughters, he conferred wit and wisdom on a handful of voters. "I don't know whether I'm going to make any showing or not, but I'm having a lot of fun."

New Hampshire itself was improbable, a political cyclotron created by press and television bent on demonstrating that a hundred thousand or so voters in this remote corner of the North could name the principals in the Presidential contest. New Hampshire was the first state in the union to have an official lottery, and its primary was another sort of lottery, with many more losers than winners having paid their entry fee.

I spent a day campaigning on the main street of Concord with George Romney, whom I had known in Michigan. At the first stop, outside a bank, he solicited the support of a drunk. "You're drunk," said the righteous Mormon. "You can't prove it, I'm not drunk," the man retorted. Torn away by his handlers from this debate, the Rambler Man moved on to encounter a more sober adversary. In a sporting goods store he approached a sturdy, crusty looking character. "I'm George Romney, I'm running for president, and I want your support." Said the crusty character, "I wouldn't vote for you if you were the last man on earth." Half an hour later Romney was still talking, demanding to know why anyone could be so perverse, and the crusty character was telling the candidate that surely he must have a better way to spend his time. That was also the strong feeling of his handlers, who had been for twenty minutes tugging on his sleeve. Shortly afterward Romney announced his withdrawal.

To the surprise of practically everyone, McCarthy came close to defeating a slate of delegates pledged to Lyndon Johnson. Naturally, on the Republican side, Richard Nixon was the victor in conservative New Hampshire, with 80 percent of the vote. Were these two, the dreamer-schemer, and the hard-line, never-say-die politician, to oppose one another in November? Surely not. In spite of the setback in New Hampshire and the decline in all the political indicators, the widespread belief was that Johnson would run for a second full term as he was free to do since he had served little more than a year after Kennedy's assassination. You couldn't keep him from running. As far as I can recall, only my old friend Irving Dilliard, former editor of the editorial page of the *Post-Dispatch* and then lecturer at Princeton, challenged this belief. He had been saying for weeks that Johnson would retire, forced out by the mounting unpopularity of the war.

The renunciation scene was Johnsonian in its contrived drama. A press conference was called for a Saturday afternoon. Held in the Rose Garden on a sun-filled April day, it was sparsely attended. As I listened to him talk about the war, an impending conference with the military command, his hopes for a compromise peace with Hanoi, I found he had nothing to say about his own plans. I doubt that any of us there had the slightest suspicion of what was to come the next evening when, on nationwide television, he announced he would not run for a second term. His decision was irrevocable. In a session with the press that followed he said he might have made the announcement on the previous afternoon if the attendance had not been so poor. None of us believed that. It had been a well-kept secret. Humphrey was to tell me later that he had been informed of the decision scarcely an hour before the broadcast.

One tragedy followed another that awful spring and summer. The fabric of American life was ripped and torn. The assassination of Martin Luther King brought riots, burning and looting in a half dozen cities. From my office in downtown Washington, I saw billowing clouds of smoke rise over the capital as the reserves and the National Guard turned out to halt the devastation. Then came another senseless crime, the assassination of Sen. Robert Kennedy in Los Angeles. After the loss of the Oregon primary to Eugene McCarthy, he had won in California by a bare five percent of the vote. Lawrence O'Brien, who had given him his own talent and his loyalty, knew, as he was to tell me later, that Kennedy could not have had the nomination if he had lived.

Humphrey was the man, the only Democrat who seemed to have a chance to unite a party divided by war and domestic strife. "I wanted the nomination," he said to me after Senator Kennedy's death. "I've worked very hard for it. But God knows I didn't want it this way." The only serious rival was McCarthy, and the party was not ready in 1968 for an excursion into the wild blue beyond the Liberal-Left. But there was a portent of what was to come. Sen. George McGovern of South Dakota had become an instant candidate. I found him in a suite in the Blackstone Hotel in Chicago, surrounded by the adoring young, grinning like a Cheshire cat and looking a bit surprised.

Humphrey's seemingly impossible task was to put together the elements of the old politics, the party organizers, labor, the survivors of the New Deal out of his own past, for a first ballot nomination. The new politics was rampaging wildly in the streets of Chicago. And from the Pedernales, news came that the President of the United States, a mysterious stranger, would fly to Chicago on his birthday to make a great speech, or he would not come at all. The battle between the hippies, the yippies and the police darkened the streets of Chicago, and he did not appear. As for McCarthy, the dreamer-schemer, he played the role of the spoiler, the ego tripper. From his headquarters in one of the top floors of the Hilton Hotel his ardent young followers were said to be dropping plastic bags of filth on the crowds below.

The police had set up barriers to keep the demonstrators several blocks away from the convention hall. After adjournment, I would write in the press area until two-thirty or three in the morning. Returning to the Hilton the first night I saw a field command post ringed by guardsmen in uniform and machine gun emplacements; tight security measures required identification from anyone entering the hotel. To me it was infinitely depressing. Across Michigan Boulevard in Grant Park, the demonstrators with bull horns were chanting, "Fuck you, Mayor Daley, fuck you, Mayor Daley, fuck you, Mayor Daley. . . ." They had vowed to keep it up all night. At four-thirty in the morning I took refuge with my son, Prentiss, who had a room in a quiet hotel near the Drake. On the night of Humphrey's nomination television coverage switched to the violence in the streets, missing at least two of the seconding speeches.

At the outset it seemed a hopeless undertaking. Humphrey was under the shadow of his own past: his unfailing support as a Johnson cheerleader for a war that had torn the nation apart. A more tangible shadow was the President himself. If Humphrey were to repudiate his past and the lowering, suspicious Johnson, he would risk not only public rejection by the titular head of his party but the loss of Texas and other states in the South and Southwest. With his principal advisers divided between those opposed to any modification of his position on Vietnam and those, like Larry O'Brien, arguing that, in light of his poor standing in the polls, he had to speak out, it was not until September 30 that the break came. In a speech in Salt Lake City he said that he would be willing to stop the bombing of North Vietnam in the hope that this would lead to negotiation and a shorter war. Hardly the forthright statement O'Brien and others had wanted, it did turn the campaign around with immediate gains. I have always believed that if he had broken with his past a few days after the convention he would have won. The half-million-vote difference between Nixon and Humphrey, out of the 73 million cast, was a measure of the doubt and uncertainty dividing the nation.

I had talked with Nixon when he was campaigning for the primary in New Hampshire. It was the familiar performance, carefully understated, reserved, cool, polite and unforthcoming. He said he expected to get 40 percent of the vote there, knowing, as he must have, that his share would be much larger. He won 80 percent in New Hampshire, his only competition a small write-in for Nelson Rockefeller. Throughout the national campaign, he was to walk like a cat amidst all the hazards in his path. As a matter of fact, the hazards had been screened out as completely as a skilled public relations operation could manage. The television panels were hand picked, the performances resembled a genuine news program but were really part of a skillfull selling job put together by experts. The mass rallies were stage-managed down to the last prancing Nixonette and the last soaring balloon.

Humphrey told me, as I recall it was late in 1971, that he would not run again. Muriel, he said, would not go through another campaign. That seemed to me a wise decision given the state of the Democratic party. For all the horrors of Vietnam, the Cambodian bombing, the incursion into Laos, and the demonstrations on the campuses and in the streets, Nixon was an incumbent president and incumbency is an immense advantage. But, early in 1972 Humphrey's loyal friends, like William Benton in New York, were aware that he was positioning himself for another try, and they came through with generous support. His decision divided the moderates who might have united behind Sen. Edmund Muskie. The way was open for the shambles of the McGovern campaign, the Nixon landslide and the catastrophe of Watergate. For the Presidential virus there is no effective antibiotic. Nixon had proved that himself by coming back after the great renunciation

scene he played in 1962 following his defeat in the
California gubernatorial election. As another Presidential year approached Humphrey could try again. I
had seen Adlai Stevenson, to his own sorrow, tempted
by the illusion of one more venture. With Humphrey
there was an important difference. He is a vigorous,
hard working Senator with a constituency in the country at large as well as in his own state. The causes he
champions are those many Americans believe in. For
him politics is meat and drink, and the golden apple
hangs always just out of reach.

XII

China:
The Great
Wall Breached

To telephone to Peking is now routine. The overseas operator asks which China you want, you say People's Republic, you give the number of the information section of the foreign office, and twenty minutes later you are passed through the Shanghai switchboard to Peking. The subject of my call was visas. We had been poking about in Ottawa and New York in vain for nearly two years, beginning in 1971. Yes, said Peking, we know, we have your request under consideration. Six weeks later a call from the Chinese embassy in Ottawa informed us that our visas would be ready twelve days thence at the China Travel Service in Hong Kong. Would we please wire the ministry what our special interests were and where in China we would like to travel.

It was an irresistible invitation. In my wire I listed Tibet, Inner Mongolia, Kwangsi province, the Yangtze Gorges, and even Sinkiang, the border province where the confrontation with the Soviet Union has brought a massive military buildup. I did stop short of Lop Nor,

the center of China's nuclear development. And I
included, of course, places more likely to be on the
itinerary worked out with the ministry once we were
in Peking.

On the day I was to leave for San Francisco to join
Jane for the flight to Hong Kong, I had a hearty breakfast with Henry Kissinger in his spacious office in the
West Wing of the White House. I told him that more
than anything else I hoped to have a talk with Chou
En-lai. These two, the Jewish refugee from Nazi Germany and the Mandarin turned Communist, had become
fast friends. It was an intellectual friendship based on
a profound mutual respect. Kissinger had told me of the
transcripts made in both English and Chinese of the
more than thirty hours of discussion he had had with
Chou on his five visits to Peking. This was a record that
would be invaluable for David Bruce, who was soon to
leave for China to head the United States liaison mission in the capital. Kissinger, then the President's
adviser on national security affairs, talked about Chou
with affection. The Prime Minister was without rivals,
both as intellectual and administrator. He worked
eighteen or twenty hours a day, sometimes without
sleeping. Kissinger recalled that once when he was
closeted with him they were interrupted by an aide
who brought in proofs of the front page of the following day's edition of *The People's Daily*. Apologizing
for the interruption, Chou went over the proofs. *The
People's Daily* is, of course, the chief propaganda organ
which is circulated throughout the country.

I sensed that Kissinger's China adventure meant
more to him than any of his other achievements. This
is not to say that his was a simplistic view. On the contrary, the imponderables with the generation of Chou
and Mao Tse-tung soon to pass away loomed very large,
and these same imponderables may have been part of
the fascination. On the previous day he had given his
"Year of Europe" speech at the Associated Press luncheon in New York. That was a foretaste of the com-

plexities, the troubles in every form in every sphere soon to descend on him. He was unhappy because in the question and answer period following the speech at least two-thirds of the questions had been about Watergate rather than Europe and foreign policy. This, too, was a foretaste of what was to come. He said he would send a wire to Peking informing Chou of my forthcoming visit. I was grateful; this was not sponsorship, but it would be an alert and I could not ask for more. Yet during the long, boring hours of the flight across the Pacific, China and Chou seemed as intangible, as remote, as the distant horizon.

Hong Kong is an improbable gateway to the People's Republic; the riches glitter in every shop window of the luxury hotels for the foreign visitor with foreign currency. The China Travel Service was likewise improbable. We were told on our first inquiry that they had never heard of us; it was rather dismaying to think we had come those thousands of miles for no purpose. In the exact middle of the time span given in the telegram to Ottawa, however — and this was characteristic — our visas materialized. Early the following morning we were on the commuter train to Shumchun, the border crossing point, and thence, after the bureaucratic formalities with passports, conducted with friendly courtesy, we were on the comfortable air-conditioned train to Canton.

I thought of the China that had for so long intrigued Americans, the strange land of strange people with pigtails, who live on the opposite side of the earth as though it were the far side of the moon. Children digging in the sand said they were digging to China. The illusory China of Christianity began, for me, with mite boxes handed out in my Sunday school in a small town in Iowa, to be filled for the starving Chinese. I thought of the China of Marco Polo, and later the China of the Dragon Empress, scarlet and gold, but also of the violence, death, disease, and of poor little Pu Ji, the puppet whose name happily fitted the headlines, propped up briefly on the throne. China had been romanticized for us in *The Good Earth*, the China of surviving custom and caste that we wanted to believe in. And there beyond the train window we saw the good earth, the rice paddies, the water buffalo, those patient figures (were they patient?) in a landscape cultivated down to the last inch. There was another China, that of John Foster Dulles, a quarantined land of monolithic communism controlled from Moscow. Nixon had broken the spell he had helped to cast years before. I was ill-equipped for this assignment. But that was nothing new. I had often rushed in where, if not angels, then wise and knowledgeable specialists feared to tread.

Our rooms in the Peking Hotel looked out on the gold roofs of the Forbidden City and, when the day was clear, to the mauve shapes of the western hills. Once established with our guide and mentor, Fu Fung Kwei, who was to be with us during our entire stay, the first official encounter was with Ma Yu-chen, deputy director of the information division of the foreign office. Mr. Ma was small, almost diminutive, and handsome, his eyes the striking feature. But above all, and it was true of many Chinese we met, the quality we noted was intellect tempered by humor. We told him we wanted to be in Peking when our friends David and Evangeline Bruce arrived. Since that was a week away, a trip might be in order. While boating with Mr. Ma on the lake at the Summer Palace the next day, it was arranged. We were to go to Shanghai and Hangchow.

The last stop of the Nixon party, Hangchow is famous for its scenic setting, a misty lake surrounded by green hills, the shoreline planted with graceful willows. One of our expeditions was to the Dragon Well tea brigade, which produced, so we were told, the finest tea in China. Young girls were picking the bright green leaves off the top of the plants, the top leaves making the best tea. We sat down with the young vice-chairman of the Dragon Well brigade in his commodious office and were served, naturally, Dragon Well tea. The office was in the center of what had once been a handsome private compound. I asked him who had owned the plantation before liberation. (Liberation was the word used invariably for what had happened in 1949 when Chiang Kai-shek and the remnant of his armies were driven off the mainland as the Communists took over.) It had been owned by three landlords. And where were they? One was shot at once. He had killed so many peasants that there was no choice. The other two were being "reeducated"; one was doing quite well, the future of the second, a laggard, was uncertain.

This was the frankest answer we got to the question about the flotsam and jetsam of a corrupt and degenerate society. The past had been erased so successfully in the bright cheerful present one saw everywhere that it seemed as though it had never existed. An old China hand, in the best sense of that much abused phrase, who spent more than forty years in China before and then following a stretch in jail when the Communists took over, estimated that 2.5 million had been killed. That is probably a conservative estimate. They are gone. That is the answer. As we were several times reminded, the contrast with India, the second most populous nation, is great. In India, the landlords, the usurers, the hoarders, the corrupt officials are in place, and famine, mass death and breakdown are the order of the day.

Back in Peking in time to greet the Bruces, we again sought out Mr. Ma. Would another trip be in order? he inquired. Would we like to see Yenan, the cradle of the revolution, perhaps. We were firm. We wanted to stay in Peking in anticipation, so we hoped, of an interview with Chou En-lai. That was our goal as we had said at the first meeting. But we could always be summoned back, he said. No, we would wait.

It was a waiting game enlivened by various diversions arranged by our hosts. Before our trip we had had a two-hour session with Chiao Kuan-hua, the deputy minister for foreign affairs. We felt we were being given a kind of test to determine whether we qualified for a session with the Prime Minister. Tall, strongly built, looking much younger than his middle years, Chiao, as he had proved at the United Nations, is highly articulate with a sturdy sense of humor. This was a new kind of journalism. Chiao, his interpreter, Jane and I were seated in a big conference room in the center of a semicircle formed by a dozen observers from the ministry. Conducting an interview in the presence of so many silent onlookers made me self-conscious at first. Chiao's responses came without hesitation in a booming voice often underscored by laughter. China did not want to be a superpower, he said. "You and the Soviet Union are superpowers. You are up there at the top and that is very dangerous." On nuclear disarmament the answer was the stock one. China is ready to give up all armaments but who would follow that example? No one at all. Disarmament committees and disarmament agreements are worthless. Throughout the discussion his buoyant confidence came out loud and clear. Kissinger had said China would not be admitted to the United Nations at this session of the General Assembly, but Kissinger had been wrong as he learned when he was about to board his plane and fly back to Washington. This was obviously a source of satisfaction to Chiao since he had been principally responsible for persuading the General Assembly to reject Washington's "two Chinas" policy and vote in Peking as the sole representative of the Chinese people. That vote had come on Chiao's night of triumph when delegates of the Third World paraded in the aisles in celebration as the vote was recorded. This was the new China and whatever the suffering had been in the terrible years, men like Chiao were not looking back.

We were waiting and, though Mr. Ma made no commitment, he held out a vague hope. We were shown through the winding corridors of the deep air raid shelter under the Ta Cha-lan department store. Ten thousand people could take shelter there in a matter of minutes, we were told. And given the discipline of the

Chinese, the extraordinary block-by-block organization, I did not doubt it. Despite the ever-present slo-
gans — "Dig tunnels deep, store grain, no hegemony" —
and the propaganda on the radio and on Peking's limited
television, it was hard to believe that these were a
people living under the fear of war. The 800 million
were everywhere, on the streets, in the shops, singularly
identical in sexless blue or grey pants and jackets. Only
the grandmothers, pushing small children in bamboo
strollers, and now and then an old man with three or
four strands of silky white beard, were set apart. It
would have been oppressive, this swarming mass, if it
had not seemed on the surface so good natured. Placid
may be more accurate, or self-contained; yet, as we
were to learn in our travels beyond cosmopolitan Peking,
the people were invariably curious about these strange
white creatures from the underside of the earth.

On the eighth day, the alert came without prior
warning from Mr. Ma's office: Stay in your hotel after
lunch and be ready for a summons. It was to happen
after all. All through dinner and into the early evening
we were nerved up for the meeting with the mysterious,
great khan. Shortly before ten o'clock, Mr. Ma's office
called to say it would not happen this night. But when?
The answer was vague. We were sunk in gloom. Now,
we said, it will not come about. On the following day,
a Sunday, while I was filing copy at the telegraph office
Jane, on an offchance, got Mr. Ma himself on the phone.
He was standing by even though it was a holiday, in
the likelihood that a call might come from the secretary to the Prime Minister. Our hopes rose again. But
dinner passed and nine-thirty came and went with no
call. We were preparing for bed when the order came.
Be ready not later than ten-thirty, we would be called
for and driven to the Great Hall of the People to meet
with the Prime Minister.

The overwhelming impression was of the silence of
the city. Broad Chang'an Boulevard was deserted. The
Great Hall, which was in darkness, was only ten min-

utes away. As we entered the side door, a slender figure in an immaculate, grey Mao suit came from an anteroom to greet us. He was a living legend, embodying the rebirth of a great nation that had been reduced to servitude. My first impression was of his reticence, his reserve; a friendly serious greeting with something like modesty.

In the now familiar semicircle, with even more auditors than before, the interview began. I had been told that there would be no transcript and no direct quotations would be permitted, although his remarks could be attributed to him. A discussion began, more nearly a discussion than an interview, that went on without pause for three and a half hours, covering every phase of China's relations with friends, neighbors, enemies, and with at least tangential bearing on domestic policy. Showing how well briefed he was he began by saying he understood I was working on a book about John Foster Dulles. I said this was true but I was finding it difficult, if not impossible, to bring him to life. Dulles is gone, Chou said, but his policies remain; he persisted in believing in monolithic communism long after the split between Moscow and Peking was a fact.

Why, he asked, do you think Dulles was so stubborn for so long in supporting Chiang Kai-shek on Taiwan? I said the answer seemed obvious: Dulles hoped to restore Chiang to the mainland and make him the ruler of all China. You are mistaken; what he wanted was to establish Taiwan as a separate nation. And if his son, Chiang Ching-kuo, tries to do this after Chiang is gone we shall know how to deal with it. This was a new perspective. I saw what it would mean, a Republic of Taiwan with a flourishing industry and diplomatic representation independent of the Chinese past. Because I had been unaware of it I was surprised when Chou told me that Chiang's forces still held the small offshore islands of Quemoy and Matsu. I thought of how many thousands of words I had written about those foolish islands in the Dulles era. They are Taiwan's commitment to the mainland, Chou said, and we are pleased that they have that commitment. We shell them every other day, usually with shells which release propaganda leaflets, and Taiwan responds with a similar bombardment. For the long pull Chou seemed to feel that Taiwan would be no obstacle to relations with Washington, even though the United States continued to recognize Chiang's China and a Taiwanese ambassador was stationed in the American capital. Yet it was clear that the Prime Minister believed a kind of double standard still prevails as a vestige of the old "two Chinas" policy.

We had not talked for long when inevitably the Soviet Union came into the discussion. The great power to the north is central to China's outlook on the world. Chou sketched with broad strokes the nightmare that had haunted the People's Republic since 1949. There would be a three-pronged attack: Russia from the North, Japan from the South and the United States in the middle. Even India might join in. It was hard to believe he could be entirely serious until one recalled the fifty years or more of war and revolution before 1949; the Japanese invasion and the atrocities that went with it; the movement of American forces in Korea up to the Yalu River, China's boundary, and the threat of American bombing; last and most menacing, the massive Soviet force on the north and the bloody skirmishing in the late sixties along the Ussuri River. That nightmare has now been dispelled, the threat of war with the Soviet Union deterred. This has come about in considerable part by major successes in diplomacy. First came the Nixon initiative and the communiqué signed in Shanghai by the president and Chou renouncing hegemony and declaring that Chinese on both sides of the Taiwan Strait are Chinese. Next was the visit of Prime Minister Tanaka and Japan's recognition of the People's Republic and break in relations with Chiang.

Although he never raised his voice, speaking throughout in a quiet conversational tone, Chou gave the impression of supreme confidence, as though in the quiet after trials and tribulations that had seemed endless. Turning to me with a slight smile, he said, your friend Joseph Alsop writes frequently that nuclear war with the Soviet Union is inevitable. We do not believe this. While expressing unshakable confidence that an attack from the north had been deterred, he developed at length his conviction of the aggressive designs of the Soviet Union. They could never be trusted and that applied with special force to the agreements signed by President Nixon and Leonid Brezhnev in Moscow in May 1972. Perhaps his greatest emphasis was on the continuing arms race between the two superpowers. It goes up and up and up, he said, gesturing with his expressive hands. He could see no end short of total disaster. He repeated in effect what Chiao Kuan-hua had told us. China did not want to be a superpower.

About midway in our discussion he brought up Watergate, which already, on May 20, 1973, had begun to take on epic proportions. Why, he asked, half laughing, must there be a Watergate when so many serious political questions should be discussed? Yet phenomena such as Watergate are quite common in times of turbulence like the present. Could I give him an assurance, he asked with great seriousness, that the same sort of thing would not happen again in future elections? I could only reply that I could not give such an assurance. It seemed to me that he was concerned about continuity; he wanted to be assured that the turbulence reflected in Watergate would subside. The symbol of continuity was Kissinger. At least twice, and it may have been three times, Chou spoke of Friend Kissinger. Once he referred to him as my old friend Kissinger, this having special significance in Chinese. With a smile he said that his friend Kissinger wanted to be a philosopher. He criticized his "Year of Europe" speech, which called for a new and expanded relationship with Western Europe and Japan, as being too philosophic. It was evident that he saw a closer relationship with the

West, a relaxation of tensions with the Soviet Union and a possible reduction of American forces in Germany as a potential threat to the People's Republic. Then the Soviets could increase their massive force on China's border. And while Moscow might claim to have pulled back her own troops from the Western confrontation, this could never be verified.

At about one o'clock a supper with the inevitable tea was served on small tables set beside each place. Jane had been taking notes throughout, and although I was the interlocutor I did some rough shorthand of my own from time to time. The only interruptions had come from Chiao Kuan-hua, who sat on Jane's right. Occasionally he corrected the interpreter. If Chou spoke English, as reports had it, he gave no sign that he understood my questions until they had been put into Chinese. There was no indication that the Prime Minister wanted to conclude the discussion. In fact, what has seemed to me on reflection the most significant part of the talk, particularly in light of the inevitable passing of Chou and Mao, occurred toward the end. It began with my question: Do you think a second Cultural Revolution may be necessary some time in the future? There was a pause for reflection. If we do better than we did before, then it will not be necessary, he replied. But he did not rule out the possibility. History had shown that one revolution was never enough. Your American revolution removed certain feudal and colonial elements in your society and so did the French revolution, but those revolutions did nothing to change the power structure. Your Civil War was a war between slavery and slave owners and the industrial North.

The Cultural Revolution? While we were in China we learned very little about the upheaval that, beginning in 1967, tore the country apart, nearly halting production, education, transportation. Mao's goal was to try to insure against a new elite coming into being and to wipe out the vestiges of the past with renewed revolutionary fervor. After we left the People's Republic we learned of the chaos that had been worked by the Red Guards, the young inspired to destroy the relics of bourgeois life, including human relics. Mao himself had finally to go to the country to persuade leaders of the cadres to stop the revolution and get the Red Guards either back in school or into remote agricultural communes. And where had Chou En-lai been during all of this? One report is that he had consistently urged restraint. This is, of course, conjecture. We did hear of one incident while we were in Peking. A mob surrounding the British embassy compound had set fires. Coming out of the Peking Hotel, where he had been attending a reception, Chou had seen the distant flames against the sky. Learning that the embassy was threatened he immediately ordered troops to the scene and saved the lives of the staff. If they had been killed, the harm done to China's relations with the rest of the world would have been very great.

In 1974 reports coming from China hinted at the beginning of a new Cultural Revolution. Chiang Ching, Mao's wife, was said to be a leader of this new movement as she had been in the earlier one. But if another revolution was intended, it was for some unknown reason aborted. Perhaps Mao himself had intervened. The concept of a perpetual revolution contradicts the very existence of a modern state, since high technology is dependent on at least a degree of stability. The crucial question is whether, with the passing of the old leaders, the inheritors, younger men with sufficient support, can strike a balance and prevent a destructive power conflict.

Several times during our long discussion, Chou took pains to point out that all decisions were made by Chairman Mao; ping-pong diplomacy, the bid to Nixon, everything that followed originated with the great god Mao.

At two-thirty he looked at his watch and then at me. It is time that we left, I said, trying to express my gratitude for his having given us three and a half hours of continuous dialogue. He shook hands gravely in the entrance hall with a photographer recording this moment, as he had been recorded so many times with so many visitors. Once again we were moving through the silent sleeping city as though we had wakened from a long and extraordinary dream.

We were astonished to see in that morning's *People's Daily* the picture taken on our arrival at the Great Hall of the People. We had been lined up in the anteroom, the principals and the auditors, on a two-step stand. There we were, looking very solemn. Our room attendants in the hotel, who had been friendliness itself, were overjoyed at this evidence of our status. After calling on Mr. Ma, who said it was one of the most comprehensive and certainly one of the longest interviews the Prime Minister had ever given, I had to begin to write. That was the rub! As I had so often in the past, I knew I'd had a great opportunity, full of mood, color, substance, but I had to try to convey it in the conventional language of a news story. Even with the greater latitude permitted in a column, I knew I would fall short.

Having had the view at the top, Mr. Ma stipulated, there would be no interviews lower down the slope. This was disappointing since we had hoped to talk with Chiang Ching, Kuo Mo-jo, and others. Instead we began our tour of the country. The first stop was Yenan, where in caves dug into the loess hills Mao, Chou and the others had survived the Japanese and the Kuomintang. In Yenan, the young American foreign service officers stationed in Chungking, Davies, Service, Vincent, had formed their opinion of the strength of the Communist force and the possibility, indeed the likelihood, that they would prevail. For their forthrightness and their honesty they were cashiered and subjected to trial by humiliation in their own country. Mao's restored cave dwelling, with the clay *kang* and desk placed as they had been in the small room, was a shrine. The museum of the revolution was closed in order, so we heard, to clear out all traces of Lin Piao, at one point Mao's designated heir. He had died, so the official version went, in a plane crash in Outer Mongolia while presumably escaping to the Soviet Union after an attempt on Mao's life had failed.

A day spent at the nearby May 7 school established, if nothing else, how difficult, if not impossible, it is for the non-Chinese-speaking foreign visitor to comprehend a new world. The men and women spending six months in the camp were leaders in a variety of fields in the city of Sian—the chief surgeon in the principal hospital, the director of grain storage and distribution, a woman doctor in charge of a large clinic. They were digging caves, making adobe bricks, the medical personnel working with the peasants. The atmosphere was a bit like that of a camp for middle-aged boy scouts. On the surface they were cheerful enough but that could be said of almost all the Chinese we saw. Their rooms in barrack-like buildings had a military neatness and precision; thick volumes of the writings of Chairman Mao, Lenin and Marx on each bedside table. Had they elected to come here to take six months out of busy careers? The answer of the school director was unequivocal. They sought appointment to the Sian May 7 school. But would not the surgeon, for example, be serving his country far better by teaching internes and residents in his hospital his skills rather than making bricks? Not at all. Attitudes were even more important than skills. For one of the six months each man and woman was required to live with a peasant family. The elite, those with exceptional ability, were to learn what life was like at the lowest level. It was a new world and the line between retribution, punishment, and reeducation, if that was the correct term, was impossible for the passing visitor to discern.

A new world in the frame of an ancient civilization—that is the paradox of this extraordinary people. The heavy weight of history must be held off with nothing like a Confucian elite, which through the centuries served so many emperors, allowed to take

over. That, if I understand it, is the reason for the prolonged propaganda assault directed at Confucius and
the revisionists. The revolution must not revert to a
new class of the privileged. This was part of the inspiration that led youthful Red Guards to break into suspected bourgeois homes and break all old objects they
found.

The broad Sian plain sweeping down from the rugged country around Yenan produces, with extensive
irrigation and electrical pumps bringing water out of
deep wells, a crop yield said to be at least half again
as great as it was before 1949. Commune and brigade
leaders we talked with were proud of the oncoming
wheat harvest, boasting that before the end of the
decade the yield would be double that before liberation.
We had seen the loess hills terraced to the very top with
geometric precision. This was labor, most of it without
benefit of labor-saving machines, on a scale hard for a
Westerner to imagine. The 800 million were being fed.
That must be the greatest single achievement of the
new order. With so much of the country desert or
mountain, perhaps 70 or 75 percent, a constant drive is
on to bring in new cultivatable areas. And everywhere,
from the big commune outside Peking, which grows produce for the city, to the broad sweep of the wheat
fields around Sian, there is pride in the achievement.

In Sian, one of China's oldest cities, for nine centuries the capital of the Tang dynasty, the paradox of
the new order in the setting of an ancient civilization is
dramatic. It is the center of archaeological finds as
important as any in the country. We were taken to a
dig from which many of the beautiful objects in the
Sian museum, a former temple of Confucius, had come.
This was the tomb of Princess Yung Tai, who died at the
age of seventeen in 701. We went down into the princess' tomb through the long entryway with murals of
court life on either side, many of them reproductions
based on careful research, others dim fragments that
survived damp, cold and tomb robbers. If Princess

Yung Tai's dig was a success, with 1,354 pieces recovered in spite of the tomb robbers, the forthcoming work of an archaeological team headed by Chao Pei-yuan and his collaborator, Yeng Cheng-hsin is even more dramatic. Their excavation of the tomb of Emperor Li Chi occupies virtually a whole mountain. A royal way leading to the tomb of the third emperor of the Tang dynasty is lined with massive stone sculptures of birds, animals and tomb guardians. At the end of the way is a kind of royal enclosure with sixty-one stone figures representing the ambassadors and heads of state who came from far-off places to attend the emperor's funeral. In the setting of a neglected field on a hillside, with the mountain of the emperor's tomb in the distance, one can imagine the pomp and ceremony that once flourished there.

In Peking, at the end of a tour of the imperial palace museums, we were taken to a working area where restoration was going forward on objects to be part of the exhibits the People's Republic of China was sending around the world. A jade body garment, platelets of jade sewn together with gold filaments, was to be one of the principal attractions in Paris, London, Washington and the other capitals where thousands would queue up for hours. The capacity to recreate the past was also great. In Sian we had been shown in the museum a Tang horse with brilliant glaze. It was a reproduction, we were told, of one that had gone with the exhibit that opened in Paris. In a jade factory in Shanghai we watched craftsmen with ancient skills carving the old designs and training young apprentices. The artifacts would be sold abroad for foreign exchange.

Tibet, Inner Mongolia, Sinkiang were still only names on the map. Mr. Ma had smiled politely at their mention, but he had given us a reward at our leavetaking. On our list of preferred places we had included Kwangsi in south China, an autonomous region administered from Peking. We were to be the first foreigners, or at any rate the first foreign journalists, to be allowed to go to Kweilin, the center in Kwangsi of the Chuangs, one of the largest minorities. From Sian it meant a train journey of two days with a stopover for a change in the middle of the night. We saw a good deal of the country from the comfort of our compartment, which was reminiscent of the old days on American transcontinental trains, as was the dining car with a steward anxious to consult us on our preferences. With our guide-interpreter, who had long since become Hisao (good friend) Fu rather than Mr. Fu, it was a pleasant interlude.

In hot, humid Kweilin, set in the magic of the karst landscape that had been the inspiration, over centuries, of the scroll painters, we were put in a guest house in which the beds were carefully shrouded in mosquito netting. We were taken to the caves and mountains, escorted up steep slopes with great care because of our advanced age, we were told. Hisao Fu came to me on the second day with a look of concern on his normally placid face. We were to charter a barge for a trip down the Li River. I hope you will not think it is too expensive. It will be $100 for the day, lunch on the boat and the return journey by motor from Yang Suo, our destination. That seemed very reasonable. The whole trip had been an astonishing travel bargain: room, meals, cars and driver, thirty-five dollars a day; air and rail fares comparably low, though the day we left China the government announced a 50-percent increase in all travel charges.

The beauty of the Li with the fantastic karst formations in shades of green, the tall bamboo lining the shores and reflected in the dark water like great waving plumes is beyond description. The comfortable double-deck barge was pulled by a small tug with a big People's Republic flag at the stern. The countryside seemed empty; now and then we'd see a sampan with red sails, a family, young and old, on board, bamboo fishermen's rafts, here and there a village almost buried in the green. With two restored Tang pagodas on the hillside, Yang Suo had a remote, isolated look. Half the populace must have turned out to see these white barbarians helped up the steep path under umbrellas held against the drizzle.

I left China knowing that the only thing I knew was how little I knew. It had been an incomparable journey with kindness, friendship, good cheer on every hand. The Chinese, unlike the Russians, never thrust their propaganda on you. But if you ask to see a propaganda film, such as one about the building of the Red Flag Canal, they will show it and you will sit for an interminable time with the numb feeling that you yourself have hammered each rock in place. Nor do you see the heavy hand of authoritarianism that is often visible in the Soviet Union. There is one thing I must add. I left with an indelible impression of the capacity of the Chinese people to work: the memory of a woman, she might have been thirty or forty, in the streets of Shanghai pulling a four-wheel cart heavily loaded with steel shapes, straining with her whole body; in the oppressive heat of the Li valley men with great loads borne on yokes, sweating like steers; work, work everywhere, so much done by the bent back that has long disappeared with work-saving machinery in the West.

Anyone who ventures to predict the future must be a fool. When the great god has passed from the scene there will be a great empty space. How will it be filled? Our guide-interpreter, Hisao Fu, was exceptionally intelligent, a teacher of English in the Foreign Language Institute, who spoke our language without trace of an accent although he had never been out of China. He told us of having once seen Chairman Mao at an airport at a distance of about fifty yards. Although that was in 1957 he spoke of it with awe, wonder. "As soon as I could I went to Shanghai in order to share this experience with my parents." And he had felt the harsh discipline after 1967 of the Cultural Revolution; he had been sent out to work in the rice paddies, separated from his family for a year and a half.

As we left Canton there were reports of damaging floods in the rice-growing areas in the south and a threatening drought in the north that could cut back the wheat crop. The ever-present concern was feeding the 800 million. There had been grain purchases abroad and they had taken scarce foreign exchange. We heard in Peking and later in Hong Kong reports of China's great offshore oil deposits and the interest of American oil companies in developing those deposits. Chou En-lai had said during our discussion that the People's Republic wanted American technology and American know-how. We are a backward nation, he had said, and this had come from others, we need your help. But are the Chinese prepared to work in partnership with an American corporation and American technicians? Secrecy, suspicion, and pride in self-reliance prevail over so many areas. Adapting to the high technology of the West would mean breaking down defensive barriers.

A good beginning has been made. The appointment of David Bruce, America's preeminent diplomat, the first head of the liaison mission in Peking, and Peking's selection of Huang Chen, a member of the Politburo and a distinguished scholar, to head their mission in Washington give evidence of the mutual desire to promote a lasting relationship. The staff assembled under Bruce was outstanding, virtually all speaking Chinese fluently and with a long background of knowledge. But in the last analysis Kissinger was the link that meant continuity and growth.

Back in Washington I reached Kissinger at San Clemente to give him messages that Chou En-lai had asked me to pass on. Although he was grateful I could tell that his interest was elsewhere. The traps that had been laid for him in the White House and that he in turn had laid were making life hazardous, not only for him but for his closest colleagues. He spoke bitterly of one of the intriguers, describing him as "that svine." Survival was the highest priority. I told him that Chou looked forward to seeing him in Peking in the near future. Yes, he wanted to go at the first opportunity. China at this moment of Watergate must have seemed a distant mirage.

XIII

The Man, the System

In the northwest wing of the White House is a small reception room. I spent hours there waiting to see Henry Kissinger when he was the President's adviser on national security affairs. On one wall was a painting on loan from the Boston Museum of Fine Arts that showed William Penn landing in the new world and exchanging greetings with an Indian chief; Penn's ship stood off-shore. These two lonely, symbolic figures were painted with the realism of the last century. Running out of reading matter I studied the painting with special care since my forebears had come to America with Penn. But more often my gaze fell on the pretty, blond reception-ist—she might have been picked from a model agency—waiting dutifully at her desk for a signal from the interior.

Now and then one of the mafia—Haldeman, Ehr-lichman, Ziegler—would pass through on their way to or from the President's office. I tried to be as unobtrusive as possible since I thought that recognition and later identification with something I might write would support the charge of a Kissinger leak. The web of intrigue had already begun to give the President's house an air that was slightly sinister and wholly unreal, peopled by shadowy shapes of anonymous power.

At last the pretty blond receptionist would say, "Dr. Kissinger can see you now." Someone would come out to escort me into the inner sanctum through the maze of small offices. There I was in the presence. These encounters were always worth the waiting. They produced not so much any startling inside secrets as a perspective on what was likely to happen, whether in the interminable peace talks with Hanoi, the outlook for the SALT talks or another concern with which this tireless weaver of the threads of foreign policy was taken. Almost invariably as we talked the light on his direct phone to the President would go on and he would ask me to step out for a few minutes. But more than the journalistic reward was the impression of a great mind, a limitless ego tempered by remarkable judgment of men and events. He seemed to me one of the few authentic geniuses I had ever encountered. I think I understood how I at this remove, the petitioner for light from the murky depth, saw only a small part of the artful practitioner of an abstruse trade. For I had heard from certain of his dedicated acolytes of his tempers and his impossible demands, demands that matched his own capacities and his own drive and stamina. As the dark stain of the Watergate scandal spread, it seemed to me that Kissinger was almost the only remaining solid point relatively free of the web of intrigue. At the same time, survival in a nest of vipers was a constant hazard. My theory was that the wire taps, whether condoned or ordered, had been authorized in the interest of survival. He had to show that he could use fair means or foul to establish his own status with the mafia, which was jealous of his eminence and bent on bringing him down.

This gave him the benefit of every doubt. One night at a small dinner party, Gerard Smith, who had felt

Kissinger's arrogant hand at the unhappy climax of SALT I, rounded on Chalmers Roberts, of the Washington *Post*, and me. "You are responsible. You in the press built him up too high. No one could survive that kind of buildup." The accusation had a certain truth. I would mitigate my plea of guilty, or perhaps *nolo contendere*, with what I considered extenuating circumstances. The aim as the Watergate drumbeat grew louder and louder was to bring down everyone—or so it seemed to me. Hardly anyone who had played a part in public life, at whatever level, in a time of immense complexity with money so freely splashed about, could emerge unsullied. I felt outrage at the Mr. District Attorneys who went after Kissinger at his first press conference upon returning from his shuttle diplomacy in the Middle East, having achieved at least the partial success of military disengagement. Expecting to be asked about the Middle East, he was, after the first few questions, like a prisoner in the dock pressed for a plea of guilt.

Nelson Rockefeller, Kissinger's first sponsor and patron, faced a similar trial by interrogation. This was a far more complex business since the Rockefeller money had spread out through so many channels. I had thought that the Rockefeller wealth would be a target when he first considered running for President. I saw him then in Albany in the Governor's office to tell him I had an idea for a book that would put on the record the Rockefeller wealth, the philanthropies, the public spending, the private way of life. I could see that he was daunted. But I would have to get the consent of all the members of my family, he said. Couldn't that be done with a series of telephone calls? No, not at all, it would take a family council. That was the end of the idea. Returning to Washington with McGeorge Bundy, then Lyndon Johnson's adviser on security affairs, I described the incident. He laughed and said, "Come now, you didn't think Nelson Rockefeller would do a fan dance for you, did you?" I have continued to believe that if the whole account, or most of it, had been put on the record then,

Rockefeller would have had far less trouble in the confirmation hearings for Vice President.

That triangle, Nixon, Rockefeller, Kissinger, was one of the strangest alignments or nonalignments in American political history. I had an early encounter with Kissinger on the plane that took Rockefeller around the country in search of delegates to the Republican convention in spring 1968. He had for several years been head of the Rockefeller brain trust that had come up with atomic oddities such as a limited nuclear war and the rationale for home-built air raid shelters. In the welter of press and politicians on the plane he was an incongruous figure; still, he managed to be at home as he does in any environment.

Rockefeller apparently had no realization that the 1968 game was over even as he was tossing in more Rockefeller money. Nixon had corralled a majority of delegates to give him the nomination on the first ballot. Rather than Rockefeller's indiscriminate gift-giving, the real handicap of the Rockefeller wealth was that it became a barrier that shielded him from unpleasant truths. Truth-tellers whose word he would accept were rare in his entourage. One was Jamie Jamieson, the AP reporter who joined up when Rockefeller was FDR's coordinator for Latin-American affairs during the war. Jamie's death left a gap that was never filled. In 1964, as in 1968, Rockefeller had sailed into the uncharted waters of a party in which the keepers of the harbor rights regarded him as an alien. Despite the complication of his marital troubles, he nevertheless came close to winning the California primary which would have put him ahead of Barry Goldwater.

That Kissinger should have failed to realize the lost hope of that final swing was hardly surprising since he was an amateur in a game where professionalism ruled. He is said to have wept when Nixon was nominated at Miami Beach. That the loser prompted the winner to take Kissinger on board is speculation. It was an unlikely partnership that functioned with few breaches. When

Nixon made the decision to bomb Hanoi and mine the harbor of Haiphong, Kissinger not only dissented, or so he gave it out, but recommended that the impending summit in Moscow be called off or at least postponed since no room for maneuver would be left in light of the assault on North Vietnam and the possibility that a Soviet ship in the harbor would be sunk. His critics charged that he actually favored the bombing and leaked the word of his alleged dissent to win favor with dovish friends.

The stricture of secrecy had transformed the Washington I had known. It was betwixt and between the open society of pre-Pearl Harbor and the closed circuit of a nuclear power. The Central Intelligence Agency was at the heart of the uncertainty. For the Left, for civil libertarians, the CIA became the embodiment of secret machinations involved in overthrowing legitimate governments of which Washington disapproved. This was an instrument that contravened all the principles of freedom on which America had been founded, or so the civil libertarians believed. A compact with the CIA for anyone professing independence of opinion was a compact with the devil.

From the beginning I had known, in one degree of closeness or another, the successive directors of the agency. The most public and flamboyant was Allen Dulles, Foster's brother. The two served in tandem with an authority over American policy in the cold war that had few, if any, parallels. Allen initiated the huge white structure in McLean, Virginia, that made the agency only slightly less conspicuous than the Lincoln Memorial. Enlivened by his hearty laughter, his background sessions made us privy at three or four removes to the agency's inmost secrets, or so we thought. He resigned following the Bay of Pigs disaster. His successors have tried to lower the agency's profile.

The first professional director of the Agency was Richard Helms. The embodiment of discretion itself, he had, in his tight-lipped way, put me on to agents in various capitals, and I had been impressed with their ability and the low profile they maintained. That was true particularly of Ted Shackley, the station chief in Saigon, when I stopped there on a round-the-world trip in 1969. Both the embassy and the American military had warned me that an upcoming weekend would see the Communist underground in the streets. To venture out of the hotel would be to court sudden death. Because this seemed improbable, I mentioned it to Shackley. His response was a broad grin. Pay it no heed, he said, nothing like that will happen. And it didn't.

In a furious assault not unlike that which preceded the Watergate scandal, a storm broke around the CIA with charges of domestic spying in violation of the agency's charter. The accusation came in a series of articles by Seymour Hersh in the *New York Times*. The principal target was Helms, who had been appointed by Nixon ambassador to Iran. Whether, as Hugh Sidey suggested in *Time* magazine, the real issue was the fact of a super-secret agency with a department of dirty tricks, so contrary to the American conviction of openness and basic fair play, might or might not be determined by a Senate investigation. That investigation, certain to be full of sound and fury, a kind of game of truth and consequences, gave no promise of what the ultimate consequence might be of the demise or the drastic curtailment of the CIA. And for some of us who had felt that Helms was, within the context of the spying game, a useful public servant, it promised personal tragedy.

I had last been in Saigon when the French still ruled over a charming colonial city. Though their rule was vaguely threatened, Indochina was still a source of riches in rubber and other exportable commodities. They deeply resented the warning of Sen. John F. Kennedy, who had learned from a source in the American embassy how precarious their hold really was. Virtually nothing remained of the broad, tranquil, tree-lined avenues. The city had become an American power base. The GIs were everywhere. The little people who had been compliant, or so the French believed, were making it now with the vast infusion of dollars from America; the traffic jams rivaled those in New York or Paris. When at midnight I walked the seven or eight blocks from the Caravelle Hotel to United Press International to drop copy, a half dozen or more pimps seated in their own cars offered me their fourteen-year-old sisters at bargain rates because of the lateness of the hour.

In the president's palace, at a guess about twice as big as the White House, Nguyen Van Thieu was the emblem of democracy ordained by Washington. When I saw him the prospect had been floated of a reduction of perhaps 100,000 American troops by the end of the year in light of the likely success of peace talks with Hanoi. This was taken seriously by the American military. It could not be, Thieu told me. Consider the offensive the Communists were waging at the time. They could double and triple their attack, his intelligence told him. It might develop into something as serious as the Tet offensive of 1968 when they had broken into the American embassy compound. You wouldn't want to risk that, would you? A small, fragile-looking man, he seemed always to be pulling up his pride, as a man would pull up his socks, determined not to be dwarfed by the invaders. Part of his pride was the palace adorned with rare Oriental art.

On that day he was to receive the American proconsul, who was about to return to Washington to report on the state of this outpost of the nation. The title of ambassador did less than justice to the function performed by Ellsworth Bunker. He was perfect in every way for the proconsular role. Slender, tall, with a quiet dignity belied by his droll Yankee humor, he was the calm center of the strife and struggle. He could recount with laughter how, when the Communists had broken into the compound, Secretary of Defense Melvin Laird had been his house guest and together they had taken refuge in Bunker's bunker. What he may actually have thought about this far-reaching military adventure, so fearfully divisive at home, I would probably never know. He was doing his duty and that, too, was a Yankee trait.

If Saigon and half-ruined Hue bore little trace of the elegance of the past, one sanctuary remained more or less unharmed. That was Dalat where the French had gone to escape the withering tropical heat of the coast. I flew there with William Colby, who was then head of the pacification program and Operation Phoenix, which sought to root out the Viet Cong infrastructure in villages in the south which had theoretically been restored to Saigon control. Phoenix used somewhat rugged methods, such as those used by the VC, including beheading and disembowelling. Colby was all crisp business, going over during the hour-and-a-half flight to Dalat reports on the situation there. A Saigon colonel was retiring as chief of operations to be replaced by another Saigon colonel. At an altitude of a mile above sea level, it was a pleasant place where the French had lived well as the French almost always managed to do, their villas little touched by the war. Except for their servants they had allowed no one from the south to live in Dalat. In the mountains were the montagnards, the primitive tribes offbounds to civilization and the rubber plantations of the jungle lowland. Part of the American effort was to bring the montagnards into the mainstream of Vietnamese life, a chilling prospect if these simple tribespeople had had any knowledge of what that life had become with the terrible dislocation of the war and hundreds of thousands of refugees living in squalid camps.

Put up in the comfortable house of Colby's man in Dalat, we had hardly finished dinner when, with a half dozen Americans in the area, the pacification director canvassed in detail the prospects just ahead. I gathered that with encroachments from the VC they were not too good. I could hear their voices, these serious conscientious Americans engaged in an enterprise that for the distant future was doomed to failure, long after I had gone to bed. I was awakened some time in the night by heavy firing, as if in confirmation of the gloomy reports. I was a novice in these matters, and to me it sounded like incoming mortar fire. I spent an uneasy two hours counting the clump, clump, clump. After all, Colby would have been a great prize. In the morning the pros said it was only outgoing artillery in support of a little dustup with the VC about five miles down the road. All the way back to Saigon Colby pored over the records he had been given in Dalat. I was not surprised when he was named director of the CIA following Helms, after an interval when James Schlesinger, later to be Secretary of Defense, filled in the slot.

This was part of the mad gallop touched off by the Saturday Night Massacre when Elliot Richardson and Archibald Cox were sacrificed to the ritual of secrecy and concealment in the White House. The invisible man appeared only on rare occasions, his press conferences as carefully stage managed as a soap opera. In retrospect it seems to have been just that, a ghastly soap opera with disastrous consequences. A kind of point, counter-point began; a revelation in the Washington *Post* of more skulduggery, a bland denial by Ronald Ziegler. What made the charade in the White House so hard to understand was that Nixon, as a veteran of the political wars, had from the beginning never doubted the outcome of the 1972 campaign. In an interview with John Horner of the Washington *Star* in San Clemente two days before the vote, and embargoed until the day after, he said, "The election was decided when George McGovern was nominated." That was one of the few truths he spoke during the year. My own belief is that once Nixon gave so much authority to Haldeman, Ehrlichman & Co. and at the same time entrusted the Committee to Reelect the President with virtually full power to raise and spend monies he lost whatever control he had previously exercised. This was compounded by Dr. Strangeloves like E. Howard Hunt and G. Gordon

Liddy who lived out their fantasies with props sup-
plied by the White House, the CIA and the election
committee.

In all this the question certain to trouble historians
is Nixon's psyche. He gave every evidence of a dualism
in his person so pronounced as to suggest schizophrenia
or psychopathy. When the tapes in all their squalor were
pouring forth Kissinger told me that in his many intimate talks with Nixon he had never heard him use the
four-letter expletives that peppered the President's
conversations with the mafia in the Oval Office. He
checked this with Arthur Burns, chairman of the Federal
Reserve Board, who had known Nixon as long as anyone in Washington, and Burns reported that he, too,
could not recall such language. With these scholarly
men the President kept the tone at quite another level
than that to which he descended with his henchmen.

On the surface, putting aside the cloud of Watergate, everything seemed normal. Heads of government
flitted in and out to be given the presidential treatment. When the current premier of Italy came, whether
it was Mariano Rumor or Aldo Moro or another of the
figures who chased one another in and out of the Qui-
rinale, the President obliged him with entertainment
at the state dinner by Frank Sinatra. After all, Sinatra
was Vice-President Agnew's good friend and frequent
host at the Sinatra pleasure dome in Palm Springs.

So rarely was Nixon seen outside the carefully
contrived ambience of Key Biscayne or San Clemente,
with refueling stops at the White House, that his
appearance on one very special occasion drew television cameras and crowds in the street. That was the
ninetieth birthday party of Alice Roosevelt Longworth
on February 12, 1974.

With a loving eye for frauds and at the same time a
fondness for the accoutrements of power, she had known
Dick Nixon at least since he had been Senator and Vice-
President. A guest at the wedding of Tricia and Edward
Cox, she had been asked by a reporter if her wedding

to Speaker Nicholas Longworth, when she had been given away by her father, Theodore Roosevelt, resembled the Nixon ceremony. No, she replied, that was before the era of Hollywood. In her house on Massachusetts Avenue just above Dupont Circle, encroached upon by hotels and boarding houses as the city moved westward, Mrs. L. had been an institution for many years. Warren Harding, whom she described as a good-natured slob, came for all-night poker parties with Mrs. L. doing scrambled eggs and bacon in the early morning. Along the stairway from the entrance hall on the first floor were hung skins of animals her father had shot on his African safari. They were so laden with dust that they seemed about to disintegrate. Stewart Alsop, her cousin, liked to tell how he had pulled gently on the tail of a tiger skin and it had come off in his hand. At tea on many afternoons, Mrs. L. received guests, usually few in number, while seated on a small sofa in a sitting room just off the drawing room. On her left hung a photograph of the dowager empress of China. Princess Alice, as she was known in her White House years, had been a guest of the empress when traveling in the Far East in 1905 under the chaperonage of her father's then protégé, William Howard Taft, and Mrs. Taft. One morning during breakfast in her guest pavilion, she had seen a dozen courtiers in court dress approach bearing a palanquin. In the palanquin was the photograph, a present from the empress. Her laughter encompassed the absurdity of all human behavior. With it went the benign malice that she bestowed on friend and foe alike.

Would the Nixons come to the birthday party? Of course they would come. The television cameras on the sidewalk recorded their entrance with Julie Eisenhower. They came bearing gifts — a large container of caviar, a very special music box. The scene that followed could have happened only in Washington and only at that particular moment. The Nixons established themselves in one of the reception rooms while the

guests, among them many columnists and reporters
who had been rough on the President, confined themselves for the most part to adjoining rooms, peering in
now and then, as though to establish that the relics
rarely taken out of the shrine were real. Having seen him
only in his staged appearances at the increasingly rare
press conferences, when he was heavily made up, I had
thought this figure out of a citadel under siege would be
the worse for wear. Not at all. In the brief chat my wife
and I had with him, he was the familiar Nixon, courteous,
no single hair out of place. We recalled the great Kremlin
reception at the end of SALT I. Yes, and what a remarkable occasion it was, he said. They do know how to do
that sort of thing so well in that beautiful setting. He
hoped that we would be in Moscow for SALT II in May
again. We hoped so, too. The relics then returned to the
shrine.

Spiro Agnew had already fallen with a dull thud.
When he finally appeared in federal court in Baltimore
to plead no contest to a charge of income tax evasion,
with a memorandum of thirty-eight charges of bribery
and other crimes before the judge, it was an anticlimax.
He was so sleazy, so muffled in self-importance, that
the only mystery was why his petty criminality had not
been exposed long before, or for that matter why Nixon
had tapped him in the first instance.

Under the Twenty-fifth Amendment to the Constitution the President was required to nominate a
candidate to fill the vacancy in the Vice Presidency,
the nominee to be approved by a majority of both houses
of Congress. Rep. Gerald R. Ford of Grand Rapids,
Michigan, the minority leader in the House, was a
welcome relief after Agnew. He was clean cut, straight-
forward, the all-American center grown older, yet with
the same athletic build, the same determined jaw. His
record was solid, undeviating conservative. Without a
challenge to the Democrat in the White House, he had
voted for the massive appropriations for the escalation
of the Vietnam war. Hints from dubious sources about

his financial machinations were never explored by the committees examining his record. We wanted to believe after the Agnew disaster that here was a man good and true representing the virtues of his midwestern constituency. Of one thing Nixon could be sure: Ford would be confirmed if only because of the clubbable spirit in the Congress, where for twenty-five years he had been a member in good standing. One jarring note was the performance Nixon put on in the East Room when he anointed Ford. With the Marine band and an assemblage of the Washington great, the President carried on like the emcee of a posh nightclub. It was another episode in the Nixon soap opera.

Ford was the average man as Truman, on inheriting the office of President, had been judged the average man. But Ford's wife, Betty, is considerably more than that. Sensitive, intelligent, she was consigned to be the politician's wife in a society in which the male, for all the talk of women's lib, still ruled; to be seen always cheerful and smiling, to be heard infrequently and then on subjects personal or in the woman's domain. The women libbers say all this is changing. There are eighteen women in the Ninety-fourth House of Representatives and one woman, Ella Grasso in Connecticut, was for the first time elected Governor of a state with no inheritance from a husband. But the women who serve as wives lead restricted, even lonely lives. They bear some resemblance to pioneer women, keeping the household and looking after the children while the man is on the road, detained at a late session on the Hill or drinking whiskey with his cronies in his well-upholstered capitol hideout. One has only to sit next to Mrs. Ford at dinner to learn that her talents, her interests, are broader than that, broader perhaps than those of her husband.

The Vice President was certainly on the road. At least two or three times a week he was out across the country speaking at some public ceremony or appearing in behalf of congressional candidates in districts where the Republican margin was doubtful. Talking with him on rare occasions, I felt that he was a realist who understood that if he should inherit the office he would have no choice but to run for a full term in 1976, this despite his statement after he was nominated Vice President that he would seek no public office two years thence. At the press conference at each stop on the road he had to straddle questions about the President's impeachment or resignation and the growing seriousness of the charges of cover-up and obstruction of justice. It was a thin line and Ford at times fell over on one side or the other. He could not repudiate the man who had named him to high office, not least because he might appear to be trying to force the way to his own accession. It seemed to me that on the whole he handled himself in this difficult position as well as could have been expected.

Then, without warning, the last barrier gave way. The Supreme Court ruled unanimously that the President had to yield the tapes demanded in a subpoena by the Special Prosecutor. Nixon had concealed from his own lawyers and even his family the damning evidence on the tape of June 23, 1972, that he had been directly involved from the start in the cover-up and the effort to buy the silence of the Watergate burglars. Ron Ziegler, drained of all pretensions of omniscience, white and tense, passed out transcripts of the tape in the crowded briefing room, allowing us time to read it before announcing that the President would make a statement on the following morning. We poured out of the hot, crowded room to sit on the grassy slope just outside and read the incriminating dialogue that brought about Nixon's resignation in order to forestall the certainty of conviction by the Senate on a resolution of impeachment adopted by the House.

That night, as it happened, Huang Chen, head of the Chinese liaison mission in Washington, was giving a dinner in honor of Kissinger. The irony could hardly have been greater. The opening to China had been

Nixon's initiative, a radical break with the hopeless policy of isolation for which Nixon himself had been in part responsible. Now with the self-destruct mechanism he had built into the Presidency he was in disgrace, the first President ever to resign the office. If the Chinese were surprised or dismayed by the coincidence they gave no sign of it. The guests, including the top command of the State Department, talked about nothing else. Huang Chen, his outwardly cheerful, smiling self, and the members of his staff dispensed friendship, varied at the lower levels by discreet questions to the few press present as to what this momentous event might ultimately mean. It was a superb Chinese dinner, course after course, with Chinese protocol prevailing, the men on one side of each of the three big tables, the women on the other. Rockefeller had come down from New York to honor his friend Kissinger. He was soon to be the center of a raging controversy that would end with a President and a Vice President of the United States who had never been elected by the voters of the nation.

We had watched on television on August 20 the simple ceremony in which the President nominated Rockefeller Vice President. Staying with friends in Northeast Harbor, Maine, we had driven over that evening to Seal Harbor, hoping to have a word with the new Vice President-designate just returned from Washington. At the entrance to the Rockefeller place we gave our names to a guard and in a few minutes Nelson, his wife, Happy, and their two young sons came out of the boathouse. The Secret Service had already installed powerful lights trained on the path to the residence, a sprawling house designed for comfort, with a splendid view of the harbor. One thing that had impressed Rockefeller in the many exchanges he had had in the White House and on Capitol Hill was the stress on the importance of his living as Vice President in the official Vice-Presidential residence recently established by Congress. It had been the quarters of the Chief of Naval Operations on a high elevation in the grounds of the

Naval Observatory, with a commanding view down
Massachusetts Avenue. The alternative would be the
Rockefeller estate of twenty-four acres in the Foxhall
Road area of northwest Washington. That had given
Rockefeller a base in the capital, with carefully pre-
served privacy, since he had acquired it during his
World War II service under FDR. Of course he would
live in the official residence no matter what his personal
preference might be. This was said in a tone of gentle
resignation. Happy went up to see the boys into bed.
When she returned we had a glass of champagne in celebration and then, knowing how tired they were, we left.

I believe at that moment he hadn't the slightest
inkling of the ordeal that lay ahead. For nearly forty
years in official life he had served every president,
beginning with FDR, in one capacity or another. He
had been four times elected governor of New York when,
one might have supposed, every bit of his record down
to the smallest detail had been gone over. His great
wealth was surely no secret. An inquiry began first
before the Senate Rules Committee and then the House
Judiciary Committee and it was to go on for four months
before his confirmation. His record was examined in the
greatest detail, with his gifts and loans to associates
coming under the closest scrutiny. Purse-mouthed
Sen. Robert Byrd of West Virginia, the majority whip,
was the persistent inquisitor, boring in again and again
on the circumstances of the most unfortunate incident
to come to light, the book about Justice Arthur Goldberg underwritten by Laurance Rockefeller during the
New York gubernatorial campaign of 1970. Nothing
could more aptly illustrate the folly of so much of what
passes for political strategy. Goldberg had been a weak
candidate against Rockefeller seeking a fourth term and
spending his own and his family's money with his customary flush generosity. Though he had a distinguished
record, the former Justice, new to elective politics, was
ill at ease on the hustings. The polls consistently showed
him running behind. How the Rockefeller strategists
could believe that a hack book would influence the out-

come is impossible to understand. Several false starts by Nelson before he took full responsibility for having given Laurance the signal to put $60,000 into the wretched book compounded his troubles with Senator Byrd. By insisting that it was an investment rather than frankly calling it a campaign document the brothers Rockefeller heightened the absurdity.

As a prelude, indeed also as an accompaniment, to the hearings the press conducted its own intensive inquiry. This, it seemed to me, was one consequence of Watergate. Eager reporters were lurking behind every hedgerow. If one could bring down a President, then a Secretary of State or a Vice President-designate would be easy game. What could be a better target than a malefactor of great wealth, to use a hoary expression out of another and simpler age? The difficulty was in proving that, although he was wealthy, Nelson Rockefeller was also a malefactor. Mistakes he had certainly made in the course of a long public career—pursuing air raid shelters far beyond any reasonable belief in their efficacy in a nuclear holocaust; failure to move in the Attica prison confrontation—but what public figure could have come under such intense scrutiny without having serious blemishes revealed?

I saw him in his office in New York just after he had announced he meant in the future to tell his story to the Rules Committee rather than the press. There were constant leaks about the income and gift tax returns he had submitted and about FBI reports. "All I want," he said, "is to tell my story under oath on the record. I've asked them to give me a couple of days. That seems to me reasonable enough. I thought it was against the law to disclose information from tax returns." A majority of the committee could not be persuaded to return, and Rockefeller had to wait until the end of the election recess. The Senate committee voted unanimously for his confirmation. On the floor of the Senate the vote was 90 to 7, in the House 287 to 128, and the new Vice President was off to a sprinter's start.

Spiro Agnew was valid enough reason for a thorough

inquiry, stopping short of an inquisition, which sought in Rockefeller's wealth of and by itself cause to deny him the office. Another reason was Sen. Thomas Eagleton of Missouri, whom McGovern had picked as his Vice President at the last minute during the chaos of the Democratic convention in Miami Beach. One telephone call! *Do you have anything on your record that might cause you embarrassment?* I had seen Eagleton at a large splashy luncheon just as the convention opened. He radiated confidence. "You're looking at the Vice-Presidential candidate." How he could have failed to realize that the record of his psychiatric troubles was bound to come to light is one of those mysteries of the political temperament I shall never understand. Having to replace him was one more blow to a deeply divided party.

With the office vacant during the prolonged Rockefeller controversy, the heir to the Presidency was Speaker Carl Albert. A well-meaning man, elected and reelected and reelected again from the third district of Oklahoma with a population of a half million, he lived in dread of having to assume the burdens of an office for which he knew he was unfit. Uncertainty and irresolution plagued the capital and the country; the recession deepened and the indicators of inflation climbed steadily. The President had spent much of his capital of goodwill by his pardon of Richard Nixon, helping to send Republican candidates down to defeat. In California I had been impressed by Houston Flournoy, then state controller, running for Governor. With an academic background, he was the kind of moderate who could help to shape the Republican party in a less rigid direction than that laid down by Ronald Reagan. His Democratic opponent was Edmund G. Brown, Jr., whose father before him had been Governor for two terms. On the night after losing the election, Flournoy said on television, "We were moving up. No doubt of it. Then came the pardon. That did it. I think if the President had waited until Christmas I would have been elected."

With fewer than 40 percent of registered voters going to the polls the question was whether the election, any election, could end the uncertainty. Kissinger's personal diplomacy came into serious question later as he flew from capital to capital. Was he a Merlin with the magic that was a solvent for the ills of a time of troubles? Or was he merely playing a clever shell game at the country fair with the prize of peace never under the same walnut shell? Secretaries of State have long been whipping boys for failures that had their roots in political commitments made by ambitious politicians, in profound currents of opinion having little or no relation to the realities of power and diplomacy beyond America's shores. The Spenglerian gloom Kissinger often expressed, as in his searching interview with James Reston, was an implied recognition of his own limits as well as a vision of the diminished powers of the West. Yet he could be light-hearted, humorous. He gave a small luncheon for Françoise Giroux, the brilliant woman whom Giscard D'Estaing had named Minister of the Feminine Condition. The setting was the Madison Room on the eighth floor of the State Department where the artifacts of the period of that other Secretary of State seemed curiously irrelevant. As though he hadn't a care in the world, Kissinger laughed about the ready-made jokes with which the journalists had provided him at the end of his previous trip. "You kiss the Arabs but you screw the Israelis." "You're going to Japan, so you chew the gum and let the President do the talking. Or maybe it should be the other way, let him chew the gum and you do the talking." In a somber vein he had spoken before lunch to several of us about how Israel had resisted negotiation with King Hussein and now faced a dire confrontation with the Palestine Liberation Organization.

Kissinger did not impose his gloom on others. The pictures sent by satellite from Peking showed him laughing uproariously with the new foreign minister, Chiao Kuan-hua. He had to believe that a way would be found through the perils which he understood far better than anyone else. While his detractors began to sound the kind of dirge that in the past had marked the decline and fall of a Secretary of State, he continued to seem to me the only figure in a desolate landscape with both knowledge and the capacity to implement that knowledge. At the edge of the precipice he was Mr. Valiant, a pilgrim late in the day when the fate of a pilgrim was as uncertain as the will of the nation for which he spoke. As uncertain, it must be added, as the capacities of the President whom he served.

Having gone through the horrendous experience of the decline and fall of Richard Nixon, we had to believe that Gerald Ford was the answer to our prayers, the good, solid citizen from Grand Rapids who would speak the truth and shame the devil. But having put off the difficult decisions, he was faced at the end of his first six months with a threatened collapse of the economy as inflation ran a furious footrace with unemployment. The President surrendered the first article of his conservative creed, a balanced budget, and stared down a cumulative two-year deficit of $75 billion. For the conservative Republican who had spent his years in the House of Representatives happily nay-saying to the Democrats, those reckless spenders, it was confronting the Medusa.

The times called for a Machiavelli, a Franklin Roosevelt, a Keynes, and Ford was none of these. In the first surge of relief after the Nixon demise we told ourselves and our readers that the system had worked to cast up an honest man. This was naive, to say the least. The condition that Ford confronted was far more threatening than thirty years ago when Truman took over in the flush of victory. Then we had great reserves of military and industrial strength, of money, food, the urgent needs of a stricken world; today the cupboard is all but bare. Even if Ford were a Machiavelli, a Roosevelt, a Keynes, rolled into one, he would be hard put to find a way out of the pit. The test is not so much of the man as of the system itself. And politics as usual, under a system that puts the legislative and the executive in opposing parties, is no answer to perils that are short of war, but only by a margin that does not in the end exclude war itself.

Epilogue

Walter Lippmann's death at the close of 1974 marked the end of an era in American journalism. He had maintained throughout his long career a balance between privilege and responsibility. As an editor and commentator for more than five decades, he had passed judgment on passing events, always with restraint, acknowledging the privileged position that was his. After a brief taste of official life as a consultant to Woodrow Wilson at the Versailles peace conference, he concluded that government service was not for him, that the line between the government official, at whatever level, and the journalist commentator should not be breached. Yet from time to time, as he reached a preeminent position, when asked by leading public figures for advice and counsel he gave his private view of what course he believed they should follow. This was to him part of the responsibility that went with his privilege. It did not matter whether his advice was heeded, since in any event he was free to comment on whatever course the public figure might subsequently choose to follow.

Both his work and his personal life were an exercise in civility. One came down the two steps from the entrance hall into the long, handsome drawing room of the Lippmann house across from the National Cathedral on Woodley Road, and there were Helen and Walter greeting the movers and shakers of the time along with many of us who were the chroniclers of the time. He was invariably interested in what others had reported. I want to talk to you about your trip, I read your columns but I'm sure you will have something more to tell me. The atmosphere was relaxed, pleasant, even though their parties drew men and women diametrically opposed on the issues of the day. Allen Dulles, then director of the CIA, and Senator Fulbright, chairman of the Senate Foreign Relations Committee, could exchange not merely pleasantries but their divergent views on the cold war and a peaceful arrangement with the adversary in the East. Lippmann's critics, particularly the cold warriors, derided his style as magisterial, presumptuous. That style had evolved from convictions deeply held, unshaken by the turbulence of the age. I saw the Lippmanns in Paris on one of their last visits to their beloved France. Logic, esprit, ordered beauty — these held them as they had in the past, in spite of a disastrous attempt to acquire a part-time home in a small château near Fontainebleau. Not only France but de Gaulle, one of the few great men Lippmann had come to venerate, had brought them back.

To celebrate his eightieth birthday, Helen assembled for dinner in their house in Seal Harbor, Maine, friends from across the country. He responded in fine form to the toasts. That day President Nixon called to congratulate him. The call was in tribute to the decision Lippmann had taken the year before. In 1968 he declared for Nixon over Hubert Humphrey. That choice seems to have been based on the belief that welfarism had gone too far and too fast, and a pause with a Republican President was desirable. On his eighty-fifth birthday, when close friends gathered in the nursing home on Park Avenue where he spent his last months, he was asked if he thought Nixon was the worst President we ever had. His answer was, "No, the most embarrassing." By supporting Nixon he illustrated once again that labels, whether liberal or conservative, would not fit.

The dilemma of privilege and responsibility in relation to public acceptance of a free and independent press had been foreseen by Lippmann as long ago as 1922, in his classic work, *Public Opinion*. The question he raised was whether the power assumed by the press, when government was incapable of or unwilling to take measures to correct serious abuses, might not be too great for the grant conferred by the First Amendment. A skeptical public might see the independence of the press not as a blessing linked to the other freedoms of a free society but as a threat to the legitimacy of government, a force greater than that of the people's representatives duly elected under the Constitution. Would it not be wise, he asked, to create a monitor made up of concerned citizens as well as journalists to appraise the responsibilities of the press and assess how these responsibilities were being fulfilled? This was a tentative proposal growing out of his prescient concern for the future of a free press and the public doubt that could erode the base of that freedom.

Fifty years later Spiro Agnew exploited the public doubt for the political purposes of the Nixon administration. His highly selective attack was aimed at critics of the administration whom he put down as Eastern seaboard elitists arrogating to themselves the power over what the public should see and hear through the mass media. As if to confirm the doubts in the public mind, an initial poll showed that more than half the respondents agreed with the Vice President. Network executives acknowledged the cautionary effect the Agnew attack had had on television programming. With the Vice President's disgrace and resignation his allegations were seen to be part of the shabby charade of trickery and corruption. But the response they had drawn in the first instance was in itself disturbing, and soon the issue of privilege and responsibility was to take on a new and greatly enlarged dimension.

The triumph of investigative reporting by Woodward and Bernstein in the Washington *Post* had few if any parallels. A debauchery of the political process striking at the roots of representative government was uncovered. While other elements were at work—the Senate inquiry, investigative forces in the executive— the exposure by the press was considered, certainly in the public mind, to have been primarily responsible. The press had assumed a role of far-reaching power and privilege that the men who drafted the First Amendment, guaranteeing the freedom of a private enterprise dependent on the profit motive, could hardly have foreseen. Was this broad warrant of authority justified in public opinion? A backlash, that convenient cliché, was part of the answer. In the immediate aftermath of Watergate indignant readers expressed outrage that the press had, so it was charged, pulled down a whole administration. Vindictive reporters and commentators, long cherishing their hatred for him, had been determined to destroy Nixon. Letters repeating this accusation, often with an overtone of threatened violence, poured into editorial offices. The rating of the press in a Harris poll testing the degree of confidence in a wide range of institutions dropped five points.

This reaction, linked in some instances with the charge of monopoly control, caused concern among more sensitive publisher-owners, who were aware of what it might eventually mean to an independent press. One was Katharine Graham, publisher of the Washington *Post*. Under her direction—she took over following the death of her husband—a complex has grown up consisting of the *Post, Newsweek* and four television stations, one of them WTOP, which, with its radio affiliate, is the most powerful station in Washington. The latest acquisition was the Trenton (New Jersey) *Times*, purchased for a reported $14 million. Other newspaper acquisitions are in view. When she was honored by a feminist group hailing her as the most powerful woman in America, Mrs. Graham made a sober response: It was not personal power but the power of the press as an institution that should be recognized as a force for good. She was repudiating the concept of the press lord of another day. Given an aroused public opinion, such a concept is surely a relic of a past long gone.

Two colleagues in the commentating business seemed to me in this time of testing to be at opposite poles. One is Joseph Alsop. He held a position of remarkable authority in Washington, owing not a little to his character which is half eccentric, half scholar. An indefatigable worker with friendships in high places over the years, he announced at the age of sixty-four that he would stop writing his column. In a series of valedictory columns he expressed a tormented despair that made even his frequent past prophecies of doom seem almost optimistic. Most revealing was his essay on "the reporter's trade," in which he lamented the rise of advocacy journalism. More often than not Alsop had seemed to me an advocate, and a powerful advocate, rather than a reporter-commentator. He concluded that the danger to the press had worsened because "nowadays . . . too many people in my trade think the best way to make a big reputation is to convict a major public figure or institution of some sort of wrongdoing. . . ." The label conservative fitted him as well as any, and in his jeremiads at the end of his career, he blasted the weakness, the slackness, of an America undermined by the liberals and the Left.

At the opposite pole is James Reston, foremost in the field today. Rejecting the gloom and pessimism of the time, he sounds a note of hope built on his belief in the strength of the nation and the productivity of the American free enterprise system. With no trace of arrogance, his columns express the conviction of an earlier America when, as in Reston's own instance, one could rise from a modest beginning to a preeminent position, a more sophisticated version of the log cabin-to-White House tradition. With his continuing support during the long struggle over confirmation, he showed himself ready to forgive Nelson Rockefeller for his inherited wealth. This was an interesting contrast with the two *bona fide* liberal columnists on the *New York Times*, Anthony Lewis and Tom Wicker, who directed a continuous fire at the Vice-Presidential nominee. Reston's style is a reflection of his judicious temperament, his pleasant equable way with people which has helped to win him not only influence but a broad company of friends. An admirer of Lippmann, whose writings he quotes frequently, he is an inheritor of the discipline of privilege and responsibility.

My judgments have been tempered over the years by a growing awareness of the hazards of power. It may not be literally true that all power corrupts, but the more it is exercised the more likely it is for the individual to deceive himself into believing that he is infallible. And when it comes to absolute power we have seen in this grisly century all too many examples of what that can mean.

At one remove those of us chronicling the lives of the great and the near great may be tainted by this same corruption. We have a kind of intimacy based on the premise that we are observers beyond the rules of the game. But as I have suggested here, from time to time we persuade ourselves that our superior knowledge, our intuitive understanding, entitles us to play a direct part with our identity only thinly disguised. I know what this temptation is and what it means to succumb to it. It is, I have come to feel, a dangerous illusion. It jeopardizes the integrity, the independence, of the observer-reporter. Granted that this is heady wine and granted, too, that often demonstrable clods who have risen to power seem to invite beneficent intervention, yet it is a masquerade that at best adds little to the sum total of reasoned conduct and at worst merely confuses the matter in hand. The right word is the powerful agent, and those of us who traffic in words should know that if we have any strength, any influence, any force, it is in the word.

But it is a discipline increasingly difficult to maintain in a world ridden by the furies of hatred, fear, hunger and despair. No one can escape the pressures of a time of troubles magnified in this last quarter century to a degree threatening consequences more dire even than what has gone before. I have tried to weigh the figures I have known around the world during the past four decades in the balance of our time of troubles. What Hamlet said in warning to Polonius about actors being the mirror of their time is true of us who presume not only to record but to judge. I hope I have judged with understanding and compassion and with a realization that the demands have been such as to be almost beyond the capacity of mortal men, however gifted.

Index

Abs, Herman J., 122
Acheson, Dean, 41, 67, 96, 116, 133–134, 180, 194
Adenauer, Konrad, 121–126, 181
Afghanistan, 140
Agnew, Spiro, 250, 252, 257–258
Agricultural Adjustment Act (AAA), 32, 36
Albania, 77, 79
Albert, Carl, 258
Allison, John, 187–190, 193
Alsop, Joseph, 2, 166, 231, 267
Alsop, Stewart, 251
American Civil Liberties Union, 42
American University, 182
Anderson, Jack, 2
Anderson, Paul Y., 39
Arafat, Yasir, 162
Arnold, Henry H. ("Hap"), 56
Astor, Lord and Lady, 56–57
Attlee, Clement, 88–89
Ayub Khan, Mohammed, 140

Baltimore *Sun*, 17
Bangladesh, 138, 144
Bankhead, William B., 16
Barkley, Alben, 46
Baruch, Bernard, 92, 95–99
Baruch, Herman, 98
Bay of Pigs disaster, 108, 174–175, 245
Beitz, Berthold, 71–72
Ben-Gurion, David, 152
Benton, William, 220
Berle, Adolf, 172
Berlin, Isaiah, 85, 196
Berlin, Germany, 124–125, 177–178
postwar, 73–74
Berman, Jakub, 75
Bernstein, Carl, 265–266
Bevan, Aneurin, 87–88
Bevin, Ernest, 85–86
Black, Hugo La Fayette, 37–40, 47–49
Blackmun, Harry, 52
Blair, William McCormick, Jr., 92
Blankenhorn, Herbert, 121–122
Block, Paul, Sr., 23–24
Bloomington *Pantagraph*, 110
Bohlen, Charles, 191, 199–201
Boston busing controversy, 184
Bovard, O. K., 4, 39, 195–196
Bradley, Omar, 175

Brandeis, Louis Dembitz, 32–35, 41
Brandt, Raymond P., 9
Brandt, Willy, 74, 124–129, 160, 181
Brentano, Heinrich von, 124
Brezhnev, Leonid, 192–193, 194, 195, 203, 231
Brosio, Manlio, 153
Brown, Edmund G., Jr., 258
Bruce, David, 223, 225, 230
Bruce, Evangeline, 225
Bryan, William Jennings, 2
Bulganin, Nikolai A., 120, 123, 137–138
Bullitt, William Christian, 16–17
Bundy, McGeorge, 173, 243
Bunker, Ellsworth, 247–248
Burger, Warren, 52
Burns, Arthur, 250
Burton, Harold, 49
Butler, R. A., 86
Byrd, Harry, 63–64, 98
Byrd, Robert, 256–257
Byrnes, James F., 95–96

Cairo Conference (1943), 60
Cambodia, 10, 115
Carraway, Mrs. Hattie, 3
Castro, Fidel, 174, 176
Central Intelligence Agency (CIA), 174, 245–246, 250
Chao Pei-yuan, 237
Chapman, Oscar, 45
Chase, Samuel, 50
Chiang Ching (Mao's wife), 233–234
Chiang Ching-kuo, 229
Chiang Kai-shek, 10, 55, 114, 132, 229, 266
Chiao Kuan-hua, 226–227, 232, 259
Chicago *Daily News*, 27
Chicago *Tribune*, 25–26
Childs, Jane, 127, 223, 232
Childs, Mark, 173
Childs, Prentiss, 210
Childs, William H., 1
China Travel Service, 222, 224
Chinese-American relations, 222–240
Chinese Communists (*see* People's Republic of China)
Chinese Nationalists, 55
Chou En-lai, 112–115, 131, 143, 223, 226, 228–234, 240
Churchill, Winston, 10–11, 88, 97, 157

Clark, Tom, 36
Clay, Lucius D., 73–74
Clifford, Clark, 173, 209
Clifton, Ted, 173, 175
Clockwork Orange, A (film), 129
Cohen, Ben, 18, 35
Colby, William, 248–249
Coleman, Thomas, 67
Collins, Leroy, 107
Columbia University, 61
Committee for Economic Development, 179
Communist scare, 41–42, 48, 65–69, 71
Confucius, propaganda assault on, 236
Congo, 170
Connally, John, 101
Conners, William J. ("Botchy"), 92
Coolidge, Calvin, 41
Corcoran, Tommy (Tommy the Cork), 18–19, 35, 40
Cox, Archibald, 249
Cox, James, 20
Cox, Tricia and Edward, 251
Cuba-American relations, 172, 174–176, 179–180
    Bay of Pigs, 108, 174–175, 245
    missile crisis, 175–176
Cummings, Homer, 34

Daley, Richard, 92
Damaskinos, Archbishop, 79
Daniels, Josephus, 11, 20
Davies, Joseph, 197, 201
Democratic Conventions, 21–22
    1936, 21–28
    1948 (Philadelphia), 62–63
    1964 (Atlantic City), 208
    1968 (Chicago), 218–219
Department of Justice, 36, 164
D'Estaing, Giscard, 259
Dies Committee, 41
Dilliard, Irving, 217
Dillon, Douglas, 173
Dirksen, Everett, 82
di Vittori, Guiseppe, 80
Dixon, Pierson, 153
Dobrynin, Anatoly, 194, 198
Dodd, Thomas, 208
Donovan, Robert, 169
Douglas, Helen Gahagan, 194
Douglas, William O., 44–45, 47–52
Dove, Thomas and Marguerite, 145
Dulles, Allen, 245, 264
Dulles, John Foster, 111–123, 139, 148, 157, 176, 185, 190, 198, 225, 229
    Middle East policy, 146–154
Dussehara (Indian festival), 135–137

Eagleton, Thomas, 258
Eaker, Ira, 57
Early, Steve, 7, 17
Eastland, James, 164
Eden, Anthony, 86, 113–114, 117–119, 154, 155–157
    and Suez Canal takeover, 147–151, 154–158
Egypt and Suez Canal, 146–154
Ehrlichman, John, 241, 249
Eisenhower, Dwight D., 42–43, 61–68, 92, 101–102, 116–117, 120, 152, 154, 157, 167, 174, 190–192
    president of Columbia University, 61–63
    presidential campaigns, 66–67, 100, 103, 105
    relationship with General Marshall, 56, 60, 66–69
    summit meeting in Paris, 170
    tour of Western Europe and India, 139–141
    war years, 56, 58–64
Eisenhower, Julie, 251
Elizabeth, Queen of England and Prince Philip, 69
Elliston, Herbert, 148
Europe, postwar recovery plans, 70–90
Evans, Rowland, 176

Faisal, King, 162
Farley, James A., 13–14, 26
Federal Bureau of Investigation (FBI), 50
Field, Stephen J., 50
Flanders, Ralph, 65
Flournoy, Houston, 258
Flynn, Ed, 21
Ford, Betty, 253
Ford, Gerald R., 50–51, 162, 179, 203–204, 252, 260–261
    pardon of Richard Nixon, 258, 260
Fortas, Abe, 209–210
France, 9, 79–85, 177–178
    Algerian problem, 158
    communist threat, 79–81, 83–84
    Suez Canal takeover, 146, 149, 158
    Vietnam and, 115, 117–118, 132–133
Francis, David, 201
Franco, Francisco, 70–71
Frankfurter, Felix, 40–43, 48
Franks, Sir Oliver, 168
Frederika, Queen of Greece, 79
Fritchey, Clayton, 101
Fu, Fung Kwei, 225, 238–239
Fuchs, Klaus, 48
Fulbright, William, 264

Gaitskell, Hugh, 151
Galbraith, John Kenneth, 143
Gandhi, Mahatma, 130–131
Gandhi, Mrs. Indira, 143–144
Garner, John Nance, 17–18, 171
Garst, Bob, 191
Gaulle, Charles de, 84–85, 139, 156,
  159, 177–178, 191–192, 264
Geneva:
  Indochina conference of 1954, 112–118
  summit conferences, 101, 119, 123
Germany, postwar, 15, 71–75, 89, 120–
  122, 124, 128
  (*See also* Berlin; West Germany)
Giroux, Françoise, 259
Goldberg, Arthur, 210, 256–257
Goldwater, Barry, 205, 244
Göring, Hermann, 47
Graham, Katherine, 266
Graham, Philip, 170–171
Grasso, Ella, 253
Great Britain, 85–90
  lend-lease to, 85, 98
  nationalization of industry, 86–89
  Suez Canal takeover by Egypt, 146–158
Greece, economic and military aid,
  77–79
Gridiron Dinner (1936), 27–28
Griswold, Dwight, 77
Gromyko, Andrei, 190
Grosjean, Alice, 2–3
Guillaume, Günter, 128

Hagerty, James, 102, 191–192
Hague, Frank, 21–22, 24, 95, 104
Haldeman, H. R. ("Bob"), 241, 249
Hannegan, Robert, 44
Harding, Warren, 251
Harriman, W. Averell, 92, 103–104, 201–
  203
Hearst, William Randolph, 17
Heikel, Herr, 188
Helms, Richard, 245–246
Hersh, Seymour, 246
Herter, Christian, 82, 86
Hillenbrand, Martin, 127
Hiss, Alger, 48, 194
Hitler, Adolf, 15, 66, 71–72, 122
Ho Chi Minh, 132–133
Hong Kong, 223–224
Hoover, Herbert, 17, 32
Hoover, Herbert, Jr., 154
Hoover, J. Edgar, 50
Hopkins, Harry, 14–15, 19, 21
Horner, John, 249
House Committee on Un-American
  Activities, 71

Huang Chen, 240, 244–245
Hughes, Charles Evans, 31–32, 35
Hull, Cordell, 15–17
Humphrey, George, 156–157
Humphrey, Hubert, 168–169, 182–183,
  195, 208–209, 218–221
Hunt, E. Howard, 249
Hurley, Patrick J., 55
Hussein, Ahmed, 146
Hussein, King of Jordan, 162, 259
Hyde, Henry, 17–18

Ickes, Harold, 14–15, 44–45
Ikeda, Hayato, 173
India, 130–145
  industrial development, 131, 135
  Pakistan war, 143–144
Indochina, 10–11, 132
  See also Vietnam War
Iran, 140, 202
Ireland, Kennedy's visit to, 181–182
Israel, 149, 152, 157, 159–162, 259
  Six-Day War (1967), 159
  Yom Kippur War (1973), 161
Italy, postwar, 79–81
  communists, 79–80
Ives, Mrs. Irving, 109

Jackson, Henry, 203–204
Jackson, Robert H., 46–49
  Nürnberg trials prosecutor, 47
Jaipur, Maharaja and Maharani, 135–137
Jamieson, Jamie, 244
Japan, 89, 230
  China policy, 230
Jefferson, Thomas, 1
Jenner, Albert, 66–67, 115
Johnson, Ladybird, 207, 210
Johnson, Lyndon, 43–44, 51, 101, 108,
  170–171, 178, 192, 205–219, 243
  New Hampshire primary, 216–217
  trip to Southeast Asia, 211–215
  Vietnam disaster, 206–207, 212–213
  withdrawal from Presidential race,
  217–218
Johnson, U. Alexis, 112–113
Jones, Jesse, 197
Jouvenel, Bertrand de, 94

Kansas City *Star*, 23
Kashmir, 138
Keating, Kenneth, 36
Kefauver, Estes, 103
Kelly, Edward J., 21–22, 24–25
Kennedy, Edward M. ("Teddy"), 169,
  183–184

Kennedy, Jacqueline ("Jackie"), 109, 167-168, 177-178
Kennedy, John F., 106-108, 164-182, 210, 246
 approach to the press, 169, 172, 176-177
 assassination, 44, 182
 cabinet members, 172-173
 Cuban policy, 174-180
 hatred for, 164-165, 184
 1960 campaign, 168-172
 Pulitzer prize for *Profiles in Courage*, 166, 173
 trips to Europe, 177-178, 180-182
Kennedy, Joseph P., 165-166, 169-170, 182
Kennedy, Robert F., 170, 172-173, 177, 182-183
 assassination, 183, 218
Kennedy, Rose, 167
Kenny, John V., 104
Keynes, John Maynard, 12, 97-98
Khrushchev, Nikita, 120, 137-141, 176-177, 185-187, 200
 at Paris conference, 191-192
 visits to U. S., 139-141, 190-191
Kiessinger, Kurt Georg, 126
Kilpatrick, James Jackson, 2
King, Martin Luther, 218
Kissinger, Henry, 162, 194, 198, 202, 241-245
 China policy, 222-223, 227, 231, 240, 254-255, 259-260
 Middle East diplomacy, 161-162, 243
 Nixon and, 241, 250
 shuttle diplomacy, 148, 161, 259-260
 wire taps, 242-243
 "Year of Europe" speech, 223-224, 231
Knowland, William, 113, 115
Knox, Frank, 27
Korea, 214-215
Korean War, 66
Kreisky, Bruno, 160
Krock, Arthur, 166-167
Krupp, Alfred, 71-73
Krupp Complex, 71-73, 89
Ku Klux Klan, 37
Kuo Mo-jo, 234
Kuznetsov, Vasily, 186
Kwangsi province, China, 237-238
Ky, Nguyen Van, 212

Labor Relations Act, 36
La Follette, Robert M., Jr., 12, 64
La Follette, Robert M., Sr., 35
Laird, Melvin, 193, 247-248
Landon, Alf, 23-24, 26, 27
Leahy, Admiral William Daniel, 11

Legelin, Philip, 208
Lemnitzer, Lyman, 58
Lewis, Anthony, 267
Lewis, John L., 13
Liddy, G. Gordon, 249-250
Lilienthal, David, 96
Lin Piao, 234-235
Lincoln, Abraham, 91
Lincoln, Mrs. Evelyn, 166
Lippmann, Helen, 263-264
Lippmann, Walter, 2, 173, 263-265
Literary Digest poll, 26
Litvinov, Maxim, 196-197
Lloyd, Selwyn, 151
Lodge, Henry Cabot, 165, 207
London, England, 56-57, 71, 85, 90
Long, Huey, 2-3
Longworth, Alice Roosevelt, 250-252
Look magazine, 7
Lutyens, Sir Edwin, 130

Ma Yu-chen, 225-228, 234
MacArthur, Douglas, 60-61, 132
McCardle, Carl, 113, 152-153
McCardle, Dorothy, 206
McCarran, Pat, 41-42
McCarthy, Eugene, 182-183, 208, 215-218
McCarthy, Joseph, 41, 64-69, 116, 172, 199
McClellan, John, 172
McGovern, George, 218, 220, 249, 258
McLeod, Scott, 199
McMahon line, 142-143
Macmillan, Harold, 120, 155-158, 192
Macomber, William, 152-153
McReynolds, James, 31
MacVeagh, Lincoln, 78
Malraux, André, 85
Manila summit, 211-212
Mao Tse-tung, 55, 223, 233-235, 239
Marshall, George Catlett, 53-56, 60, 66-69
Marshall Plan, 74, 82-83, 85-86
Meany, Mr. and Mrs. George, 173-174
"Meet the Press" program, 65-66
Meir, Golda, 160
Mellon, Andrew, 46
Mencken, H. L., 32
Mendès-France, Pierre, 84, 118
Menshikov, Mikhail, 197
Mercer, Lucy, 19-20
Merrell, George, 135
Meyer, Mrs. Agnes, 93, 106
Meyner, Robert, 104
Middle East problems, 146-162, 243
Mikolajczyk, Stanislaw, 75-76
Miller, Merle 36, 68

Mirabelle, Elizabeth de, 84–85
Mollet, Guy, 154, 158
Molotov, Vyacheslav M., 86, 96, 113, 120, 155
Monnet, Jean, 83–84
Morgenthau, Ellie, 12
Morgenthau, Henry, 12
Morro, Aldo, 250
Morse, David, 117
Mountbatten, Earl and Viscountess, 134
Moyers, William, 215
Murphy, Robert, 147
Murray, Philip, 63
Murrow, Edward R., 65
Muskie, Edmund, 220
Mussolini, Benito, 71

Naidu, Mrs. Sarojini, 131
Nasser, Gamal Abdel, 147, 149
Nation magazine, 39
National Press Club, 39, 93
National Security Council, 180
NATO (North Atlantic Treaty Organization), 159
Negro press, 93
Nehru, Jawaharlal, 130–135, 138–139, 141–142
Nenni, Pietro, 80–81
Neuberger, Richard, 168
New Deal, 4, 19
New York *Herald Tribune*, 176
New York Times, The, 1–2, 166, 180, 246, 267
Niemeyer, Harry, 4
Nitze, Paul, 193
Nixon, Richard M., 43, 53–54, 217, 220, 244, 264
   anti-communism, 48, 67, 194
   China policy, 225, 230, 233
   corruption and political power, 95
   distrustful of the press, 172
   dualism in personality, 250
   foreign policy, 194–195, 202
   landslide victory, 220
   in Moscow, 194–195, 231
   ordered bombing of Hanoi, 127, 245
   public appearances, 249–252
   relationship with Rockefeller and Kissinger, 244–245
   resignation, 254–255, 258, 260
   SALT talks, 252
   Supreme Court appointments, 52
   Vice President, 102–103, 117
   Watergate (*see* Watergate scandal)
Nong Kimny (Cambodian ambassador), 115
Normandie (French liner), 93–94

Nuclear bomb threats, 175–176, 190, 192–193, 198, 203–204
Nuclear test ban agreement, 105–106, 182
Nürnberg trials, 47

O'Brien, Lawrence, 165, 218, 219
O'Donnell, Kenneth, 165
Oil, 87, 154
   Arab embargo, 162
"Open skies" plan, 119–120
Oumansky, Constantine, 195–196

Pakistan, 138, 140, 143–144
Palestinian Liberation Organization, 161–162, 250
Pandit, Madame, 139
Pannikar (Indian ambassador), 131
Papastratos, Madame, 77
Park Chung Hee, President of Korea, 214–215
Parvin Foundation, 50
Patterson, Joseph C., Jr., 56–57
Paul, King of Greece, 79
Pavlichenko, Ludmill and Ivy, 197
Peace Corps, 173
Pearson, Drew, 39–40, 173, 208
Pearson, Lester, 113–115, 138
Pendergast, Tom, 21–22, 93–95
Pentagon Papers, 51
People's Daily, The (Peking newspaper), 223, 234
People's Republic of China, 55, 72, 131–132, 222–240
   border conflicts with India, 142–143
   Cultural Revolution, 232–233, 239
   at Geneva, 112–116
Perkins, Frances, 13
Pershing, John J., 60
Philippines, 211–212
Phumipol, King of Thailand, 214
Pinay, Anthony, 149
Pinchot, Gifford, 19
Pinchot, Leila, 19
Poland, postwar, 9, 75–76, 199
Pope Pius XII, 81
Post-Dispatch (*see* St. Louis *Post-Dispatch*)
Potsdam Conference, 88
Powell, Lewis, 52
Press and television, 180, 263–269
   attacks by Agnew, 265–266
   responsibility and privilege, 263–269
Public Utilities Holding Co. Act, 19, 35
Pullman, George Mortimer, 196

Quemoy and Matsu, 229–230

Rabin, Yitzhak, 161
Radziwill, Prince, 76
Rather, Dan, 2
Rauh, Joseph L., 62
Rayburn, Sam, 171
Reagan, Ronald, 258
Reconstruction Finance Corporation, 197
Redfield, Malissa, 167
Reed, Stanley, 40
Rehnquist, William, 52
Reid, Escott and Ruth, 138
Reston, James, 1–2, 259, 267–268
Reuter, Ernst, 74, 124
Richardson, Elliot, 249
Roberts, Chalmers, 243
Roberts, Roy, 23
Robertson, Walter, 114
Rockefeller, Laurance, 256–257
Rockefeller, Nelson, 119, 179, 220,
    243–244
  Congressional hearings, 256
  Kissinger and, 243–244
  nominated Vice President, 255–257
  public career, 243–244, 256–257
  treatment in the press, 267–268
Rogers, William P., 127, 198
Rome, Italy, 79–80
Romney, George, 216–217
Ronning, Chester, 113
Roosevelt, Eleanor, 12–13, 19–22, 93,
    97, 106
Roosevelt, Franklin D., 5, 7–29
  Assistant Secretary of the Navy, 11
  brain trust, 30, 35
  Cabinet Officers, 12–14
  court packing plan, 31–36, 38–39
  economic problems, 12–13
  on the Far East, 10, 55
  fireside chats, 9, 14
  first campaign, 12–13
  foreign policy, 15–17
  fourth term plans, 8–9
  hatred for, 26–27, 164–165
  historical perspective, 8–9
  infantile paralysis, 20
  lend-lease program, 85, 98
  1936 Campaigns, 21–28
  personality, 10–12
  press conferences, 7, 13
Roosevelt, Franklin D., Jr., 169
Roosevelt, James, 22, 62
Roosevelt, Sara Delano, 21
Roosevelt, Theodore, 251
Rosenberg, Julius and Ethel, 48
Ross, Nancy Wilson, 56
Rostow, Walt, 173, 182, 215
Rowley, James, 66

Rumor, Mariano, 250
Rusk, Dean, 108, 173, 198

Sacco and Vanzetti case, 40
St. Louis *Post-Dispatch*, 2–4, 9, 38–39,
    93, 217
Salinger, Pierre, 173, 176
SALT (Strategic Arms Limitation Talks),
    193–194, 198, 252
Saudi Arabia, 162
Scheele, Walter, 127
Schlesinger, Arthur, Jr., 109, 173
Schlesinger, James, 249
Schmidt, Helmut, 128
Schneider, Murray, 102
Schniedwind, August, 122
Schulz, Robert L., 61, 63
Securities Exchange Act, 19
Semenov, Vladimir, 193
Senate Judiciary Committee, 164
Shackley, Ted, 246
Shriver, Sargent, 173
Sidey, Hugh, 246
Sinatra, Frank, 250
Skouras, Spyros, 190
Smathers, George, 116
Smirnovsky, Vladimir, 197
Smith, Gerard, 176, 193–194, 242–243
Smith, Walter Bedell, 118
Social Security, 36
Socialist International, 160
Sokolovsky, Gen. Vasily, 74
Sophoulis, Themistocles, 78
South Korea, 131, 214–215
Soviet Union, 9, 16, 41, 49, 96, 185–204
  arms talks, 192–193
    (*See also* Nuclear bomb threats;
      SALT talks)
  détente, 195, 200–201
  Geneva summit talks, 119, 123
  nuclear test ban agreement, 105–106,
    182
  postwar policies, 65, 74
  World War II, 201–202
Spanish Civil War, 70–71, 85
Spivak, Lawrence, 66
Stalin, Josef V., 9, 48, 79, 86, 88
Stassen, Harold, 103
Stevenson, Adlai, 67, 91–92, 95, 99–110,
    131, 194, 208, 221
  ambassador to the U.N., 108–109
  presidential campaigns, 99–110, 170
Stone, Harlan, 38–41, 47
Strachey, John, 88
Strategic Arms Limitation Talks (*see*
    SALT talks)
Strauss, Franz Joseph, 126

Suez Canal takeover, 146–149, 154–158
Sukhodrev, Viktor, 187
Summersby, Kay, 62
Supreme Court, 254
  FDR's "court packing" proposals,
    31–36
  Nixon and, 52
Sweden: The Middle Way, 3–4
Symington, Stuart, 170
Syria, 159

Taft, Robert A., 65
Taft, William Howard, 31, 251
Taiwan, Republic of, 229
Tanaka, Prime Minister, 230
Taylor, Maxwell, 182
Teapot Dome scandal, 39
Tehran Conference, 9, 11
Television, effect on politics, 110, 180
  (*See also* Press and television)
Tennessee Valley Authority, 96
Thailand, 213–214
Thanarat, Prime Minister Sarit, 214
Thayer, Charles, 58
"They Hate Roosevelt," 26–27, 165
Thieu, Nguyen Van, 212, 247–248
Third World powers, 162, 227
Thompson, James, 213–214
Thompson, Llewellyn, 188, 191, 199–201
Thurmond, Strom, 63
Tibet, 133
Time magazine, 246
Tito, Marshal, 79
Togliatti, Palmiro, 80
Tokyo, 170
Totalitarianism, 3–4
Truman, Harry S., 36, 44–46, 85, 88,
    92–93, 95, 99, 101, 131, 133–134
  China problem, 55
  reelection campaign, 62–64
  and Stevenson, 103–104
  use of atomic bomb, 175–176
Tsaldaris, Constantine, 78
Tugwell, Rexford, 12
Turkey, 77
Tzulc, Tad, 180

U-2 spy plane, 139, 170, 191–192
United Nations, 95–96, 131
  atomic-energy control proposals, 95–96
  Chinese Communists, 227
  peace-keeping troops, 159, 161
  Suez Canal resolution, 150–153
  Yasir Arafat at, 162

Van Devanter, Willis, 31, 35–36
Vietnam War, 51, 109, 182

bombing of Hanoi, 127, 245
CIA operations, 246–249
Geneva conference (1954), 112–118
Ho Chi Minh, 132–133
Humphrey and, 219
Saigon, 246–249
Vinson, Fred M., 47–49
Vladivostok meeting (1974), 203–204
Voorhis, Jerry, 194

Wall Street Journal, 207
Wallace, George, 183
Wallace, Henry, 14, 32, 63
Warren, Earl, 42–44, 210
Warsaw, 75
Washington, George, 50
Washington, D.C., 163–164
  fire and riots, 218
Washington *Post*, 148, 170, 206, 249,
    265–266
Washington *Star*, 69, 249
Watergate, 195, 202, 220, 224, 240, 249
  Kissinger and, 242
  reaction of Chinese, 231
  revelations in Washington *Post*, 249,
    265–266
  Saturday Night Massacre, 249
  tapes, 51, 250, 254
Welles, Orson, 15
Welles, Sumner, 16–17
Wendell Willkie Awards for Negro
    Journalism, 93
West Germany, 121–129
Westmoreland, William C., 212
Wheeler, Burton K., 34–36
White House:
  concealment and secrecy, 241, 249
  tapes, 51, 250–254
Wicker, Tom, 267
Willkie, Wendell, 7, 11, 93, 101
Wilson, Woodrow, 31–32, 97
  Versailles peace conference, 263
Wilson, Mrs. Woodrow, 168
Wolfson, Lewis, 210
Woodward, Robert, 265–266
Woolton, Lord, 86
Works Progress Administration, 14–15

Yalta conference, 199
Yamani, Sheik, 162
Yeng Cheng-hsin, 237
Yugoslavia, 56–57, 77, 79
Yung Tai, Princess, 236–237

Zhukov, Marshal, 191
Ziegler, Ronald, 241, 249, 254
Zionists, 203

ABOUT THE AUTHOR

Marquis Childs, winner in 1969 of the first Pulitzer Prize for distinguished commentary, for his coverage of Washington, has been a witness to power since his first days with United Press in Chicago and the St. Louis *Post-Dispatch*. Since 1944, he has written a syndicated column on the affairs of state around the world for United Feature Syndicate. He was chief of the *Post-Dispatch* Washington bureau in the critical period of the Sixties. He is author of a number of books, including the best-sellers, *Sweden: The Middle Way, Eisenhower: Captive Hero*, and *The Peacemakers*, and, with James Reston, he edited *Walter Lippmann and His Times*. He has recently been engaged in a Ford Foundation study on the press and television and the attitudes of audiences He lives in Georgetown, in Washington, D.C.